Z
1035
73

DATE DUE

*Books
That
Changed
the South*

Books That Changed the South

by Robert B. Downs

The University of
North Carolina Press
Chapel Hill

Copyright © 1977 by
The University of North Carolina Press
All rights reserved
Manufactured in the United States of America
ISBN 0-8078-1286-2
Library of Congress Catalog Card Number 76-13181

Library of Congress Cataloging in Publication Data

Downs, Robert Bingham, 1903–
  Books that changed the South.

  Bibliography: p.
  Includes index.
  1. Books—Reviews. 2. Southern States—Civiliza-
tion—Addresses, essays, lectures. I. Title.
Z1035.A1D673   028.1   76-13181
ISBN 0-8078-1286-2

For
Elizabeth

Contents

Acknowledgments

Particular gratitude should be expressed to a number of individuals who advised on the selection of books to be included in the present work. Valuable guidance was received from Professor John T. Flanagan of the University of Illinois; Clarence Gohdes, Jay B. Hubbell, and John Alden of Duke University; Lewis Leary and Louis Rubin, Jr., of the University of North Carolina; and Jane B. Wilson, former director of Durham City Libraries and North Carolina State Library public library consultant. Appreciation should also be expressed to Dean Edward. G. Holley for a semester's appointment on the University of North Carolina School of Library Science faculty, enabling me to make full use of two great Southern libraries, those of the University of North Carolina and Duke University.

Published works that proved particularly helpful in the preparation of the work were Jay Hubbell's *The South in American Literature*, Louis Rubin, Jr.,'s *A Bibliographical Guide to the Study of Southern Literature*, and Clarence Gohdes's *Bibliographical Guide to the Study of the Literature of the U.S.A.*. Also suggestive and useful were two articles by Professor Thomas H. English of Emory University: "On Choosing a Southern Hundred" (*Princeton University Library Chronicle*, volume 27, pages 45–53, Autumn 1965) and revised in "A Basic Southern Book List" (*Southeastern Librarian*, volume 18, pages 88–91, Summer 1968).

Essays in somewhat different form on several of the books included in the present work appeared previously: W. J. Cash's *The Mind of the South* in my *Books That Changed America* (Macmillan, 1970), and Smith's *Generall Historie*, Byrd's *Histories of the Dividing Line*, Weems's *Life of Washington*, Washington's *Up from Slavery*, and Du Bois's *Souls of Black Folk* in my *Famous American Books*

(McGraw-Hill, 1971). I am grateful to the two publishers for permission to incorporate material from these publications in *Books That Changed the South*.

The preliminary research for the titles selected for *Books That Changed the South*, and aid in making the final choices, was done by Elizabeth C. Downs, to whom the author feels a deep sense of appreciation.

Two long-time associates prepared the manuscript for publication: Clarabelle Gunning and Deloris Holiman. Their assistance was indispensable, as it has often been in the past.

Robert B. Downs

Urbana, Illinois

Introduction

The proposition advanced in the present work, with supporting evidence, is that the culture and civilization of the Southern region of the United States have been deeply affected by the printed word, or, more specifically, that certain seminal books have played key roles in shaping the South as it exists in the twentieth century. A basic premise is that the section's economic and social thought, political actions, and overall history clearly stem from the influence, direct or indirect, of specific published works issued from the seventeenth to the twentieth centuries.

It should be noted that the thesis adopted here follows the pattern of the writer's previous works: *Books That Changed the World*, *Books That Changed America*, *Famous American Books*, *Molders of the Modern Mind*, and *Famous Books Ancient and Medieval*. In each case, the books selected for discussion and critical analysis were chosen for their historical effect. Literary merit was generally a secondary consideration. The measurement of influence is of course a complex matter. Books which sell in the millions of copies may make little permanent impact on popular thought or behavior, while other works of limited circulation may shake the world. A reasonable theory is that most ideas are formulated by a few thinkers and then communicated in a variety of ways, often indirectly, to the masses of people.

The emphasis in the selection of titles for *Books That Changed the South* is on history and the social sciences, rather than science and the humanities. The several works of fiction included—Cable's *Old Creole Days*, Dixon's *The Clansman*, Harris's *Uncle Remus*, Longstreet's *Georgia Scenes*, and Page's *In Ole Virginia*—are of chief interest today as reflections of certain ways of life for their periods. In short, they are historical and sociological treatises in fictional form.

No limitations were placed on dates of publication for the books included. The range is from 1624 to 1951. Historical perspective of at least twenty-five years, it was decided, was needed for proper objectivity. The general arrangement adopted is chronological by date of publication. Two exceptions are William Byrd's *History of the Dividing Line*, which was not published until more than a century after it was written, and Fanny Kemble's *Journal of a Residence on a Georgian Plantation*, which was delayed some twenty-five years.

Neither are there any restrictions with reference to the place of birth of the authors included nor to place of publication. As it turns out, nineteen of the twenty-five books reviewed were written by Southern-born authors, four by Northerners, and two by English writers. Only six of the titles were issued by Southern presses—in Georgia, Louisiana, North and South Carolina, Virginia, and Tennessee—while nineteen first appeared elsewhere: nine in New York, three in Boston, three in Philadelphia, two in London, and one in Hartford, Connecticut. The preponderance of non-Southern publishers is indicative of two facts: the controversial nature of a number of the books, which prevented their publication in the South, and the scarcity, until recent years, of strong publishing firms in the Southern states.

A tragic theme running through the history of the South for three hundred fifty years has to do with problems of race. Since the first Negro slaves were landed in Virginia in 1619, the Southern states have been preoccupied with the Negro, with slavery, and the traumatic issues growing out of race and race relations. Scarcely any works issued after 1800 are unconcerned with these matters, and for a majority it is a central motif: for Cable, Calhoun, Cash, Dixon, Douglass, Du Bois, Harris, Helper, Kemble, King, Odum, Olmsted, Page, Phillips, Washington, and Woodward, in particular, and to a lesser extent, Bartram, Byrd, Clemens, Crockett, *I'll Take My Stand*, Jefferson, and Longstreet.

A new dimension was added to the question of the economics of American Negro slavery by the publication in 1974 of *Time on the Cross*, a two-volume work by Robert William Fogel and Stanley L. Engerman. The authors apply sophisticated computer methods to question several traditional assumptions: that slavery was generally an unprofitable investment, or depended on trade in slaves to be profitable, except on new, highly fertile land; that slavery was economically moribund; that slave labor and agricultural production based on slave labor were economically inefficient; that slavery caused the economy of the South to stagnate, or at least retarded its growth, during the antebellum era; and that slavery provided extremely harsh material conditions of life for the typical slave. By electronically sifting a mass of slave-sale invoices, plantation records, census figures, and customs manifests from Southern ports, the authors shed doubts on standard beliefs and interpretations concerning the profitability of the slave system and its effects on the slaves themselves. Heated debate on the validity of the Fogel-Engerman findings is expected to continue for years to come. A new work, announced for publication in 1976 by the University of Illinois Press, *Slavery and the Numbers Game* by Herbert G. Gutman, challenges most of the Fogel-Engerman conclusions. According to Gutman, many of the interpretations of *Time on the Cross*—for example, that the use of harsh punishment, the break-up of families, and the sexual exploitation of slaves occurred much less frequently than historians have assumed—are to a substantial extent based on nonfacts, pseudostatistics, and the misuse of quantitative data. And so the debate goes on.

A new school of revisionists among American historians in recent years has also been reexamining popular conceptions of the Reconstruction era. C. Vann Woodward concludes, for example, that "it is quite possible that the Carpetbagger and the Scalawag have been allotted by the historians a share of attention out of all proportion to their importance in the revolutionary process." Woodward points out that in no Southern state did Radical rule last as long as a decade, and in the average state it continued less than three and a half years. "It was not the Radicals nor the Confederates but the Redeemers," Woodward asserts, "who laid the lasting foundations in matters of race, politics, economics, and law for the modern South."[1] Another Southern historian, Norman A. Graebner, adds: "Radical governments, whatever their weaknesses, wrote into the record a considerable body of social and economic legislation destined to stand the test of time. They established programs of compulsory education; they expanded the social services in poor relief and public works; and they created constitutions, largely on

Northern models, which long survived the return of white rule to the South."[2] Graebner describes the Fourteenth and Fifteenth Amendments as "the lasting monuments to black rights erected on the ashes of Radical Reconstruction."[3]

Some of the most enlightening and readable books among the selected twenty-five are accounts by travelers, beginning with the earliest. Notable examples are Captain John Smith's descriptions of his explorations of the area surrounding the Jamestown colony, William Byrd's observations of the Virginia–North Carolina country from the coast to the mountains, William Bartram's extensive travels through the Southeast from Philadelphia to Florida, Fanny Kemble's graphic picture of travel conditions between Philadelphia and Georgia, and the far more detailed and widely ranging chronicles of Frederick Olmsted and Edward King. Mark Twain's *Life on the Mississippi* reveals much about river travel and traffic in the 1850s and later.

Inevitably, there will be differences of opinion about the selection of titles for the present work. No two persons would choose the same list. Rigorous standards were required to reduce the total to twenty-five. Among works seriously considered for inclusion, but eliminated because they failed to meet the criteria established, were the following:

Baldwin, *Flush Times of Alabama and Mississippi*
Caldwell, *Tobacco Road*
Catesby, *Natural History*
Chesnutt, *Diary from Dixie*
Chopin, *The Awakening*
Cooke, *The Virginia Comedians*
Dodd, *Cotton Kingdom*
Ellison, *The Invisible Man*
Faulkner, *Absalom, Absalom!*
Glasgow, *Barren Ground*
Harris, *Sut Lovingood's Yarns*
Hooper, *Simon Suggs*
Lawson, *New Voyage to Carolina*
Mitchell, *Gone With the Wind*
Percy, *Lanterns on the Levee*
Scott, *Waverly* and other novels

Stowe, *Uncle Tom's Cabin*
Taliaferro, *Fisher's River*
Wolfe, *Look Homeward, Angel*
Wright, *Native Son*

The possibilities appear endless. Some of the above and other titles were rejected because of their largely local interest or limited appeal. Others are difficult to measure as to their influence on the South. There can be no question, of course, of the tremendous impact of Harriet Beecher Stowe's *Uncle Tom's Cabin* on Southern history, and Mark Twain charged that Sir Walter Scott's Waverly novels were responsible for bringing on the Civil War. To avoid overlapping, a few titles were dropped because they seemed to cover ground similar to those included. For example, Longstreet's *Georgia Scenes* was considered a more significant work than Baldwin's *Flush Times of Alabama and Mississippi*, and Dodd's *Cotton Kingdom* resembles Olmsted's *The Cotton Kingdom* in various respects. Catesby's *Natural History of Carolina* and Lawson's *New Voyage to Carolina* are less comprehensive and less scientific than William Bartram's *Travels*, which deals with some of the same subjects, though the former contain much of absorbing interest about life and natural history in the early colonies.

As one reviews these twenty-five influential books, one is inclined to wonder: Did the times make the book, or vice versa— that is, did a particular work have an impact chiefly because the time was ripe for it? Would the book have been equally significant in another era, or could it even have been written at any other date? The conclusion is inescapable that the times produced the book in nearly every instance. In some other period, the work would not have been produced at all, or, if it had appeared, would have attracted little attention.

An unfortunate tendency has spread in recent years to downgrade the importance of books. Denigrators would have us believe that books are obsolescent and have been superseded by newer media. The twenty-five titles considered in the present work demonstrate conclusively that books have been dynamic and powerful instruments for generations, and many newer works are equally effective in showing the influence of the written word.

R.B.D.

*Books
That
Changed
the South*

1.

The First American

CAPTAIN JOHN SMITH'S *The Generall Historie of Virginia, New-England, and the Summer Isles*

Captain John Smith, a contemporary of Shakespeare, was a true Elizabethan in spirit. He belonged to the breed of adventurers who were exploring new worlds and beginning to establish a wide-flung British empire. Smith was born in 1580 on a Lincolnshire farm in the same year that Francis Drake was homeward bound from the Pacific Ocean, on his voyage around the world.

Smith's thirst for adventure began early. From 1597 to 1599, while still in his teens, he served with English troops in the Netherlands, helping the Dutch Protestants to free themselves from Spanish rule. After a truce had been reached, he decided to fight against the Turks in Hungary. After various misadventures and visits to Alexandria and Greece, he finally reached Vienna and joined the Imperial Army as captain of 250 horsetroops. In continued service against the infidels, Smith killed three Turks in duels, but was later wounded, captured, and sold into slavery in a wild region beyond the Black Sea. Rebelling against mistreatment, he killed his master, escaped northward to Muscovy, then to Poland by way of Hungary, and finally back to England, after visiting every country and nearly every city of any consequence in central and western Europe. For all these events, we have substantiation mainly through Smith's own account, but recent historical research has validated his principal claims.

Thus, at age twenty-four John Smith had experienced a series of spectacular adventures, personal perils by land and sea, and numerous escapes from tight places. Still unsatisfied, he began to look around for more excitement. In some manner he became associated with a group sponsored by the Virginia Company of London, which was planning to establish a new colony in Virginia. The company had received a royal charter for the discovery and occupation of lands in North America between the French possessions in Canada and the Spanish colonies in Florida and Mexico. Smith became an active promoter of the new company and was appointed one of seven members of the Council to take charge of the settlement.

Arthur Innes, English historian, accurately describes the group of 105 would-be settlers who landed in Virginia in 1607 as "gentlemen, artificers, labourers, loafers and rapscallions. There were good men among them, but they could scarcely be called a select company; they were without training or discipline, all the members of the council were jealous of each other, there was no supreme authority, and few of them had any practical experience."[1] Instructions given by the London Company, prior to the adventurers' sailing, were unrealistic in terms of the conditions that would be encountered in the American wilderness. The choice of the site that became Jamestown was fortuitous—the expedition's three ships were driven by a storm into Chesapeake Bay.

The prospects were decidedly inauspicious. The gentlemen had quarreled among themselves during the four-month voyage, and Smith's behavior had been so obstreperous that he was accused of mutiny and barely escaped hanging. The president of the Council, Edward Wingfield, lacked force and the qualities of leadership essential to inspiring or enforcing obedience and discipline. The marshy peninsula selected for the settlement, some fifty miles up the James River, had serious drawbacks. It generated malaria, but the land was fertile and water supplies were ample. In any event, the first permanent colony of the British Empire was being launched.

The story of the first year of the English occupation of Vir-

THE
GENERALL HISTORIE
OF
Virginia, New-England, and the Summer
Isles with the names of the Adventurers,
Planters, and Governours from their
first beginning An: 1584. to this
present 1624.

With the Proceedings of those Severall Colonies
and the Accidents that befell them in all their
Iournyes and Discoveries.
Also the Maps and Descriptions of all those
Countryes, their Commodities, people,
Government, Customes, and Religion
yet knowne.
DIVIDED INTO SIXE BOOKES.
By Captane IOHN SMITH sometymes Governour
in those Countryes & Admirall
of New England.

LONDON
Printed by I.D. and
I.H. for Michael
Sparkes.
1624.

ginia is one of mutual suspicion, distrust, confusion, and anarchy. As Smith summed up the case some years later, "There is no misery worse than to be conducted by a fool or commanded by a coward." From the beginning, the fainthearted wished to abandon the colony and return to England's material comforts. Because Wingfield opposed any fortification and insisted on treating the aborigines as civilized Europeans, the settlement narrowly escaped being wiped out in an Indian massacre. When manpower was urgently needed to build shelters and to cultivate corn and other crops in preparation for winter, the whole colony went mad with gold fever. The London Company had assumed that Virginia had a year-round summer climate and tropical abundance; hence it neglected to supply the necessities for survival. After the ships' provisions were exhausted, the colonists were to raise their own food. Game and fish were available, but the settlers lacked the Indians' expertise in exploiting the natural resources. Thus, with the supplies left by the departing ships soon consumed or spoiled, and a trifling acreage of Indian corn having been planted, the settlers were soon reduced to half a pint of barley meal per day per person and were dying of malnutrition. Neither by temperament nor talent were most of the men qualified to make a success of a plantation in the Virginia wilds.

For a time, John Smith was barred for insubordination; eventually he was admitted as supply officer. From June 1607, when he assumed that responsibility, until September 1608, he concerned himself with the difficult problems of feeding the adventurers, looking after their safety and defense against the Indians, and exploring the Chesapeake Bay area. As noted, the settlers themselves had no experience that would fit them for the difficulties or dangers they would meet in the New World. Perhaps a majority had embarked on the expedition under the delusion that they would find gold mines and unlimited wealth, as the Spanish had done in Mexico and Peru.

Because he lacked formal authority during these perilous early months, John Smith absented himself frequently from the settlement to engage in his favorite occupation—leading exploring expeditions in the surrounding country. In the course of his explorations he learned something of the Indians' languages, their trading methods, and their social customs. Indeed, Smith showed considerable talent for anthropology, as is evidenced by his excellent descriptions of Indian society in all its aspects. He was the one man in the colony who knew how to deal effectively with the natives, for he seems to have had an intuitive understanding of when to trust them and when to be on guard against treachery. Thus he fought them, made treaties of peace and friendship, forced them to trade for corn to feed the starving colonists, and mapped their territory. The Indians were still mainly nomadic in habits, hunters by inclination, who had only lately begun to settle in villages and to cultivate the soil.

While Smith was on an expedition in December 1607 there occurred one of the most famous episodes in early American history—if we can rely upon the captain's account. Smith had gone off up a tributary river with a small party. He and one of the guides went ashore and at once found the woods full of concealed Indians. Resistance and escape being impossible, Smith surrendered and was taken to the camp of the great Powhatan, principal chief of the Chesapeake Bay Indians. Fortunately, Smith was carrying a compass which he demonstrated as a magic instrument to the fascinated chief. Even so, Smith was kept prisoner for about three weeks while the Indians were debating how to dispose of him. The story of his rescue first appeared in print in the *Generall Historie*, seventeen years later. Captain Smith tells the story in the third person:

Having feasted him [Smith] after their best barbarous manner they could, a long consultation was held, but the conclusion was, two great stones were brought before Powhatan: then as many as could layd hands on him, dragged him to them, and thereon laid his head, and being ready with their clubs, to beate out his braines, Pocahontas the Kings dearest daughter, when no intreaty could prevaile, got his head in her armes, and laid her owne upon his to save him from death: whereat the Emperour was contented he should live to make him hatchets, and her bells, beads and copper.[2]

This is Smith's own version of his adventure. Its truth has been questioned on the theory that it was a bit of picturesque fiction, unattested by any eyewitness. One reason for questioning Smith's story is that it was published long after the event, though the captain maintained that it had been included in a letter addressed to the queen eight years earlier. In further substantiation, John Gould Fletcher notes in the biography *John Smith—Also Pocahontas*: "It was the universal practice among Indian tribes to grant the life of a captive, white or red, only at the instance of some favorite squaw; and Pocahontas was notoriously Powhatan's favorite daughter."[3] Arthur D. Innes adds: "Smith may have been giving rein to his imagination when he said in after years that the 'princess' intervened at the risk of her own life, but otherwise there is no real reason to doubt the story."[4]

Subsequent happenings lend further credence to the legend. Smith was escorted back to the fort by a dozen of Powhatan's warriors. Afterward, Pocahontas is reported to have often visited the fort, always bringing with her a fresh supply of provisions, thereby helping the colonists to survive. She was perhaps no more than twelve or thirteen years of age at the time of the celebrated rescue. A satisfying conclusion for the romantic tale would have been for the young heroine to have married John Smith, but in fact she wed another Englishman, John Rolfe, and was taken to London, where she died some ten years later.

In the fall of 1608 Smith was elected president of the council at Jamestown and began the most important phase of his career. By this time there were about four hundred Englishmen in Virginia, of whom only thirty were survivors of the original company. It was a disorganized, faction-ridden, mutinous crowd, hostile to the London Company and fearful of the Indians surrounding them. Smith assumed control in masterly fashion. His hard work and decisive actions saved the colony from starvation and perhaps extermination during the winter of 1608–9. The Indians were ordered by Powhatan not to trade for corn with the English; Smith changed the chief's mind by threatening war. By a continual show of force, Smith avoided open hostilities and obtained the food needed by the colonists. He was, perhaps by necessity, an autocratic ruler, and his dictatorial methods were resented by the unruly men under him, at least half of whom were unacquainted with hard manual labor and unwilling to do the essential work of clearing and cultivating the land.

On three occasions the discontented made plans to abandon the colony and return to England. Each time Smith turned the fort's guns on the ships and threatened to sink them. Just as the situation appeared to be improving and there was a stock of food-stuffs sufficient to see the settlers through their second winter, they discovered that most of the corn had rotted in the poorly con-structed granaries, and the unspoiled portion had been attacked by a plague of rats brought by the ships. For the remainder of the winter, the men had to live off the land, mainly subsisting on fish and wild berries. Nevertheless, Governor Smith brought the colony through with the loss of only seven men—and these from sickness rather than starvation.

Another crisis during Smith's administration was created by the return of Captain Christopher Newport, who commanded the original fleet in 1607 and represented the London Company in its dealings with the Jamestown colony. Newport was instructed to bring back some tangible return for the investment the London Company's directors had made in the enterprise. The captain, according to his directions, was not to return to England without accomplishing at least one of the following missions: finding a passage to the South Seas, bringing samples from gold mines which he was ordered to discover, or locating survivors of Raleigh's "lost colony" at Roanoke. Further, Powhatan was to be crowned king, to assure his cooperation and support, and the London in-vestors demanded a return cargo worth at least £2,000 to cover the cost of the voyage. The only part of his instructions which New-port was able to carry out was the crowning of Powhatan in a ridiculous, and what Smith rightly regarded as a futile, ceremony. Newport stayed on in Virginia until December 1608, by which time his sailors had consumed most of the food brought from England for the colonists.

Back on the Jamestown front, Smith was adopting strong measures to bring into line the gentlemen who were allergic to labor. He gave orders that those who did not work would not eat. Soon pitch, tar, and ashes for making soap were being produced, a well was dug within the fort, defenses against Indian attacks were strengthened, about forty acres were prepared for crops, fishing operations were made more efficient, and livestock, mainly chick-ens and hogs, was being bred and raised.

Meanwhile, complaints against Smith's authoritarian methods

began to reach the London officials, who were dissatisfied in any case by the lack of immediate profits from their venture, and the governor was ordered removed from office. At about the same time, Smith suffered a serious wound when a bag of gunpowder exploded. In the early fall of 1609, he sailed for England, ill and disappointed over the developments at Jamestown. Smith never returned to Virginia, though his keen interest in the colony's progress was frequently shown during the remaining twenty-two years of his life. That the first permanent English settlement in the New World survived its first two years is due largely to the endurance, courage, administrative ability, intelligence, and indomitable will of young Captain John Smith.

How important Smith's leadership was to the Jamestown colony was revealed soon after his departure for England. In the winter after Smith left, the misruled colony barely survived, all but sixty of the colonists died, and Jamestown would have been abandoned had not fresh supplies from England arrived at the last moment. Several years later, in 1622, hundreds of colonists were wiped out in an Indian massacre. After his return to England, Smith made vain efforts to persuade the colonial authorities to send him back to Virginia in command of a small military force to protect the settlers.

Smith's interest in colonization did not end with the Jamestown venture. His attention was turned next to New England. The name of the region, which first appeared in print in Smith's tract *A Description of New England* (1616), was apparently inspired by Drake's *Nova Albion* on the Pacific coast. The first recorded appearance of the name "Massachusetts" is also found in Smith's writings.

In 1614 Smith was placed in command of a small pioneering expedition to the New England area, with two ships and a crew of about fifty. Under the sponsorship of the Northern Virginia Company, the captain was directed to search for whales, furs, and gold mines, though his own interests were primarily in geographical discovery and the establishment of colonies. Much of the New England coast was explored, and Smith wrote glowing descriptions of the region's natural resources, with its cornfields, extraordinary plenty of fish, fruit, and fowl, good harbors, and healthy, invigorating climate. An eloquent plea was made for colonization for the greater glory of the English nation. Smith's map of the region and his writings made him a kind of press agent for New England and provided essential information for the use, a few years later, of the Pilgrims and the Puritans.

A year after his first voyage, Smith sailed again for New England in a small ship carrying four guns. A series of adventures ended in capture by four French privateers. Following a landing on the French coast, Smith eventually made his way back to England, thus ending the last of his seagoing expeditions.

Smith's active efforts to promote the colonization of New England continued, however, after his return from the second voyage. "I am not so simple to think," he wrote, "that ever any other motive than wealth, will ever erect there a Commonweale; or draw company from their ease and humours at home, to stay in New England." In that assumption Smith was mistaken, for religion was the prime incentive for the establishment of five commonwealths in New England. The captain offered his personal services to the Pilgrims, in 1619, to command the emigrating party. The bid was declined, ostensibly "to save charges," but more likely because Smith was a staunch member of the Church of England. The rebellious Pilgrim Fathers would never have agreed to place themselves under the leadership of one who disliked factions and believed in church unity. Smith recognized that "my books and maps were much better cheap to teach them, than myself," though he might have saved both the Pilgrims and the Puritans some of their costly errors in pioneering a new land.

All that Smith ever received for his cooperation and longtime efforts to develop colonies in the Northeast was the title of admiral of New England. He had the satisfaction before his death of knowing that his work was bearing fruit, as increasing numbers of emigrants sailed for the English colonies in the north and south.

Throughout his colorful and varied career Captain John Smith displayed a liking and talent for writing. A report of his first year in Virginia, a forty-four-page pamphlet, is entitled *A True Relation of Such Occurrences and Accidents of Noate as Hath Happened in Virginia Since the First Planting of That Collony* (London, 1608). Four years later, a second work relating to the Virginia colony, *A Map of Virginia, with a Description of the Country* (Oxford, 1612), was issued in two parts, the first a thirty-nine-page *Description of the Country, the Commodities, People, Government, and Religion*, and the second an account of "the proceedings and accidents" of the colonists from 1608 to 1612, including a map of Virginia.

Smith's largest and most ambitious literary production was his *Generall Historie*. A four-page prospectus for the book was printed in 1623. Shortly thereafter a patron, the wealthy Duchess of Richmond and Lenox, was found to finance publication. The dedication is "To the Illustrious and Most Noble Princesse, the Lady Francis." The large handsome volume of 248 pages came off the press in London in 1624 with the full title *The Generall Historie of Virginia, New-England, and the Summer Isles with the Names of the Adventurers, Planters, and Governours from their first beginning, Anno: 1584 to this present 1624. With the Proceedings of those Severall Colonies and the Accidents that befell them in all their Journyes and Discoveries. Also the Maps and Descriptions of all those Countryes, their Commodities, people, Government, Customes, and Religion yet knowne*. The work is divided into six parts. The first describes the first settlement of Virginia and voyages there to 1605; the second is a reprint, with revisions, of the *Map of Virginia* (first part), describing the country and its people; the third part is also a reprint, with some variations, of the second part of the *Map of Virginia*, relating occurrences during Smith's voyage and the settlement of Jamestown from December 1606 to 1609; the fourth continues the Virginia history from the planting of Point Comfort in 1609 to the dissolution of the Virginia Company in 1624; the fifth includes the history of the Bermudas or Summer Isles (which Smith never visited), from 1593 to 1624; and the sixth and last contains the history of New England, 1614–24, made up of reprints of Smith's earlier writings, *A Description of New England* (1616) and *New England's Trials* (1620), with some added material.

The beginning of Part Four of the *Generall Historie* is a graphic description of the Jamestown colony's "starving time," in 1609, after Captain Smith's departure, when the number of settlers had been reduced to about fifty, "most miserable and poor creatures," who survived for the most part by eating roots, herbs, acorns, walnuts, berries, some fish, and even resorting to cannibalism.[5]

A momentous event in American history, the introduction of black slavery in the continental United States, is mentioned casually, merely in passing, by Smith in the *Generall Historie*. He records that "about the last of August [1619] came in a dutch man of warre that sold us twenty Negars."[6] W. O. Blake's *History of Slavery and the Slave Trade* emphasizes that it was not an English ship but a Dutch one that brought the first slaves. The Dutch ship had chanced to touch the coast with some Negroes on board bound for the Spanish colonies.[7]

In the *Generall Historie* Smith aimed to present a complete account of English explorations and settlements in America, beginning with the Cabots in 1497 and continuing with the story of Raleigh's "lost colony" at Roanoke, of Jamestown and Plymouth up to 1624, and of Bermuda to 1623. It is a highly personal narrative, for Smith wrote fully about his own experiences as an explorer and settler, his observations on Indian culture, and his views on the economics of colonization. A considerable part of the work is not original but rather is a collection of travels and voyages. In addition to reprinting his own earlier writings with revisions, Smith extracted passages from the writings of some forty-five books and documents by other authors, mainly sixteenth- and earlier seventeenth-century works.

Smith's historical writings did not end with the *Generall Historie*. His story was continued in *The True Travels, Adventures, and Observations of Captaine John Smith*, published in London in 1630, the year before Smith's death. From a literary point of view his last book is generally rated his best: *Advertisements for Unexperienced Planters of New England, or Anywhere* (London, 1631).

Captain Smith concludes his account of the Jamestown experience in the *Generall Historie* on a note of explanation and defense. It reads in part, with spelling modernized:

Thus far I have traveled in this wilderness of Virginia, not being ignorant for all my pains this discourse will be wrested, tossed and turned as many ways as there is leaves; that I have written too much of some, too little of others, and many such like objections. . . . I thank God I never undertook anything yet any could tax me of carelessness or dishonesty, and what is he to whom I am indebted or troublesome. . . . But here I must leave all to the trial of time, both myself, Virginia's preparations, proceedings and good events, praying to that great God the protector of all goodness to send them as good success as the goodness of the action and Country deserves, and my heart desires.[8]

In one of the best of the twenty or more full-length biographies of John Smith (starting with Henry Wharton's in 1685), Bradford Smith's *Captain John Smith: His Life and Legend* offers an acute observation: "The material Smith likes best to deal with is that which has action in it—exploring new rivers, adventuring into Indian villages, sailing along unexplored coasts, escaping from pirates, hacking homes out of the wilderness, surviving Indian massacres, planting crops, or finding a fortune in ambergris."[9] His writing style has been criticized, but he was a man of action rather than a man of letters; even so, his narratives are clearly expressed, straightforward, and hold the reader's interest. A perceptive evaluation comes from the pen of Alexis de Tocqueville, who comments: "That which is most remarkable in Captain Smith is that he mingles with the virtues of his contemporaries qualities which were rare in most of them. His style is simple and clear, his narratives have the seal of truth, his descriptions are not ornate. Upon the state of the Indians in the era of North America's discovery he throws precious light."[10] Another highly relevant statement appears in John Lankford's *Captain John Smith's America*: "Smith was one of the first to fall in love with the land and to see its potential. Beyond the forests and Indian fields, Smith envisioned growing towns and cities and thriving trade and commerce. To him, America was the setting for a new civilization."[11]

2.

An American Pepys

WILLIAM BYRD'S *History of the Dividing Line
Betwixt Virginia and North Carolina*

William Byrd's *History of the Dividing Line Betwixt Virginia and
North Carolina* has become accepted as a classic of the colonial
period of American literature. It is a valuable source for the social
history of the time, especially as a description of the frontier region
along the Carolina-Virginia border. Jay Hubbell, American literary
historian, concludes that after Benjamin Franklin and perhaps Jona-
than Edwards, Byrd was the most important of the colonial writers.
Byrd's literary reputation grew slowly, because of the tardiness
with which his works were published; even so, as Hubbell comments, "some of our earlier critics and literary historians were
inexcusably blind to his merits."[1]

In many respects, Byrd was the most remarkable of early
Southern planters. He belonged to one of Virginia's leading families.
His early years were spent in England, first as a student and later as
a colonial politician, but he was devoted to his native province and
his hospitable Westover mansion. William Byrd, I, his father, had
left him an estate of 20,000 acres, which the son increased before
his death to nearly 180,000 acres. He experimented with various
methods of farming and mining. His library numbered some 4,000
volumes, said to be the largest and best in the colonies. He collected

specimens for, and became a member of, the Royal Society of London, a rare honor for a colonial. Byrd also found time to serve in various capacities in the colonial government and to found the cities of Richmond and Petersburg. It has been remarked of Byrd that he could never resist an old book, a young girl, or a fresh idea. He lived splendidly, conceived large schemes, and was perpetually in debt.

According to family traditions, Byrd always kept a detailed journal in shorthand when absent from home—a habit which has won for him the title of "the American Pepys." His most significant work, *The History of the Dividing Line Betwixt Virginia and North Carolina*, received limited circulation in manuscript form during the author's lifetime and after. Thomas Jefferson, for example, was a warm admirer. Not until 1841, nearly a century after Byrd's death, was the first edition of the *History* issued, by Edmund Ruffin in Petersburg. Another lengthy period passed before a companion work, *The Secret History of the Line*, was published in 1929, though Lyman C. Draper had called attention to the manuscript in the library of the American Philosophical Society as early as 1851. A third manuscript was discovered in 1925 in the University of North Carolina Library and subsequently published in 1942 under the title *Another Secret Diary of William Byrd of Westover, 1739–1741*.

Other less well known writings by Byrd, *A Journey to the Land of Eden* and *A Progress to the Mines*, are also narratives of business travels through the frontier country, graphically describing places and people observed.

In 1727, on his fifty-third birthday, Byrd accepted the most arduous assignment of his life. Virginia and North Carolina had a long-standing quarrel about the dividing line between the colonies, which had never been surveyed. Previous plans for defining the boundary had been aborted. As a consequence, a strip of land somewhere between fifteen and thirty miles wide had become a refuge for criminals, runaways, and other undesirables who recognized the authority of neither colony. A contemporary writer, Hugh Jones, states that the tract in question constituted a sort of "American mint whither wicked and profligate persons retire, being out of the certain jurisdiction of either government, where they may pursue any immoral or vicious practices without censure and with impunity." Both the Virginia and North Carolina governments had attempted with little success to collect taxes from the disputed territory. When King George II came to the throne, he ordered the governors and councils of the two colonies to appoint commissioners to survey the dividing line and make it definitive. William Byrd, William Dandridge, and Colonel Richard Fitzwilliam were appointed as Virginia's commissioners to run the line. Four commissioners were appointed by Governor Everard of North Carolina: Christopher Gale, John Lovick, Edward Moseley, who was surveyor general of the colony, and William Little, the attorney general.

Byrd's *History* opens with a historical sketch. He notes that the creation of certain British colonies out of Virginia was the source of the dispute over the line between Virginia and North Carolina. Byrd surmises that the misunderstanding had arisen because Weyanoke Creek, one of the reference points used in the king's charter of 1665, had disappeared, at least under that name, and had probably become the Nottoway River. He shows how Virginia by successive royal grants had been greatly reduced from its original size—developments which Byrd as a loyal Virginian viewed with regret. As a member of the commission, he was prepared to resist further encroachments.

The *Dividing Line* is appropriately titled, literally and metaphorically, for Byrd is obviously a prejudiced witness, repeatedly recording the scorn of the prosperous and efficient Virginia planter and landowner for what he considers the poor white trash of North Carolina. His satirical comments on some of the North Carolina commissioners, and upon North Carolinians as a class, understandably irked sensitive citizens of the colony. Byrd's amusing but biased views on the Tar Heel's laziness have been often quoted:

Surely there is no place in the World where the Inhabitants live with less Labour than in N Carolina. It approaches nearer to the Description of Lubberland than any other, by the great felicity of the Climate, the easiness of raising Provisions, and the Slothfulness of the People.

Indian Corn is of so great increase, that a little Pains will Subsist a very large Family with Bread, and then they may have meat without any pains at all, by the Help of the Low Grounds, and the great Variety of Mast that grows on the High-land. The Men, for their Parts, just like the Indians, impose all the Work upon the poor Women. They make their Wives rise out of their Beds early in the Morning, at the same time that they lye and Snore, till the Sun has run one third of his course, and disperst all the unwholesome Damps. Then, after Stretching and Yawning for half an Hour, they light their Pipes, and, under the Protection of a cloud of Smoak, venture out into the open air; tho', if it happens to be never so little cold, they quickly return Shivering into the Chimney corner. When the weather is mild, they stand leaning with both their arms upon the corn-field fence, and gravely consider whether they had best go and take a Small Heat at the Hough: but generally find reasons to put it off till another time.

Thus they loiter away their Lives, like Solomon's Sluggard, with their Arms across, and at the Winding up of the Year Scarcely have Bread to Eat.

To speak the Truth, tis a thorough Aversion to Labor that makes People file off to N Carolina, where Plenty and a Warm Sun confirm them in their disposition to Laziness for their whole Lives.[2]

Elsewhere in *The Dividing Line*, further characterizing North Carolinians, Byrd satirizes the Carolinians' lack of religion: they "live in a climate where no clergyman can Breathe, any more than Spiders in Ireland. . . . They count it among their greatest advantages that they are not Priest-ridden" Byrd adds: "One thing may be said for the Inhabitants of that Province, that they are not troubled with any Religious Fumes, and have the least Superstition of any People living. They do not know Sunday from any other day, any more than Robinson Crusoe did, which would give them a great Advantage were they given to be industrious. But they keep so many Sabbaths every week, that their disregard of the Seventh Day has no manner of Cruelty in it, either to Servants or Cattle."[3]

The Carolinians were great pork eaters, Byrd reported, and he attributed certain unfortunate maladies to their monotonous diet. These and similar observations created a distorted picture of North Carolina civilization in the colonial period. Thought to be based on what Byrd had seen of the border inhabitants, they were accepted as authentic by later historians, including Parkman.

After a formal exchange of correspondence, the two commissions agreed to meet at Currituck Inlet on the coast on 5 March 1728. Even before the commissioners came together, a controversial note had been sounded. The Virginians assumed that they would set standards for the expedition and therefore, as stated in Byrd's *Secret History*, wrote the North Carolina commissioners as follows:

It is very proper to acquaint You in what manner we intend to come provided, that so you, Gentlemen who are appointed in the same Station, may if you please do the same Honour to Your Government. We shall bring with us about 20 men furnish't with Provisions for 40 days. We shall have a Tent with us & a Marquis for the convenience of ourselves & Servants. We shall be provided with much Wine & Rum as just enable us, and our men to drink every Night to the Success of the following Day, and because we understand there are many Gentiles on your Frontier, who never had an opportunity of being Baptized, we shall have a chaplain with us to make them Christians. For this Purpose we intend to rest in our Camp every Sunday that there may be leizure for so good a work. And whoever of your Province shall be desirous of novelty may repair on Sundays to our Camp, & hear a Sermon. Of this you may please to give publick notice that the Charitable Intentions of this Government may meet with the happier Success.[4]

To this somewhat boastful and patronizing communication the North Carolina commissioners replied with mock humility and not too subtle irony:

We are at a loss, Gentlemen, whether to thank you for the Particulars you give us of your Tent, Stores, & the Manner you design to meet us. Had you been Silent, we had not wanted an Excuse for not meeting you in the same Manner, but now you force us to expose the nakedness of our country, & tell You, we can't possibly meet you in the Manner our great respect to you, wou'd make us glad to do, whom we are not emulous of out doing, unless in Care & Diligence in the Affair we came about. So all we can answer to that Article, is, that we will endeavour to provide as well as the Circumstances of things will admit; And what we want in Necessarys, we hope will be made up in Spiritual Comfort we expect from Your Chaplain, of whom we shall give notice as you desire; & doubt not of making a great many Boundary Christians. To conclude, we promise, to make ourselves as agreeable to you as possibly we can; & we beg Leave to assure you that it is a Singular Pleasure to Us, that You Gentlemen are nam'd on that Part, to see this business of so great concern & consequence to both Governments determin'd which makes it to be undertaken on our parts more cheerfully, being assured your Characters are above any artifice or design.[5]

Byrd notes, "This Letter was without date they having no Almanacks in North Carolina, but it came about the beginning of January."[6]

When the commissioners finally convened, their work inevitably began with a dispute. The official instructions of the Virginia delegates empowered them to carry the survey to a conclusion even if North Carolina's representatives should delay or refuse to co-operate. The North Carolinians interpreted the orders as "too lordly and positive." After lengthy and acrimonious arguments, the commissioners agreed that Weyanoke Creek in North Carolina's 1665 charter referred to the Nottoway River.

Across rivers and islands, over creeks and marshes, through wild land and some settled areas, the surveying party proceeded. They were often up to their waists in icy water. The marshy country near the ocean was so damp, according to Byrd, that they became as used to water as beavers and otters. At times they rode on horseback, occasionally hiked through "intolerable quagmires," and where the water was too deep took to large Indian canoes. At night, they camped in the fields of plantations along the way, got drunk, and trifled with any available women.

On 14 March the Dismal Swamp was reached. There lay ahead the most arduous part of the task. No one knew the size of the swamp and none had penetrated its forbidding interior. When the surveyors reached the Dismal, Byrd reports that they "laid eyes on no living creature; neither bird nor beast, insect nor reptile came in view." His graphic description continues:

Doubtless the Eternal Shade that broods over this mighty Bog, and hinders the sun-beams from blessing the Ground, makes it an uncomfortable Habitation for any thing that has life. Not so much as a Zeland Frog cou'd endure so Aguish a Situation.

It had one Beauty, however, that delighted the Eye, tho' at the Expense of all the other Senses: the Moisture of the Soil preserves a continual Verdure, and makes every Plant an Evergreen, but at the same time the foul Damps ascend without ceasing, corrupt the Air, and render it unfit for respiration. Not even a Turkey-Buzzard will venture to fly over it, no more than the Italian Vultures will over the filthy Lake Avernus, or the Birds in the Holy-Land over the Salt Sea, where Sodom and Gomorrah formerly stood.[7]

The commissioners were advised that the swamp was impass-able, but several men volunteered to try getting through. With two men cutting a path for the surveyors, they plunged in. Byrd reported that the surface was like a thin crust floating on liquid mud. A dense growth of tall reeds interwoven with bamboo briars had to be cut away as the men proceeded. In some places juniper trees or large white cedars grew among the reeds or had fallen and their rotting trunks blocked the way. The surveying party disappeared for nine days, but eventually surfaced with hair-raising tales of having to sleep in water every night, ploughing through stinking junglelike morasses, running out of food, and suffering from fevers and chills.

From that point the project proceeded rapidly as the uplands were reached. The line was driven straight through a wilderness with few plantations along the way. Dissention among the commissioners continued. Especially troublesome to Byrd was his fellow commissioner, Richard Fitzwilliam, whom Byrd considered not only unreasonable and vulgar, but a traitor because he fraternized with the North Carolina surveyors and seemed to favor their cause. Nevertheless, by 5 April, a month after the expedition started, it had gone more than seventy-three miles, as far as Isle of Wight County on the Meherrin River. The spring was hot and dry and rattlesnakes infested the country. A unanimous agreement was reached to postpone completion of the survey until September.

The commissioners met again on 20 September. Byrd decided, because of the difficulty of carrying food, that the party should live off the country. Ned Bearskin and another Indian were hired to do the hunting; they brought in a plentiful supply of wild turkeys, deer, and fat bears. The line followed the Roanoke River in general. When thick underbrush was encountered, the surveyors could travel only two or three miles a day. Where the way was reasonably clear, they could make ten miles or more. As the Allegheny Mountains were approached, the country became wilder and rougher, panthers and wolves were seen and heard, Indian campfires were spotted, and the expedition was far beyond any white habitation.

As the mountains became higher and steeper, Byrd decided that the commission had gone far enough to satisfy the king's orders; the season was getting late, the horses were worn out, and the supply of bread was near exhaustion. A red oak tree was blazed to mark the spot where the dividing line was temporarily ended. From start to finish, the party had traveled, on a straight line, more than 240 miles. The arduous trip home began; Byrd brought his party back in good health and without the loss of a man. The boundary controversy was resolved and its location determined, though later surveys were needed to correct certain errors.

One of the most valuable features of the Byrd *History* is the author's observations on animal and plant life encountered along the border. He was fascinated by the curiosities of nature. When he found some new or interesting specimen, he drew upon his own knowledge and wide reading of ancient authorities, such as Pliny, as a basis for comment. Certain accounts are in the realm of tall tales: alligators swallowing rocks in order to make themselves heavy enough to pull a cow under water and drown her, thereafter spewing up the rocks; Indians capturing sturgeon by riding them bareback; squirrels crossing rivers on pieces of bark, using their tails as sails; and a louse guiding a settler lost in the Dismal Swamp, by pointing north. It is a moot question whether Byrd intended these fanciful yarns to be accepted as fact.

But when Byrd relied upon his direct knowledge, his observations were accurate and are still useful to students concerned with the plant and animal ecologies of colonial Virginia and North Carolina. His *History* contains excellent descriptions of the elk, opossum, buffalo, bear, turkey, wildcat, polecat, and rattlesnake. The woods teemed with deer, bears, and turkeys.

Byrd's acquaintance with plants was even more expert and scientific. His prime interest was in plants potentially useful for materia medica. Of all the plants found in the course of the survey, Byrd was most enthusiastic about ginseng, which other American travelers found the Indians drinking as a tea to guarantee a long life. Other favorite medicines were "snakeroot stewed in wine" and ipecac, or ipecacuanha, used as an emetic. Byrd fancied himself a doctor, though some of his stock remedies appear as likely to kill as to cure—for example, sweating, bloodletting, vomiting, and swimming in cold water.

As the surveying expedition proceeded, many Indians were met along the route. Byrd's views on the natives are revealing. Despite his cavalier background, he was highly tolerant of the Indian civilization and free of race prejudice. In his judgment, there was "but one way of converting these poor infidels and reclaiming them from barbarity, and that is charitably to intermarry with them, according to the modern policy of the Most Christian King Louis XIV, in Canada and Louisiana." Byrd adds:

It was certainly an unreasonable nicety that prevented their [the English] entering into so good-natured an alliance. All nations of men have the same natural dignity, and we all know that very bright talents may be lodged under a very dark skin. The principal difference between one people and another proceeds only from different opportunities of improvement. The Indians by no means want understanding and are in their figure tall and well proportioned. . . . I may safely venture to say that the Indian women would have made altogether as honest wives for the first planters as the damsels they used to purchase from aboard the ships. Tis strange, therefor, that any good Christian should have refused a wholesome, straight bedfellow when he might have had so fair a portion with her as the merit of saving her soul.

In the course of their travels Byrd and his companions visited several Indian villages. As a result of these encounters, Byrd is able to describe the Southern Indian's way of curing deer hides, his superstitions, his marriage customs, his endurance, and his hospitality. On one occasion, Byrd talked at length with his chief hunter, Ned Bearskin, about his religious faith; he discovered that Bearskin believed in a supreme god who had made the world a long time ago and had created many worlds before this one, all of which had been destroyed for various reasons.

Byrd's character sketches are lively. The frankest descriptions are in *The Secret History*, where the author's respects are paid both to the North Carolinians and to individual members of the Virginia delegation. John Lovick, one of the North Carolina commissioners, was "a merry, good-humored man," who "had learnt a very decent behavior from Governor Hyde, to whom he had been *valet de chambre*." William Little, another North Carolinian, "had degenerated from a New England preacher, for which his godly parents designed him, to a very wicked but awkward rake." Byrd also speaks his mind freely about two of his Virginia associates, Richard Fitzwilliam and Alexander Irvine, whom he accuses of siding on all possible occasions with the Carolina commissioners.

Southern poor whites first emerge into literature in the *Histories*. The wild border folk turned out en masse to see Byrd's party as it passed their way, convinced that the whole crew was insane to undertake such hardships and perils. As Byrd amusedly observes, "The men left their beloved chimney corners, the good women their spinning wheels, and some, of more curiosity than ordinary, rose out of their sick beds to come and stare at us. They looked upon us as a troop of knights-errant, who were running this great risk of our lives, as they imagined, for the public weal; and some of the gravest of them questioned much whether we were not all criminals condemned to this dirty work for offenses against the state."

From Byrd's point of view, the border people were extremely bizarre. A picturesque specimen was a mariner, living near the coast, who "modestly called himself a hermit, though he forfeited that name by suffering a wanton female to cohabit with him." The description continues:

His Habitation was a Bower, cover'd with Bark after the Indian Fashion, which in that mild Situation protected him pretty well from the Weather. Like the Ravens, he neither plow'd nor sow'd, but Subsisted chiefly upon Oysters, which his Handmaid made a Shift to gather from the Adjacent Rocks. Sometimes, too, for Change of Dyet, he sent her to drive up the Neighbour's Cows, to moisten their Mouths with a little Milk. But as for raiment, he depended mostly upon his Length of Beard, and She upon her Length of Hair, part of which she brought decently forward, and the rest dangled behind quite down to her Rump, like one of Herodotus's East Indian Pigmies.

Thus did these Wretches live in a dirty State of Nature, and were mere Adamites, Innocence only excepted.[8]

Though Byrd's most scathing comments were directed at North Carolinians, his prejudices showed plainly in his attitude toward Puritans, Quakers, Catholics, and non-Virginians in general. The New Englanders he considered mercenary, mean traders who drove hard bargains, were often unscrupulous, and were flooding the South with Negro slaves. While professing utmost godliness, the Puritans were selling their "kill-devil" rum up and down the coast and carrying off Carolina tobacco without paying duty on it. As for the Quakers, Byrd held them in contempt for being overly religious. William Penn, it is reported, "in his earlier days, had been a man of pleasure about the town" and was the father of an illegitimate daughter. To be excessively mercenary or religious was a despicable trait, in Byrd's view.

On the other hand, Byrd was inclined to accept unreservedly the concept of the "noble red man," taking the Indians as they were and maintaining that their further perfectibility merely depended upon education. "All nations of men have the same natural dignity," asserts Byrd; "very bright talents may be lodged under a very dark skin." Slavery Byrd regarded as a liability. He wrote to Oglethorpe congratulating him on his exclusion of Negroes and rum from Georgia, but predicting that both laws would be frustrated by the profiteering proclivities of "the Saints of New England."

The *History of the Dividing Line* and the *Secret History* are complementary. The first contains a basic account of the surveying mission, including much information not included in the *Secret History*. Its highlights are a sketch of British colonization in America, descriptions of the region traversed by the surveying expedition, including its flora and fauna, the customs of the Indians and the life of the pioneers, and characterizations of North Carolina and its people. The *Secret History* is hardly more than half as long as the *History*, but contains considerable information regarding the expedition not given in the latter work, for example, a number of letters exchanged between the North Carolina and Virginia commissioners, five speeches delivered by Byrd, and a detailed schedule indicating the distances between places in the territory covered by the commissioners.

The use of fictitious names in the *Secret History* makes it easy for Byrd to express frank opinions about the leading personalities in the survey party, though the individuals characterized are easily identifiable. The *Secret History* is much more explicit than the *History* in dealing with the men taking part in the expedition, their quarrels and conflicts of interest, and their attitude toward the women of the frontier. A half-dozen episodes are noted wherein members of the group were guilty of violence toward women met in the course of their travels. Such conduct Byrd condemned and made some effort to prevent—with little success, indicating a lack of discipline and control.

Byrd's diaries are the most extensive of any originating in the South during the early eighteenth century and perhaps during the whole colonial period. They have counterparts, of course, in a number of New England journals. Altogether, Byrd's various accounts represent thirty years of Virginia history, written by a person prominent in the colony's government. Through the Byrd chronicles we gain a better understanding of the colonial leaders of his time, and of the way in which they lived, as well as their attitude toward servants and other people they rated inferior. We also get a clear picture of manners and customs and of economic and political conditions. Here, for example, is Byrd's record for an ordinary day, 12 August 1710:

I rose at five o'clock and read a chapter in Hebrew and some Greek in Lucian. I said my prayers and ate boiled milk for breakfast. I danced my dance. I had a quarrel with my wife about her servants who did little work. I wrote a long and smart letter to Mr. Perry, wherein I found several faults with his management of the tobacco I sent him and with mistakes he had committed in my affairs. My sloop brought some tobacco from Appomattox. Mr. Bland came over and dined with us on his way to Williamsburg. I ate roast shoat for dinner. In the afternoon Mr. Bland went away and I wrote more letters. I put some tobacco into the sloop for Captain Harvey. It rained and hindered our walk; however we walked a little in the garden. I neglected to say my prayers, but had good health, good thoughts, and good humor, thank God Almighty.[9]

William K. Boyd, first editor of the *Secret History*, summarizes William Byrd's character and career: "Cosmopolitan, intellectual, and devoted to the public service, he is the best type of Virginia gentleman of the Eighteenth Century; few, if any, were his equal in personality and wealth of ideas until the days of the Revolution."[10]

3.

American Statesman

THOMAS JEFFERSON'S *Notes on the State of Virginia*

In reviewing a recent work on Thomas Jefferson, Robert E. Spiller, historian of American literature, comments: "Before the age of forty-five he had produced three works which go down in literary history as among the great documents of political and cultural thought: *A Summary View of the Rights of British America* (1784); *The Declaration of Independence* (1776); and *Notes on the State of Virginia* (1784–1785)."[1]

The last of the three titles, the only original full-length book ever written by Jefferson, was conceived almost by chance. The work was designed to answer a series of twenty-three questions propounded by the Marquis François de Barbé-Marbois, secretary of the French legation in Philadelphia. This "foreigner of distinction," as Jefferson referred to him, was seeking information about the various ones of the American states for the benefit of his own government. Jefferson's assignment was specifically to describe Virginia, but similar inquiries were directed to other states. No one replied in such detail as Jefferson, who set out to provide a comprehensive view of his native state—its history, activities, physical aspects, and resources. The Marbois questions ranged from the boundaries, rivers, seaports, mountains, climate, military and marine forces to laws, constitution, religion, slavery, agriculture, education, manners, manufactures, and commerce.

The writing of the *Notes* was not an impromptu, off-the-cuff affair for Jefferson. He had long been making notes on Virginia on loose sheets of paper, which he had bundled together without attempting to place them in order. As he mentions in an autobiographical sketch, "I have always made a practice whenever an opportunity occurred of obtaining any information of our country, which might be of use in any station public or private to commit it to writing." The inquiry from Marbois provided a suitable occasion to embody the substance of the memoranda in organized form. Unexpected leisure for the undertaking came when Jefferson was confined to his home for several months because of a fall from his horse.

Marbois's first query was: "An exact description of the limits and boundaries of the state of Virginia?" At the time that Jefferson was writing, Virginia was by far the largest state in the new confederation embracing territory that was subsequently divided into numerous states, about one-third of the continent. The area was beginning to shrink, for in 1781 Virginia offered to the government the territory north and west of the Ohio. Jefferson's account was not limited to the boundaries of Virginia. In discussing rivers, he wrote not only of the Potomac, the Rappahannock, the York, the James, and the Appomattox, but also of the Ohio, "the most beautiful river on earth," the Mississippi, Missouri, Illinois, Wabash, and other rivers of the wild interior.

In replying to the fourth and fifth questions on Marbois's list, concerning mountains and caverns, Jefferson combined the scientist and the poet. His description of the junction of the Potomac and Shenandoah rivers at Harpers Ferry is memorable: "The passage of the Patowmac through the Blue ridge is perhaps one of the most stupendous scenes in nature. You stand on a very high point of land. On your right comes up the Shenandoah, having ranged along the foot of the mountain an hundred miles to seek a vent. On your left approaches the Patowmac, in quest of a passage also. In the moment of their junction, they rush together against the mountain, rend it asunder, and pass off to the sea."[2]

Gilbert Chinard, his French biographer, notes that "Jefferson

NOTES

ON THE

STATE of VIRGINIA.

WRITTEN BY

THOMAS JEFFERSON.

ILLUSTRATED WITH

A MAP, including the States of VIRGINIA, MARY-
LAND, DELAWARE and PENNSYLVANIA.

———————

LONDON:

PRINTED FOR JOHN STOCKDALE, OPPOSITE
BURLINGTON-HOUSE, PICCADILLY.

M.DCC.LXXXVII.

was truly the first to discover and depict to Europeans the beauty of American natural scenery and to proclaim with genuine American pride that 'this scene is worth a voyage across the Atlantic—and is perhaps one of the most stupendous in nature.'"[3] After a detailed description of the Natural Bridge of Virginia, for example, Jefferson concludes, "It is impossible for the emotions, arising from the sublime, to be felt beyond what they are here; so beautiful an arch, so elevated, so light, and springing, as it were, up to heaven, the rapture of the spectator is really indescribable."[4]

In proportion to the space allotted to it, Jefferson apparently considered the sixth query of utmost importance: "Productions mineral, vegetable and animal?" It is this section which justifies the statement that the *Notes on Virginia* is probably the most important scientific book written by an American before 1785. Jefferson displays his vast learning by detailed treatment of "the mines and other subterranean riches" of the state, "its trees, plants, fruits, etc.," and then proceeds to a discussion of the quadrupeds of Europe and America, of slaves and slavery, and the American Indian. The trees, plants, and fruits of Virginia are divided into the medicinal, edible, ornamental, and useful for fabrication; the Linnean terms and popular names for each are given. It is noted further that the English found tobacco, maize, potatoes, pumpkins, cymlings, and other types of squash when they came to the New World. Jefferson concludes with mentioning what grains the Virginia farms grow, the produce of gardens, and the yields of the orchards.

Turning to animals, Jefferson begins with the subject of paleontology, a science that he found of endless fascination. Europeans had first observed vertebrate fossils in America as early as 1519. Mastodon bones had been discovered by Le Moyne in 1739 and taken to Europe for study. Jefferson's lively interest was instrumental in stimulating study of the field in his own country.

A large part of the sixth section is devoted by Jefferson to refuting erroneous and misleading statements by the eminent French naturalist Buffon and other European scientists concerning American animals. The Comte de Buffon, according to Jefferson, had advanced the opinion: "1. That the animals common both to the Old and New World, are smaller in the latter. 2. That those peculiar to the New, are on a smaller scale. 3. That those which have been domesticated in both, have degenerated in America, and 4. That on the whole it exhibits fewer species."[5] Buffon believed that heat and dryness are requirements for the production and development of large quadrupeds—elements more friendly to animal life in Europe than in America.

Buffon's theories grew out of a curious belief among European scientists in New World degeneracy, extending even to mankind. The New World, they held, had emerged from the flood later than had the other continents, and was still afflicted with dismal swamps, impenetrable forests, and extremes of heat and cold. To disprove these fallacious conclusions, Jefferson drew up three tables: first, quadrupeds found on both continents; second, those found in only one; and third, those which had been domesticated in both. Actual or estimated weights were given for each animal. In the first group, Jefferson found that "of twenty-six quadrupeds common to both countries, seven are said to be larger in America, seven of equal size, and twelve not sufficiently examined."[6] A comparison of quadrupeds found in but one of the two continents demonstrated that there were eighteen peculiar to Europe and seventy-four to America. Thus Jefferson presented convincing evidence that animals and plants reached a development hitherto unknown under the different conditions and the favorable American climate.

Throughout Jefferson's differences of opinion with Buffon, there was no rancor, and Jefferson maintained friendly relations with the great French naturalist, whom he admired. He showed considerably less tolerance, however, for other European critics of America. "The least vigorous European," de Pauw wrote, "is more than a match for the strongest American." Even Buffon is quoted by Jefferson as asserting that the American Indian "is feeble and has small organs of generation; he has neither hair nor beard, and no ardor whatever for his female." Compared to the European, "he is also less sensitive, and yet more timid and cowardly; he has no vivacity, no activity of mind."[7] In substance, the American aborigines—weak, indolent, lacking strength and courage, wanting interest in the opposite sex and therefore unable to reproduce themselves—scarcely deserved to be called men.

Jefferson reacted vehemently to such arrant nonsense. Of Buffon's diatribe he comments, "An afflicting picture indeed, which, for the honor of human nature, I am glad to believe has no original."[8] The many meetings and associations which Jefferson had enjoyed with the Indians qualified him to refute the charges of defective ardor, impotency with the female, lack of bravery, honor, and general sensibilities, inequalities between the sexes, fewness of children, and overall indifference and weakness. Probably no American knew Indians better than Jefferson, who had studied assiduously their character and their history. Through the years he had collected some fifty Indian vocabularies. In the *Notes*, he emphasizes that the Indian was a product of climate and over the centuries had adapted himself perfectly to that climate. The Indian, Jefferson maintained, was ardent and brave, strong and agile, resourceful and sagacious, living in complete harmony with his environment.

In further defense of the aborigine, Jefferson cites his talent for oratory, offering as an example the pathetic protest of Logan, the red chief, whose family had been wantonly exterminated by the white man's cruelty. "I may challenge the whole orations of Demosthenes and Cicero," wrote Jefferson, "to produce a single passage superior to the speech of Logan, a Mingo chief to Lord Dunmore, when Governor of this State."[9]

Incensed over the slanders directed toward Indians, Jefferson reacted even more strongly to the attempts by other European writers to apply similar animadversions to white Americans. For example, de Pauw made the flatfooted charge that "through the whole length of America, from Cape Horn to the Hudson Bay, there has never appeared a philosopher, an artist, a man of learning whose name has found a place in the history of science or whose talents have been of any use to others." Equally damning was the Abbé Reynal's remark, "One must be astonished that America has not yet produced one good poet, one able mathematician, one man of genius in a single art or a single science."[10] And the learned Dr. William Robertson, rector of the University of Edinburgh and author of a *History of the Americas*, added further insult: "The same qualities in the climate of America which stunted the growth of its native animals [a baseless theory ridiculed by Jefferson, as noted] proved pernicious to such as have migrated into it voluntarily." To these misguided critics, Jefferson replied:

When we shall have existed as a people as long as the Greeks did before they produced a Homer, the Romans a Virgil, the French a Racine or Voltaire, the English a Shakespeare or Milton, should this reproach be still true, we will inquire from what unfriendly causes it has proceeded. . . . In war we have produced a Washington, whose memory will be adored while liberty shall have notaries, whose name will triumph over time, and will in future ages assume its just station among the most celebrated worthies of the world. . . . In physics, we have produced a Franklin, than whom no one of the present age has made more important discoveries, or has enriched philosophy with more, or more ingenious solutions of the phenomena of nature. We have supposed Mr. Rittenhouse second to no astronomer living.[11]

On the basis of population, Jefferson calculated that America, "though but a child of yesterday," had produced more eminent individuals proportionately than France or Britain, in a single generation. In brief Jefferson argued that Americans were extremely fortunate in their environment, blessed with a variety of climates and soils, and living under conditions most favorable to the health and happiness of men. Given these factors, ignorant and libelous statements to the effect that New World inhabitants were naturally inferior, degenerate, feeble, enervated, and without talent or genius infuriated the patriotic Jefferson.

Consideration of the environment and its bearing on men, animals, and plants led naturally to the seventh query regarding climate, "a notice of all what can increase the progress of Human Knowledge?" In his response, Jefferson presents a detailed account of the climate of Virginia and of the country as far west as the Mississippi. The subject had long been one of Jefferson's major interests. Since early manhood, he notes, it had been his practice to "make two observations a day, the one as early as possible in the morning, the other from 3 to 4 o'clock, because I have found 4 o'clock the hottest and daylight the coldest point of the 24 hours."[12] Weather data were exchanged with various friends and correspondents around the country, as a result of which Jefferson had an exceptional knowledge of heat, cold, frost, winds, and changes of climate.

Another question of national importance comes up in the eighth query—population and the number of inhabitants. Jefferson estimated that Virginia would not reach Britain's density of population for at least a century. The 1782 census reported a total of

567,614 inhabitants in Virginia, of whom 259,230 were slaves. Because of the country's huge geographical area, thinly settled, Jefferson noted, "The present desire of America is to produce rapid population by as great importations of foreigners as possible." But, asked Jefferson, "Is this founded in good policy?"[13] He feared that unlimited immigration would dilute the quality of the native stock, then composed principally of persons of British descent. The American government, Jefferson wrote, "is a composition of the freest principles of the English constitution, with others derived from natural right and natural reason. To these nothing can be more opposed than the maxims of absolute monarchies. Yet, from such, we are to expect the greatest number of emigrants."[14]

For these reasons, and because he was anxious to protect and to preserve the republican institutions which had been won, as Churchill would have said, by so much "blood, sweat, and tears," Jefferson was adamantly opposed to having the new nation flooded by "a heterogeneous, incoherent, distracted mass" unsympathetic to democratic ideals. A policy of selective and restrictive immigration, in Jefferson's view, would produce a government "more homogeneous, more peaceable, more durable." An exception should be made, however, for "the importation of useful artificers. . . . Spare no expence in obtaining them . . . they will teach us something we do not know."[15]

In reviewing Virginia's population figures, Jefferson points out that nearly one-half of the total were slaves. The subject appears to have constantly occupied his mind, for he devotes considerable space to it in responding to three of Marbois's queries. Because of the slaves' "mild treatment" and "wholesome, though coarse, food," at least as Jefferson had observed in Virginia, "This blot in our country increases as fast, or faster than the whites."[16] During the colonial period, a duty, amounting practically to a prohibition, had been placed on the importation of slaves, but George III vetoed the measure and refused to reinstate it. One of the first acts of the new republican government was to place a complete ban on further slave imports, a step which Jefferson thought "will in some measure stop the increase of this great political and moral evil, while the minds of our citizens may be ripening for a complete emancipation of human nature."[17]

Another aspect of the slavery issue is dealt with by Jefferson in his answer to the fourteenth query. Here he examines ethnological and anthropological questions involved in slavery. Support was expressed for a proposed new law to emancipate all slaves born after passage of the act, educating the children at public expense in "tillage, arts or sciences, according to their geniuses," after which they would be colonized in an appropriate place. "It will probably be asked," Jefferson remarks, "Why not retain and incorporate the blacks into the state, and thus save the expense of supplying, by importation of white settlers, the vacancies they will leave?" The arguments against that plan, as summed up by Jefferson, were: "Deep-rooted prejudices of white settlers; ten thousand recollections, by the blacks, of the injuries they have sustained; new provocations; the real distinctions which nature has made; and many other circumstances, will divide us into parties, and produce convulsions, which will probably never end but in the extermination of the one or the other race."[18]

Jefferson advances as a theory, "a suspicion only, that the blacks, whether originally a distinct race, or made distinct by time and circumstances, are inferior to the whites in the endowments both of body and mind."[19] He remained open-minded on the matter, however, adding, "The opinion that they are inferior in the faculties of reason and imagination must be hazarded with great diffidence." Both black and red men, Jefferson concludes, should be studied as "subjects of natural history" to test such unproven assumptions.

Jefferson returns to the topic of slavery in his answer to the eighteenth query: "The particular customs and manners that may happen to be received in that state?" The whole of his reply is devoted to a consideration of the degrading effects of slavery on the white masters and their families. "The whole commerce between master and slave is a perpetual exercise of the most boisterous passions," asserts Jefferson, "the most unremitting despotism on the one part, and degrading submissions on the other."[20] Even stronger words followed for the government and its leaders: "And with what execration should the statesman be loaded, who permitting one half the citizens thus to trample on the rights of the other, transforms those into despots, and these into enemies, destroys the morals of the one part, and the *amor patriae* of the other."[21] Jefferson's hope, not to be realized, was that total emancipation would come "with the consent of the masters, rather than by their extirpation."

Jefferson was a confirmed agrarian, convinced that America should remain an agricultural country. As one of his biographers, Dumas Malone, phrased the Jeffersonian credo, "The young American Republic, richly endowed with land, should be mated with the pure damsel of agriculture; commerce was a vixen and manufacturing a diseased harlot beside her."[22] In part, it was a matter of sentiment with Jefferson. He was a skilled farmer who delighted in applying scientific methods to his ten thousand acres. He was willing to leave manufactures and trade to the Europeans, but in America for a long time to come there would be "an immensity of land courting the industry of the husbandman."[23]

In his own region of Virginia, Jefferson had observed the exhaustion of the soil by tobacco culture and advocated the cultivation of grain crops to contribute to the general welfare. He spoke as an agronomist, economist, and political scientist in stressing the merits of agriculture as a way of life. Jefferson eulogized the husbandman and revealed his own deep love of nature in these words: "Those who labour in the earth are the chosen people of God, if ever he had a chosen people, whose breasts he has made his peculiar deposit for substantial and genuine virtue. It is the focus in which he keeps alive that sacred fire, which otherwise might escape from the face of the earth. Corruption of morals in the mass of cultivators is a phenomenon of which no age nor nation has furnished an example."[24]

The vision of an America entirely devoted to agricultural pursuits was utopian, as Jefferson realized. His model society was to be arcadian rather than utopian, concerned less with crops than with the preservation of distinctive political ideals and institutions. Any great growth of industry would produce a proletariat class in the North and slavery would become a permanent institution in the South. If industry spread and slave labor became more productive, Jefferson foresaw that there would be little hope for emancipation.

His response to the seventeenth query led Jefferson into a highly controversial area, religion: "The different religions received into that state?" Here he had an opportunity to reiterate his views on the relation of religion to the state. His aim, without any hostility to either Catholicism or Protestantism, was to separate church and state and, even more specifically, to break the stranglehold of the Church of England on liberties of conscience. In the *Notes*, Jefferson described the situation in Virginia which had forced him to do battle for religious liberty and toleration: "The first settlers in this country were emigrants from England, of the English Church, just at a point of time when it was flushed with complete victory over the religions of all other persuasions. Possessed, as they became, of the powers of making, administering and executing the laws, they showed equal intolerance in this country with the Presbyterian brethren, who had emigrated to the northern government."[25]

The laws to enforce religious conformity and to punish dissident sects, such as the Quakers, were still on the statute books when Jefferson was writing, though largely nonenforced. His eloquent plea for religious freedom asserts that "our rulers can have authority over such natural rights only as we have submitted to them. The rights of conscience we never submitted, we could not submit. We are answerable for them to our God. . . . Reason and free inquiry are the only effectual agents against error. Give a loose to them, they will support the true religion, by bringing every false one to their tribunal, to the test of their investigation. They are the natural enemies of error, and of error only."[26]

The importance of an enlightened citizenry was emphasized by Jefferson in his discussion of proposed legislation for educational reforms, replying to the fourteenth query relating to "the administration of justice and description of the laws." The *Notes* describes at length the educational system Jefferson had proposed for Virginia. As summarized by him, "The ultimate result of the whole scheme of education would be the teaching all children of the State reading, writing, and common arithmetic; turning out ten annually of superior genius, well taught in Greek, Latin, geography, and the higher branches of arithmetic; turning out ten others annually, of still superior parts, who, to those branches of learning, shall have added such of the sciences as their genius shall have led them to; the furnishing to the wealthier part of the people convenient schools, at which their children may be educated, at their own expence."[27]

Jefferson's comments on international relationships, commerce, and war, included under the twenty-second query, form the real conclusion of the *Notes*. "It should be our endeavor," he advises, "to cultivate the peace and friendship of every nation, even of that which has injured us most, when we shall have carried our point against her." As an advocate of unrestricted trade, it is recommended that for America "our interest will be to throw open the doors of commerce, and to knock off all its shackles, giving perfect freedom to all persons for the vent of whatever they may choose to bring into our ports, and asking the same in their."[28] The case against war is eloquently stated by Jefferson: "Never was so much false arithmetic employed on any subject, as that which has been employed to persuade nations that it is to their interest to go to war. Were the money which it has cost, to gain, at the close of a long war, a little town, or a little territory, the right to cut wood here, or to catch fish there, expended in improving what they already possess, in making roads, opening rivers, building ports, improving the arts, and finding employment for their idle poor, it would render them much stronger, much wealthier and happier."[29]

Realistically, however, Jefferson recognized that the nation would occasionally become involved in war. Therefore, "All the wise can do, will be to avoid that half of them which would be produced by our own follies, and our own acts of injustice; and to make for the other half the best preparations we can."[30]

At the outset, Jefferson had intended merely to supply Marbois with factual answers to his twenty-three questions, but it is obvious that as he proceeded his enthusiasm carried him away and he went far afield, adding his views on politics, religion, science, education, and philosophy. William Peden, editor of a standard edition of the *Notes*, points out that Jefferson "attacks the assumption and usurpation of power by the rich, the powerful, and the well born; the tyranny of the church; the dogmas of the schoolmen; the bigotry of the man on horseback; the enslavement of man by man; the injustice of racial superiority."[31] The author's primary ideal always was the right of the individual to freedom and happiness under just laws.

The *Notes* also exhibits the amazing range of Jefferson's knowledge and interests. He felt at home in every scientific or technical field—law, medicine, chemistry, mathematics, agriculture, botany, zoology, geology, architecture, and political science—and he was equally at ease in the humanities: *belles lettres*, prosody and philology, classical languages and literature, ancient and modern history.

It had not been Jefferson's intention originally to publish the *Notes*. Manuscript copies were circulated among a number of close friends, and at their urging Jefferson had investigated the possibility of an American edition. Finding the cost prohibitive, he delayed the printing until he went to Paris. There *Notes on Virginia* was published anonymously, in 1785, at Jefferson's expense, in an edition of two hundred copies, meant strictly for private distribution. Shortly afterward, an inadequate French translation appeared (1787), authorized when Jefferson learned that an unscrupulous French bookseller was planning to publish a pirated translation. Finally persuaded that an authorized English edition for general distribution was necessary and desirable, Jefferson negotiated with a London publisher, John Stockdale. A corrected copy of the 1785 Paris edition of the *Notes* was forwarded to Stockdale, an excellent printer, who did his work quickly and efficiently. The English edition came off the press in the summer of 1787. The first American edition appeared the following year, in Philadelphia.

As could have been anticipated the controversial opinions and statements in various sections of the *Notes* aroused violent reactions. Jefferson's scientific theories collided with those of Buffon and other European naturalists. He was roundly attacked from the pulpits of reactionary federalist preachers as an enemy of Christianity because he had dared express some doubt about the story of the universal flood, specifically because he was unconvinced that the rocks on the tops of the Virginia mountains had been left there by receding waters. Later during the bitter political struggle that culminated in Jefferson's election to the presidency, his political enemies searched the *Notes* for ammunition to be used against him. Because of his interest in philosophy and science, he was tagged as a "howling atheist" and "confirmed infidel." His pleas for the common man were enough to condemn him as a traitor to his class. One passage after another of the *Notes* was taken out of context and perverted for partisan propaganda.

Jefferson and his reputation have of course survived all such assaults. Peden comments, "With the *Notes on Virginia* he produced one of America's first permanent and intellectual landmarks,"[32] and Chinard concurs by calling the *Notes* "one of the first masterpieces of American literature."[33] Historians of science generally agree in rating the *Notes* as one of the most influential scientific books ever written by an American.

4.

Terrestrial Paradise

WILLIAM BARTRAM'S *Travels Through North and South Carolina, Georgia, East and West Florida*

America's first two great botanists were father and son, John and William Bartram. John Bartram, a Pennsylvania Quaker born in 1699, was self-educated. Before he died in 1777, Linnaeus had called him "the greatest natural botanist in the world." Along with Benjamin Franklin, he was one of the founders of the American Philosophical Society, was a member of the Royal Societies of London and Stockholm, and carried on correspondence with the leading scientists of his time. His considerable scientific accomplishments included the introduction into England of such plants as the bush honeysuckle, fiery lilies, mountain laurel, dogtooth violet, wild asters, gentian, hemlock, red and white cedar, and sugar maple.

John Bartram traveled extensively in the American colonies. A trip into the Catskills in 1753 initiated his fourteen-year-old son William into botanical exploration. Bartram's long-held ambitions to travel in Virginia and the Carolinas were fulfilled in 1760 and again in 1761. In his writings, John Bartram always referred to the South as a "terrestrial paradise." The longest and most important journey of his career was undertaken in 1765, after he had been appointed "Botanist to the King," at a salary of fifty pounds a year. Taking William with him, he set out to explore eastern Florida and to travel up the St. Johns River. An account of the expedition was published in London in 1766 under the title *A Journal, Kept by John Bartram of Philadelphia, Botanist to His Majesty for the Floridas; Upon a Journey from St. Augustine up the River St. John's, as far as the Lakes.*

William Bartram was deeply influenced by his father's achievements, and the trip to Florida made a permanent impression upon him. As a youth he had displayed unusual talent for drawing natural objects. His father's friend, the English naturalist John Collinson, had shown examples of the drawings to Dr. John Fothergill, a botanist and a Quaker. At Fothergill's expense, William spent almost five years, 1773–77, exploring the southeastern region of the United States. In return, his patron was to receive curious seeds and plant specimens, drawings of birds, reptiles, insects, and plants, and journals. The story of these travels was not published until 1791, when there was issued in Philadelphia William Bartram's famous *Travels Through North and South Carolina, Georgia, East and West Florida, the Cherokee Country, the Extensive Territories of the Muscogulges, or Creek Confederacy, and the Country of the Chactaws; Containing an Account of the Soil and Natural Productions of Those Regions, Together with Observations on the Manners of the Indians, Embellished with Copper-Plates.*

The route followed by Bartram has been accurately traced, despite the disappearance or changes in names of places mentioned. He sailed from Philadelphia for Charleston, South Carolina, in April 1773; from there he took ship for Savannah, from which port he traveled by horseback through various parts of Georgia, described as "a level country, well watered by large streams . . . coursing from extensive swamps and marshes," crossing next "an uninhabited wilderness" of "high pine forests" and "dark and grassy savannas." The remainder of this season was spent "in botanical excursions to the low countries, between Carolina and East Florida." Bartram ascended the Altamaha River in a cypress canoe, and records his delight in the groves, meadows, forests, domestic herds, and other features of the country.

Part Two of the *Travels* covers Bartram's explorations of Florida, after eleven months spent in Georgia. He sailed from Fort Frederica, St. Simon Island, Georgia, and was put ashore near Amelia Island, Florida, where he bought "a neat little sailboat," and proceeded up

Frontispiece

Alico Chlucco the Long Warrior; or King of the Siminoles.

TRAVELS

THROUGH

NORTH AND SOUTH CAROLINA,

GEORGIA,

EAST AND WEST FLORIDA,

THE CHEROKEE COUNTRY,

THE EXTENSIVE TERRITORIES OF THE MUSCOGULGES

OR CREEK CONFEDERACY,

AND THE COUNTRY OF THE CHACTAWS.

CONTAINING

AN ACCOUNT OF THE SOIL AND NATURAL PRODUC-

TIONS OF THOSE REGIONS;

TOGETHER WITH

OBSERVATIONS ON THE MANNERS OF THE INDIANS.

EMBELLISHED WITH COPPER-PLATES.

By *WILLIAM BARTRAM.*

PHILADELPHIA: PRINTED BY JAMES AND JOHNSON. 1791.

LONDON:

REPRINTED FOR J. JOHNSON, IN ST. PAUL'S CHURCH-YARD.

1792.

[43] *Terrestrial Paradise*

the St. Johns River. Along the way, he admired the groves of live oaks, palms, magnolia, and orange trees. Adventures with alligators and a wild tropical storm enlivened the trip. The beauties of the landscape are described in glowing detail. At the conclusion of the expedition, Bartram returned to Charleston to plan future travels.

Part Three narrates even more extensive journeys: through the Cherokee territories and Choctaw country, through parts of Georgia and west Florida, into Alabama and Louisiana, along the Mississippi, and finally returning home by way of Charleston, Cape Fear in North Carolina, Alexandria, Virginia, and Maryland to Philadelphia, where he arrived in January 1778.

The fourth and final part of the *Travels* is in the nature of an appendix, entitled *An Account of the Persons, Manners, Customs and Government of the Muscogulges or Creeks, Cherokees, Chactaws, etc. Aborigines of the Continent of North America*—evidence of Bartram's avid interest in the Southern Indian tribes.

Bartram's descriptive powers are illustrated by his comments on the scenery along the St. Johns River in Florida: "It is very pleasing to observe the banks of the river ornamented with hanging garlands, composed of varieties of climbing vegetables, both shrubs and plants, forming perpendicular green walls, with projecting jambs, pilasters, and deep apartments, twenty or thirty feet high and completely covered . . . it is exceedingly curious to behold the Wild Squash climbing over the lofty limbs of the trees; their yellow fruit somewhat of the size and figure of a large orange, pendant from the extremities of the limbs over the water."[1]

Still more dramatic is Bartram's firsthand account of a tropical hurricane which struck while he was in the same area. The "terrific appearance" of "the approaching tempest . . . confounded me," he wrote; "how purple and fiery appeared the tumultuous clouds! swiftly ascending or darting from the horizon upwards; they seemed to oppose and dash against each other, the skies appeared streaked with blood or purple flame overhead, the flaming lightning streaming and darting about in every direction around, seems to fill the world with fire; whilst the heavy thunder keeps the earth in a constant tremor."[2] When the torrential rain began, it "came down with such rapidity and fell in such quantities, that every object was totally obscured, excepting the continual streams or rivers of lightning, pouring from the clouds; all seemed a frightful chaos."[3] The devastation was tremendous—trees blown down, nearby plantation houses razed to the ground, and valuable crops destroyed.

Other graphically described incidents in Bartram's *Travels* concern his encounters with alligators, which he sometimes refers to as "crocodiles." Ten pages are devoted to "that horrid animal." Early in his Florida stay, while camping one night on a lagoon, he observed "the subtle, greedy alligator" fishing for trout. "Behold him rushing forth from the flags and reeds," Bartram writes. "His enormous body swells. His plaited tail brandished high, floats upon the lake. The waters like a cataract descend from his open jaws. Clouds of smoke issue from his dilated nostrils. The earth trembles with his thunder. When immediately from the opposite coast of the lagoon, emerges from the deep his rival champion. They suddenly dart upon each other. The boiling surface of the lake marks their rapid course, and a terrific conflict commences."[4] Bartram himself was in imminent peril, on several occasions, from the giant reptiles. While fishing, his canoe was "attacked from all sides. . . . Two very large ones attacked me closely, at the same instant, rushing up with their heads and part of their bodies above the water, roaring terribly and belching floods of water over me. They struck their jaws together so close to my ears, as almost to stun me, and I expected every moment to be dragged out of the boat and instantly devoured."[5] Bartram went on to remark that "the alligator when full grown is a very large and terrible creature, and of prodigious strength, activity and swiftness in the water."[6]

Other land and water reptiles also engage much of Bartram's attention. He calls the coachwhip snake "a beautiful creature" and the water moccasin "a large and horrid serpent," the green and ribbon snakes "beautiful innocent creatures," and the bull snake "large and inoffensive with respect to mankind" uttering "a terrible loud hissing noise, sounding very hollow and like distant thunder." Bartram's philosophy toward wildlife was live-and-let-live. He describes with some pride that he saved the life of a "formidable" rattlesnake which had allowed him and his companions "to pass many times by him during the night, without injuring us in the least."[7]

Bartram's descriptions of common wild animals are mainly

factual. The bears of the region he explored "are a strong creature, and prey on the fruits of the country, and will likewise devour young calves, swine and sheep," although he heard of no instance of their attacking man. The wolves of Florida "are larger than a dog," but not as large as the Canadian and Pennsylvania wolves; the howls of wolf packs are "terrifying to the wandering bewildered traveler." Of another member of the canine family, he wrote, "The foxes of Carolina and Florida are of the smaller red species." Bartram also mentions the wildcat or lynx, "a fierce and bold little animal," and reports that "tygers" (actually panthers) were numerous in the region that he explored, a "very strong, mischievous animal" that preys on calves, young colts, etc. Among other animals appearing in the *Travels* are deer and elk, squirrels, raccoons, opossums, rabbits, moles, gophers, the "great land tortoise," rats, mice, weasels, polecats, and bats.

Insects are ever present in Bartram's landscape. The swarms of mosquitoes and an "incredible number" of "burning" or biting flies torment men and animals. Another innumerable insect is grasshoppers, "the favorite delicious food" of ricebirds. The rich colors of a multitude of different species of butterflies delight Bartram. He is most entranced, however, by "the small flying insects, of the genus termed by naturalists Ephemera," and devotes three pages to describing their birth, brief life span, and death. "At evening," he writes, "they are seen in clouds of innumerable millions, swarming and wantoning in the still air, gradually drawing near the river, descend upon its surface, and there quickly end their day, after committing their eggs to the deep." Bartram is amazed to observe "these beautiful and delicately formed little creatures . . . whose frame and organization is equally wonderful, more delicate, and perhaps as complicated as that of the most perfect human being."[8]

Much of Bartram's travel is by water. It is only natural, therefore, to find his observations frequently concerned with the ocean, numerous rivers, lakes, creeks, lagoons, pools, fountains, springs, and geysers. The bodies of water described swarm with animal life and are covered with vegetation. In the multiplicity of life forms are the manatee, many species of tortoise or turtle, otters, watersnakes, frogs, beavers, and of course all kinds of fish. Fishes were of special interest to Bartram, and he found that they abounded along the coasts and in sounds and inlets. He notes also that "the bays and lagoons are stored with oysters and varieties of other shell-fish, crabs, shrimp, &c." The immense quantity of fish may be judged by those observed in the St. Johns River, where "from shore to shore, and perhaps near half a mile above and below me, appeared to be one solid bank of fish, of various kinds, pushing through this narrow pass of St. Juans into the little lake, on their return down the river."[9] The fish were met by the "devouring alligators," which were attracted "in such incredible numbers, and so close together from shore to shore, that it would have been easy to have walked across on their heads, had the animals been harmless."[10]

The air and its inhabitants were also important elements in Bartram's biosphere. He was a notable ornithologist and his list of American birds, included in the *Travels*, is the most complete until publication of Alexander Wilson's *American Ornithologist* (1808–14). The Bartram list contains 215 different species of birds.[11] Among those specifically described are the crying bird, wood pelican, turkey buzzard, wild turkey-cock, savanna crane, snakebird (a cormorant), fishing hawk, jays, butcher-bird, ricebird, cedarbird, catbird, and mockingbird. Wild pigeons by the millions were seen, migrating and roosting on low trees, bushes, and in the interior parts of vast swamps. Wagonloads of the pigeons were captured by the natives, using the blaze of pine torches at night to blind the birds.

As a botanist, primarily, Bartram found the plant life of the subtropical region of absorbing interest. Among the trees, magnolias fascinated him and he devotes pages to describing different varieties. Another favorite was the red or loblolly bay, "Gordonia lasianthus," tall, with "thick foliage, of a dark green colour, flowered over with large, milk-white fragrant blossoms." Special attention was paid to uncommon species of trees with which he was previously familiar and to tropical and semitropical trees. He especially admired cypress, live oak, and palm trees. His biographer, N. B. Fagin, comments, "A complete list of all the trees Bartram describes would fill a fair-sized botanical dictionary."[12]

Even more numerous than trees in Bartram's landscape are shrubs, flowers, and other such plants. Here again the emphasis is on tropical plants or uncommon species of semitropical and temperate plants.

Not least interesting among Bartram's observations are those which relate to people—the many planters, traders, and aborigines encountered in the course of his travels. Everywhere he met with friendliness and hospitality. Typical of the reception he generally received was a visit to a tribe of Seminole Indians, normally hostile to the white traders who came among them. When the chief was informed of the nature of Bartram's work, "he received me with complaisance, giving me unlimited permission to travel over the country for the purpose of collecting flowers, medicinal plants, etc., saluting me by the name of the Flower hunter, recommending me to the friendship and protection of his people."[13] Bartram made his knowledge of medicine freely available to the aborigines, and on one occasion won their gratitude by killing a huge rattlesnake that was terrorizing a village.

Bartram's friendly feeling for the Indians is revealed throughout his narrative. He traveled and lived among them, studied their languages and customs, and became acquainted with different tribes and individuals. He was inclined to deplore the effect of civilization on the Indian. The concerns of the aborigine, he noted, closely paralleled those of the white man: to love, reproduce, care for their young, build homes, protect their persons and property, protect the aged, and to worship a Great Spirit. A telling comparison is made by Bartram between Indian "savagery" and white civilization:

The Indians make war against, kill and destroy their own species, and their motives spring from the same erroneous source as it does in all other nations of mankind; that is, the ambition of exhibiting to their fellows, a superior character of personal and national valour, and thereby immortalize themselves, by transmitting their names with honour and lustre to posterity; or in revenge of their enemy, for public or personal insults; or lastly, to extend the borders and boundaries of their territories; but I cannot find upon the strictest enquiry, that their bloody contests, at this day are marked with deeper stains of inhumanity or savage cruelty, than what may be observed amongst the most civilized nations; they do indeed scalp their slain enemy, but they do not kill the females or children of either sex.[14]

The physical characteristics of the Indians encountered are described in detail by Bartram. He observed that the males of the Cherokees, Creeks, and related tribes were "tall, erect, and moderately robust, their limbs well shaped, so as generally to form a perfect human figure; their features regular, and countenance open, dignified and placid." Their complexion was "reddish brown or copper colour; their hair long, lank, coarse and black as a raven."[15] As for the Cherokee women, they "are tall, slender, erect and of a delicate frame, their features formed with perfect symmetry, their countenance cheerful and friendly, and they move with a becoming grace and dignity."[16] The Muscogulge women were surprisingly small, the majority of them less than five feet tall. That they were daughters of Eve was revealed by their eyes: "large, black and languishing, expressive of modesty, diffidence, and bashfulness; these charms are their defensive and offensive weapons, and they know very well how to play them off. And under cover of these alluring graces, are concealed the most subtle artifice; they are however loving and affectionate."[17]

The presence of people, especially the whites, inevitably led to a damaged natural environment. Long before the advent of vast cotton and tobacco plantations, Bartram witnessed destruction caused by wasteful agricultural practices. He deplored the devastation of natural beauties that followed the white man's progress. Over two hundred years ago, Bartram expressed an increasingly popular twentieth century view that man should use his environment wisely and never abuse or destroy it. About fifteen years previously, he and his father had visited "a magnificent Indian mound" overlooking Lake George in Florida. At the time, "there were no settlements of white people, but all appeared wild and savage, yet in that uncultivated state, it possessed an almost inexpressible air of grandeur."

On the occasion of the second visit, all was changed. A large orange grove, live oaks, palms, and magnolias, "a noble Indian highway," and other extraordinarily scenic features had been cleared away to make room for cultivation. Indigo, corn, and cotton were planted, but then the land had been almost totally abandoned. As described by Bartram, "it appeared like a desert, to a great extent, and terminated, on the land side, by frightful thickets, and open pine forests."[18]

Elsewhere Bartram writes, "I have often been affected with extreme regret, at beholding the destruction and devastation which has been committed, or indiscreetly exercised on extensive, fruitful orange groves, on the banks of St. Juan, by the new planters under the British government, some hundred acres of which, at a single plantation, has been entirely destroyed to make room for the Indigo, Cotton, Corn, Batatas, etc. . . . Some plantations have not a single tree standing, and where any have been left, it is only a small coppice or clump, nakedly exposed and destitute."[19]

The paths of the great early naturalists, such as Bartram, were far from smooth, though the hazards and hardships of travel were not stressed by Bartram in his *Travels*. Settlements were few except along the coast and for a short distance inland along the rivers. Roads connecting the remote settlements were exceedingly primitive, often no more than mere trails. Camping equipment was limited to what could be carried on horseback, strapped in front of or behind the saddle. Mosquito netting and insect repellants had not yet been invented. Unfriendly Indians and renegades added to the dangers of travel. Another everpresent threat was disease such as malaria and yellow fever. Bartram describes several periods of severe illness in the course of his journey, and in the light of his subsequent career it appears that his health was to some extent permanently affected.

Within a few years after publication, Bartram's *Travels* became immensely popular in Europe. Two editions were issued in England (1782 and 1794), one in Ireland (1793), one in Germany (1793), one in Holland (1797), and one in France (1799). The literary influence of the work was extensive. Chateaubriand, Coleridge, Carlyle, Shelley, Tennyson, Southey, and Wordsworth abroad, and Emerson and Thoreau at home were among numerous writers who came under Bartram's spell. The concept of the "noble savage" was derived to an important degree from Bartram's idealistic picture of the American aborigines. A perceptive comment comes from a historian of science, J. M. Edelstein: "In an age of strong scientific curiosity and romantic interest in the far-off and the exotic, it was natural that William Bartram's book should make a deep impression and become an important influence on literature. Nature, landscape, travel, Indians—all the elements of popular interest—are in Bartram."[20]

5.

History Versus Legend

MASON LOCKE WEEMS'S *The Life*
of Washington the Great

American history, despite its relatively brief span, is filled with
myths which debunking historians regularly expose, only to have
them persist and endure, regardless of truth. None is more lasting
than the legends created by the Reverend Mason Locke "Parson"
Weems.

After a fashion, Weems is a throwback to ancient tradition.
The separation of folklore from history is one of the historian's
major tasks, and has been since ancient times. Herodotus, who
lived from about 484 to 425 B.C., is often referred to as the "Father
of History." He is also not infrequently called the "Father of Liars."
From the beginning, therefore, such history as was preserved and
later written down was simply oral transmissions. If the itinerent
singing bards exercised a certain amount of imagination and added
dramatic touches to their stories—and they unquestionably did—it
was entirely legitimate in the eyes of their audience. This is a
perfect description of Weems's approach to history.

Parson Weems has been described as a fiddling parson, an
itinerant bookseller, a sentimentalist, a corrupter of history, and an
incorrigible liar. But historian Paul Leicester Ford observed, "No
man whose writings have passed through some two hundred edi-

tions, or of whose productions some two hundred and fifty thousand [a more recent estimate is in excess of one million] copies have sold, deserves complete forgetfulness. . . . No history of the American people or their literature can be complete without noticing the man and his work."[1] Weems's writings, directed primarily at the uneducated and the young, were destined to have a permanent impact on American history.

Weems was born in 1759 at Herring Creek on the family homestead, located on the western shore of Chesapeake Bay. He was the youngest of nineteen children, offspring of a Scotsman, David Weems, said to have been the son of the Earl of Weemyss. Little is known of Mason Locke Weems's early career. He studied medicine at Edinburgh, but apparently practiced little. From Edinburgh, he went on to London to study divinity; in 1784, he was ordained a priest in the Church of England. By special dispensation, he was ordained by the bishop of London without being required to take an oath of allegiance to the king. A letter to Weems from Benjamin Franklin prophesied that a hundred years later it would be a matter of wonder that an American should be obliged to make a journey of six thousand miles to get the permission of a cross old gentleman at Canterbury before he could preach to his neighbors.

From 1784 to 1789, Weems was rector of Pohick Church, which George Washington attended, seven miles from Mount Vernon. Within eight years he gave up the ministry as a regular profession for the more irregular livelihood of bookseller and writer. For thirty years, Weems sold books for the famous Philadelphia book publisher, Matthew Carey, and for C. P. Wayne, publisher of John Marshall's *Life of George Washington*. He had no permanent clerical connections after about 1793. At the age of thirty-five, he married a colonel's daughter, considerably younger than himself, and the couple proceeded to produce ten children.

The book world provided a perfect vocation for Weems. After launching himself upon a lifetime career as promoter, seller, and author of books and pamphlets, he wandered over the Southern states preaching, fiddling, and selling books, mainly following the Eastern Seaboard from New York City to Savannah. His first publishing venture was reprinting a series of inspirational and self-

G. WASHINGTON.

THE LIFE

OF

GEORGE WASHINGTON;

WITH

CURIOUS ANECDOTES,

EQUALLY HONOURABLE TO HIMSELF,

AND

EXEMPLARY TO HIS YOUNG COUNTRYMEN.

A life how useful to his country led!
How loved! while living!—how revered! now dead!
Lisp! lisp! his name, ye children yet unborn!
And with like deeds your own great names adorn.

EMBELLISHED WITH SIX ENGRAVINGS.

BY M. L. WEEMS,

'FORMERLY RECTOR OF MOUNT VERNON PARISH.

The author has treated this great subject with admirable " success
in a new way. He turns all the actions of Washington, to the encouragement of virtue, by a careful application of numerous exempli-
fications drawn from the conduct of the founder of our republic from
his earliest life."

H. LEE, *Major-General, Army U. S.*

PHILADELPHIA:
PUBLISHED BY JOSEPH ALLEN,
AND SOLD BY LIPPINCOTT, GRAMBO & CO.,
No. 14 NORTH FOURTH STREET.

improving works by Robert Russel, Hugh Blair, Hannah More, Henry Brooke, and others. As Carey's representative, he peddled weighty works by Oliver Goldsmith, Marshall's five-volume Washington biography (the first four volumes of which managed the feat of scarcely mentioning Washington), prayerbooks, Carey's edition of the Bible, and other general and Biblical literature. Weems had a passionate faith in the value of "good books." He believed that by circulating such books he was still doing God's work as truly as though preaching from the pulpit and actually was reaching a wider mission field. In a letter to Carey in 1796, he wrote: "This country is large, and numerous are its inhabitants; to cultivate among these a taste for reading, and by the reflection of proper books to throw far and wide the rays of useful arts and sciences, were at once the work of a true philanthropist and prudent speculator. For I am verily assured that under proper culture, every dollar that you shall scatter on the field of this experiment will yield 30, 60 and 100 fold."[2]

A Weems biographer, Emily Ellsworth Ford Skeel, holds that Weems "may rightly be called the first of American book agents." She adds that he was "apt at gauging his market, prompt in changing his appeal, tireless on the road and enjoying its adventures; above all adaptive to every sort and condition of man, meeting with equal ease the crude, phlegmatic Pennsylvania-Dutch farmer and the boisterous, hard-drinking southern husbandman, the high-class city merchant and the aristocratic gentleman-planter, the dicing, brutal pot-house crew and the successful politician of many capitals." His talent for advertising was superb; Weems perhaps deserves to be called the father of the modern publisher's blurb. Mrs. Skeel notes also that Weems "chased the dollar, which was scarcer in those days than ours, with a violent vehemence which appears to us primitive."[3] His business sense is attested by a letter to Carey, dated 5 June 1809: "God knows there is nothing I so dread as *Dead stock, dull sales*, back *loads*, and *blank looks*. But the Joy of my soul is quick & clean sales—Heavy pockets, and light hearts."[4]

Lawrence C. Wroth's *Parson Weems* comments, "For thirty years there was no more familiar figure on the roads of the Southern States than this book peddler and author who, provided gipsy-like with horse and wagon, his wares and his fiddle, traveled his long route year after year, sleeping in wayside inn, farmhouse or forest, fiddling, writing, selling books, living in the open and learning some new road lore, field lore, or wisdom of the woods with each day that passed."[5] Whenever news reached him of a fair, a revival meeting, or other gathering of people, Weems would proceed thence, with his saddlebags full of books, prepared to preach, play the violin, or make sales, according to circumstances.

Works edited by or printed for Weems (before he became involved in authorship himself on a large scale), and which he added to his selling stock, carried such colorful and alluring titles as *Sure and Certain Methods of Attaining a Long and Healthy Life*; *An Estimate of the Religion of the Fashionable World*; *The History of Louisa, the Lovely Orphan*; *The History of a Reprobate*; *The American Farmer's Guide*; *The Death of Abel*; *The Immortal Mentor: Or Man's Unerring Guide to a Healthy, Wealthy, and Happy Life*; and *An Account of the Pelew Islands*. At Weems's urging, Carey printed Thomas Paine's *Age of Reason*. Weems was too sharp a bookseller not to realize the sales possibilities in Paine's controversial work, though he did not want his own name too closely linked to it.

As early as 1797, Weems wrote Carey that cheap books on Revolutionary heroes would sell; his list, which did not include the name of Washington among possible subjects, was merely suggestive. According to Weems:

Experience has taught me that small, i.e. quarter of dollar books, on subjects calculated to *strike* the Popular Curiosity, printed in very large numbers and properly *distributed*, would prove an immense revenue to the prudent and industrious Undertakers. If you could get the life of Generals Wayne, Putnam, Green, &c., Men whose courage and Abilities, whose Patriotism and Exploits have won the love and admiration of the American people, printed in small volumes and with very interesting frontispieces, you would, without doubt, sell an immense number of them. People here think nothing of giving 1/6 (their quarter of a dollar) for anything that pleases their fancy. Let us give them something worth their money.[6]

Two years later, Weems repeated his recommendation that cheap books would be a sound business venture. Early nineteenth-century American publishers were inclined to print expensive books exclusively. From his firsthand contacts with the potential market, Weems argued throughout his career for cheaper books and a larger volume of sales.

Weems was not satisfied merely to sell other men's books. He himself had an intense desire to write, in good part no doubt for mercenary rather than patriotic motives, because of the commercial possibilities he saw in popular books. There is evidence that early in 1799 he had begun work on a biography of Washington and in June of that year he announced that his work was almost completed. In a letter dated 24 June, Weems reported: "I have nearly ready for the press a piece christened, or to be christened, 'The Beauties of Washington,' tis artfully drawn up, enlivened with anecdotes." In the author's "humble opinion," the work was "marvellously fitted" to catch the public fancy.[7]

Three months later and two months before Washington's death, on 21 October, Weems again wrote that "a piece that will sell to admiration," tentatively titled *The True Patriot or Beauties of Washington*, was practically finished. Then, less than a month after Washington died, in December 1799, Weems informed Carey that his manuscript was ready for publication, and he wanted to rush it into print while the moment was favorable. The general scheme of the book is described (with spelling, punctuation, and capitalization modernized):

Washington, you know is gone! Millions are gaping to read something about him. I am very nearly primed and cocked for 'em. . . . I give his history, sufficiently minute—I accompany him from his start, through the French and Indian and British or Revolutionary wars, to the President's chair, to the throne in the hearts of 5,000,000 of people. I then go on to show that the unparalled rise and elevation were owing to his great virtues, his veneration for the Deity or religious principles, his patriotism, his magnaminity, his industry, his temperance and sobriety, his justice, etc. Thus I hold up his great virtues to the imitation of youth. All this I have lined and enlivened with anecdotes apropos interesting and entertaining.[8]

Neither the hardheaded publisher nor the exuberant author could possibly have foreseen the success of the Washington biography nor its permanent effect on the nation's view of its first president. Since its first appearance in 1800, the book has been issued in at least eighty-four editions, including French and German translations. The first two editions of the work were anonymous, though the second was "Printed for the Rev. M. L. Weems." Subsequent editions carried Weems's name as author.

The Skeel bibliography of Weems's writings, 418 pages in length, traces nine printings of the Washington life up to 1806, produced in various places and by various presses. The first edition was entitled *The Life and Memorable Actions of George Washington, General and Commander of the Armies of America*. As edition followed edition, the title grew in grandiloquence. With the tenth printing, labeled the "Fifth Edition," 1806, in many respects the definitive one, the text had doubled in size and the book had become *The Life of Washington the Great, Enriched with a Number of Very Curious Anecdotes, Perfectly in Character, and Equally Honorable to Himself, and Exemplary to His Young Countrymen*, etc. The price was increased from twenty-five to fifty cents. Only three copies of this important edition are known to survive.

Most of the famous stories of Washington's youth, including the cherry tree episode, first appeared in the 1806 edition. The legend of the cherry tree, one of the best known in American history, has played an instrumental part in fixing the character and image of the "Father of His Country" in the popular mind. The original text reads:

When George was about six years old, he was made the wealthy master of a hatchet! of which, like most little boys, he was immoderately fond, and was constantly going about chopping every thing that came in his way. One day, in the garden, where he often amused himself hacking his mother's pea-sticks, he unluckily tried the edge of his hatchet on the body of a beautiful young English cherry tree, which he barked so terribly that I don't believe the tree ever got the better of it. The next morning the old gentleman finding out what had befallen his tree, which, by the by, was a great favorite, came into the house, and with much warmth asked for the mischievous author, declaring at the same time, that he would not have taken five guineas for his tree. No body could tell him any thing about it. Presently George and his hatchet made their appearance. "George", said his father, "do you know who killed that beautiful little cherry tree yonder in the garden?" This was a tough question, and George staggered under it for a moment; but quickly recovered himself; and looking at his father, with the sweet face of youth brightened with the inexpressible charm of all-conquering truth, he bravely cried out, "I can't tell a lie, Pa; you know I can't tell a lie. I did cut it with my hatchet."—"Run to my arms you dearest boy," cried his father in transports, "run to my arms, glad am I, George, that you ever killed my tree, for you have paid me for it a thousand fold. Such an act of heroism in my son, is more worth than a thousand trees, though blossomed with silver, and their fruits of purest gold."

Thus George escaped a whipping, a celebrated myth was created, and the process of deification of our first president began. The later inclusion of the cherry tree yarn in the McGuffey Readers increased its circulation by tens of millions of copies. Close behind the story of the sad fate of the cherry tree in popular esteem came the anecdotes about the cabbage seed (to demonstrate the omnipotence of the Almighty), the heavily laden apple trees (to teach a lesson of unselfishness), and Mary Washington's dream in which she saw her little son George at the age of five extinguish a raging fire about to destroy the family home. To illustrate the belief that Washington bore a charmed life and was destined by fate for greater eminence, there is the story of the Indian warrior, told after General Braddock's disastrous defeat: "A famous Indian warrior, who acted a leading part in that bloody tragedy, was often heard to swear, that 'Washington was not born to be killed by a bullet! For,' continued he, 'I had seventeen fair fires at him with my rifle, and after all could not bring him to the ground!'"

There is little evidence to support these and similar anecdotes in Weems's account. Indeed, research has revealed that several of the stories have a base in earlier Southern traditions and were simply lifted by Weems for the purpose of moral instruction and to glorify his hero.

But Weems has his defenders. The American literary historian Jay Hubbell observes:

So much has been written about Weems' historical inaccuracies—which are numerous enough—that his literary powers have been somewhat underrated. He had as his letters show, an eye for a telling phrase. There is a crude poetic and dramatic power in his descriptive passages; and the speeches which, like the epic poets and the ancient historians, he put into the mouths of his heroes are not lacking in eloquence. His widely read biography helped to perpetuate among the masses down to our own time his conception of Washington. He did his part to create a semilegendary national hero whose name and fame would help hold together a union of diverse regions.[9]

When Weems wrote his life of Washington, the United States as a nation was only twenty-four years away from the Declaration of Independence. Democracy still had to prove its staying power and numerous skeptics doubted that it would or could survive. Threats of secession were in the air and the federal government rested on shaky foundations. What Weems did, asserts David D. Van Tassel, "was to make national symbols of his subjects, legendary giants of republican virtue and bravery for a hero-starved people, heroes of recent history for a people cut off by their own volition from their heroes of legend."[10]

And who knows? Perhaps there is a grain of truth in Weems's cherry tree story. In an essay "George Washington and Parson Weems," Robert W. McLaughlin reported that a pottery mug, belonging to the eighteenth century, had been discovered in Germany. On it is an inscription, "G.W. 1776." McLaughlin adds, "Also there is a figure with the uniform and cockade hat of an officer of the Continental army. And in the forefront is a hacked cherry tree. The presumption is that the story of the cherry tree was carried back to Germany by a Hessian, and given pictorial representation on a mug of German manufacture."[11] If true, Parson Weems did not invent the story when he wrote his life of Washington. Instead, he used a piece of prevailing folklore about the great hero. An illustration in color of the German pottery mug appears as a frontispiece in the second volume of the Skeel biography.

Washington's "Farewell Address" and "Washington's Will" conclude the life, except for several chapters eulogizing Washington's character. As a whole, Weems portrays his subject as a precocious boy, a priggish youth, a devout, solemn and sanctimonious man. He is shown as athletic, courageous, a paragon of industry, and a shrewd businessman. Among phases of his career neglected, or passed over lightly, are Washington's love of sports, especially hunting, military campaigns, and his two terms as first president of the United States.

The first edition of Weems's biography contains a portrait of Washington, but it was not until the 1809 edition that other illustrations began to be included. Starting with the 1810 edition, seven historical engravings "embellished" the book. They represent the "Defeat of General Braddock," "Battle of Lexington," the "Battle of Bunker's Hill," the "Death of General Montgomery," the "Capture of Major André," the "Surrender of Lord Cornwallis," and a portrait of Washington obviously after Stuart.[12]

An example of Weems's purple prose is his account of Washington's death:

With the resignation of a soldier he behaved like a Christian: "I am dying," he said to his physicians, "but I am not afraid." They sat around his bedside as he lay panting for breath; then they went out and the great man, feeling that the silver cord was loosing, closed his eyes for the last time with his own hands and fell asleep.

Swift on angels' wings the brightening saint ascended while voices more than human warbled and hymned the procession toward the heavenly gate, from which myriads of angels hastened forth with golden harps. High in front was seen the beauteous form of Franklin, his cheeks of celestial rosy red; his robe, like a morning cloud, streaked with gold; a heavenly star glittering on his forehead. Angels poured around in transports of unutterable tenderness to meet their Washington and embraced him while tears of joy, such as only angels weep, rolled down their rosy cheeks.

Weems was the first to recognize the avid public interest in the colonial and Revolutionary War heroes. Having discovered the gold mine with his biography of Washington, he proceeded to exploit it further with *The Life of General Francis Marion*, *The Life of Doctor Benjamin Franklin* (based mainly on Franklin's *Autobiography*), and *The Life of William Penn, the Settler of Pennsylvania*. None was as popular as the Washington work, but all went through numerous editions. The biography of Marion rivals Washington's in color and imagination. The others are less flamboyant and of lesser interest.

Weems's prolific pen was busy also in producing a series of moralizing tracts: *God's Revenge against Murder*, *God's Revenge against Gambling*, *The Drunkard's Looking Glass*, *God's Revenge against Adultery*, *God's Revenge against Duelling*, and *The Bad Wife's Looking Glass; or God's Revenge against Cruelty to Husbands*. A political sermon, *The Philanthropist; or a Good Twenty-five Cents Worth of Political Love Power* (1799), was endorsed in a letter from George Washington. All had large sales.

Abraham Lincoln, who borrowed a copy of Weems's *Washington* when he was a boy, stated to one of Weems's sons that as a lad it had been his favorite book. Another early admirer was a leading Southern author, William Gilmore Simms, who wrote:

If we deny to Weems the merit of the historian, we cannot deny that he was a man of genius. His books have had a vast circulation, have exercised a wondrous influence over the young minds of the country, have moulded many of our noblest characters. His racy and excellent frankness, his orientalisms, his fluency, the fervency of occasional passages, the spirit of the dialogues,—the cleverness with which he would make his persons swear and swagger, and rebuke them for it,—the pleasing diversity of his pictures,—the great knowledge of life which they present, and the proper morality which elevated all that he wrote—have united to exercise a greater spell over young America, in past days, than almost any collection of writings within our experience. His style was a possession of his own.[13]

James S. Purcell, in an article entitled "A Book Pedlar's Progress in North Carolina," testifies on Weems's effect on a single Southern state: "Because of his manifold activities Parson Weems had an inestimable influence upon the cultural life of North Carolina in the first quarter of the nineteenth century. His bookselling was perhaps the most telling feature. In this respect his zeal was unbounded; even his preaching was subordinate to it. . . . His enthusiasm must have lured many a laggard to literacy and his wit persuaded many a purchaser. His appeal was to all classes—from those to whom he sold the expensive calfskin-bound Marshall's *Washington* to the half-educated rank and file at whom he aimed his own sketch of Washington."[14]

The reasons for the popularity of Weems's writings are easily apparent. They were aimed at the young and uncultured, the relatively unlettered farmers, pioneers, and backwoodsmen of the new country. The books made easy, exciting reading, they were cheap, and they appealed to the people's patriotic instincts. A recent Weems critic and biographer, Marcus Cunliffe, offers convincing explanations for the parson's immense following:

American nationalism was a self-conscious creation, and George Washington was its chief symbol. Traveling widely and continuously, Weems discovered by experiment what Americans wanted to read. They were religiously minded, so they would buy Bibles, sermons, tracts. They were eager for color and excitement, so they would buy novels by the cartload. They were, when stimulated, ferociously patriotic, so they would buy works that ministered to their national pride. What better literary fare than the Weemsian biographies, which satisfied all their wants—religion (or religiosity), romanticism, patriotism—simultaneously? They were stirred by his would-be epic strain, edified by his preachments, tickled by his knockabout fare.[15]

Did it really matter that Weems exercised literary license in creating episodes, dialogue, and fictitious situations? Cunliffe suggests that Weems "despite himself may have conveyed valuable truths about George Washington and about the United States. Far from being ruined by his tales, we decide that American history would be thinner without them." Another historian, Michael Kraus, concluded, "It might not be too much to say that generations of historical scholars since his time have been unable to modify seriously the popular picture Weems created of our Revolutionary heroes."[16]

"How then," asks another historian, John K. Bettersworth, "can the historian contend against the lore of the folk? Perhaps he shouldn't. . . . Perhaps the real key to the persistence of folklore is that lore is always better than truth. It is history, not as it was, but as we wish it had been. Folklore cannot settle for less than being a *good* story. And the trouble with history is that real history so often turns out to be the sad tale of man's falling short; thus history becomes the cemetery in which man's failures are buried along with him, which may explain why history has the reputation of putting people to sleep. As for lore, it generously gives the race 'A' for effort. All that is wrong with folklore is that man's aspirations got ahead of the facts, which," Bettersworth somewhat inelegantly concludes, "is a damn sight better than never having had any aspirations at all."[17]

6.

Folk Hero

A Narrative of the Life of David Crockett of the State of Tennessee

One of his biographers, Walter Blair, argues that there are six Davy Crocketts, ranging from the historically authentic hunter in the Tennessee canebrakes, congressman, and hero of the Alamo to the fantastic, mythical demigod, hero of innumerable tall tales.[1] In the lore of the folk, it is the legendary giant, performer of superhuman feats, who endures in the popular imagination. Even before his death at the Alamo in 1836, the Crockett legend was already building, and succeeding generations have steadily added fact and fiction—principally the latter.

The Beards, in *The Rise of American Civilization*, assert that Crockett's "autobiography is one of the prime human documents for the American epic yet to be written."[2] A Crockett biographer, James A. Shackford, agrees and offers several specific justifications for his judgment:

A Narrative of the Life of David Crockett is an important document in three major areas of American culture. As a literary work, it is one of the earliest autobiographies to be published, only a decade and a half after the virtually complete version of the first of all, Benjamin Franklin's. Another American success story, it belongs in the long series of autobiographies telling similar stories. . . . It is also a very early extended example of American humor, the first of the Southwest variety. . . . It is, furthermore, a document of importance in the history of American English, being replete with dialectal usages, proverbial expressions, and spellings representing non-standard pronunciations. . . . Crockett's *Narrative* is, finally, a historical document.[3]

Still another critic, Vernon L. Parrington, in his *Main Currents in American Thought*, rates the *Narrative* as "the great classic of the Southern frontier," more significant, human, and vital than Longstreet's contemporary *Georgia Scenes*. "In its backwoods vernacular," Parrington maintains, "it purveys the authentic atmosphere of the cabin and the canebrake; it exhibits the honesty, the wit, the resourcefulness, the manly independence of a coonskin hero; it reveals, in short, under the rough exterior of a shiftless squatter and bear-hunter, qualities that are sterling in every society where manhood is held in repute."[4] Elsewhere, however, Parrington concedes that "it is a man's tale, unenriched by the emotional experiences of a woman, and as such it tells only half the story of the frontier."[5]

According to Crockett's own account, he was born in 1786, the son of an Irish father who had drifted from Pennsylvania to North Carolina and from there to Tennessee; in fact, he continued to drift farther along the frontier all through Davy's childhood. The father had fought in the battle of King's Mountain and later in campaigns against the Indians. David's grandfather and grandmother had been murdered in their cabin by the Creeks. His parents had moved, probably from Lincoln County, North Carolina, to Hawkins County, Tennessee, about three years before Davy was born, later settling on the Holston River in northeastern Tennessee, where the father kept a tavern. Davy was the fifth of six boys, none of the rest of whom was ever heard from.

The Crockett family lived on the high road from the West over the Cumberlands to Baltimore. Drovers and wagoners frequently passed by with herds of cattle or loads of wheat and flour. One of the drovers hired Davy, then about twelve years old, from his father for six dollars to help drive four hundred cattle to the sea. After a variety of adventures, he returned home and was sent to school. This period of his education ended after three days when, following a fight with another "much larger and older" boy, he decided not to return home, fearing a beating from his father. Davy was gone for nearly three years, roaming through Maryland, Vir-

A

NARRATIVE

OF THE

LIFE OF DAVID CROCKETT,

OF THE STATE OF TENNESSEE.

I leave this rule for others when I'm dead,
Be always sure you're right—THEN GO AHEAD !
THE AUTHOR.

WRITTEN BY HIMSELF.

SEVENTH EDITION.

PHILADELPHIA.
E. L. CAREY AND A. HART.
BALTIMORE:
CAREY, HART & CO.

1834.

ginia, and Tennessee, and serving as an itinerant worker for one employer after another, usually being cheated out of his fair wages. His wanderings finally brought him back home, where his family scarcely recognized their prodigal son in the stalwart youth who had "attained so advanced an age, the age of fifteen . . . without knowing the first letter of the book."[6]

Davy's improvident father was careless about incurring debts and signing promissory notes. Davy showed family loyalty by putting in six months of arduous labor working off a paternal debt of thirty-six dollars due a neighbor. A forty-dollar note, held by John Kennedy, a Quaker, required another six months of toil, during which Davy fell in love with Kennedy's niece. That romance terminated when she married another. The disappointed Crockett decided that all of his troubles, especially his lack of appeal to the fair sex, were due to his want of "learning." So Davy started going to school four days a week and working the other two to earn his board and lodging. At the end of six months, he reported: "I learned to read a little in my primer, to write my own name, and to cypher some in the first three rules in figures. And this was all the schooling I ever had in my life up to this day. I should have continued longer, if it hadn't been that I concluded I couldn't do any longer without a wife; and so I cut out to hunt me one."[7]

The first girl to whom Davy became engaged jilted him, but after various infatuations and rebuffs, he married a "little girl . . . sweeter than sugar," who brought as a dowry two cows and calves and a spinning wheel. Crockett's generous employer's wedding present was a fifteen-dollar order upon the general store for such house furnishings as the bride might pick out. With this start in life, Crockett "rented a small farm and cabin and went to work," until he became tired of paying rent and made up his mind to head for the frontier and free land. By this time, the Crocketts had two sons; as Davy remarks, "I found I was better at increasing my family than my fortune." With a capital of one old horse and a couple of two-year-old colts, the Crockett family crossed the mountains and traveled until they found land to their liking along the Mulberry Fork of Elk River, near the Alabama line. "It was here," Davy notes, "that I began to distinguish myself as a hunter, and to lay the foundation for all my future greatness."

Still searching for adventure, Crockett next served as a volunteer in the Creek War of 1813–14, under Andrew Jackson's command, enduring a considerable amount of hard marching and privation as a scout. His main assignment in the military was foraging for food for his company. He was successful in keeping the men well supplied with venison, turkey, squirrel, and an occasional cow. If Crockett killed any Indians personally, he passes over the details, though he participated in several of the militia's slaughters. In any event, he was elected a colonel of militia, and ever after used the title.

Following the war against the Indians, Crockett moved farther westward. His wife died about 1815, leaving him with three children. Several months later, he married the widow of a fellow soldier, by whom he had two more children.

Crockett's political career began on a small scale when he was informally chosen a magistrate in the community to which he had lately come; when the district was incorporated into Giles County he was appointed a justice of the peace. It was a lawless area, according to Crockett, "and so many bad characters began to flock in upon us, that we found it necessary to set up a sort of temporary government of our own." His qualifications for serving as a squire were minimal, for he candidly admits that he could just barely write his own name. Nevertheless, he worked to improve his handwriting in order to prepare warrants and to keep a record book. The *Narrative* attests his success: "My judgments were never appealed from, and if they had been they would have stuck like wax, as I gave my decisions on the principles of common justice and honesty between man and man, and relied on natural born sense, and not on law, learning to guide me; for I had never read a page in a law book in all my life."[8]

Having had a taste of government at a local level, Crockett became ambitious for a wider field of activity. He entered into a campaign for a seat in the Tennessee legislature to represent his county. Still largely ignorant of law or of the workings of government, he depended upon "laughter and liquor" rather than "law or logic" to win votes. These tactics worked: "I was elected, doubling my competitor and nine votes over," Crockett stated. Two terms in the Tennessee legislature followed.

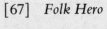 

Crockett's business ventures, however, were less smiled upon by his proverbial good luck. "I had built an extensive grist mill, and powder mill," he said, "all connected together, and also a large distillery. They had cost me upwards of three thousand dollars, more than I was worth in the world."[9] A sudden flood practically washed away the whole enterprise. Instead of declaring bankruptcy, Crockett and his wife decided to pay their creditors all that they had left, and to move on, with an empty purse, for "a brand-new start."

The next Crockett home was a spot on the Obion River in the northwest corner of the state. The site selected was seven miles away from the nearest neighbor. The *Narrative* describes the locale as "a complete wilderness and full of Indians who were hunting. Game was plenty of almost every kind, which suited me exactly, as I was always fond of hunting."[10] Here Crockett "slapped up" a cabin and provisioned it with four barrels of meal, one of salt, and ten gallons of whisky. Six bull elk were killed by Crockett in one day to provide his family with meat for a long pull. Land was cleared, corn planted, and after the crops were gathered and stored, Davy hunted for bear and deer. The year was 1822.

For the next two years Crockett operated flatboats, farmed, and hunted bears—he killed forty-seven in one season. He ran for Congress, his first attempt, and was defeated by only two votes. When the next election came around, in 1827, Davy won in a three-cornered fight, and was reelected for a second term in 1829. But then came a break with the Jacksonians, who, as Crockett put it, hunted him "like a wild varmint," and he lost the 1831 race. The chief reasons for his opposition to Andrew Jackson and his party were his vote against the Indian removal bill of 1830 and the refusal of Jackson to support a Tennessee land bill which would have protected the rights of the squatters, many of them Crockett's constituents, who had occupied much of the land before it could be offered for sale. Two years later, Davy bounced back for a third term, 1833–35. The *Narrative* was written as a campaign document to help him win reelection in 1835. The effort failed, in good part, Crockett charged, because the Jacksonians poured money into the campaign against him. Bitterly disappointed, he is reputed to have told his constituents that they could go to Hell, and he would go to Texas.

Constance Rourke, Crockett's biographer, notes that "Crockett turned his career in Congress into a gusty adventure. He attracted attention at once . · . he quickly became known in Washington as the 'coonskin congressman.' No one at all like him had appeared in office; he aroused great curiosity. His tall figure was striking. His casual speech was often repeated because of its pithy center. Tall talk was easily attributed to him."[11] In the midst of his third term, Crockett's reputation was further enhanced by a celebrated tour of the East, where he was received with great acclaim by the anti-Jackson forces of Baltimore, Philadelphia, New York, and Boston. He had now become a national figure, and his sayings and doings were being quoted throughout the land. The colonel began to take seriously the jocular suggestion that he should run for the presidency.

Crockett took a fierce pride in his political independence. The *Narrative* concludes with a ringing declaration: "Look at my arms, you will find no party hand-cuff on them! Look at my neck, you will not find there any collar, with the engraving

MY DOG
Andrew Jackson

But you will find me standing up to my rack, as the people's faithful representative, and the public's most obedient, very humble servant, DAVID CROCKETT."[12]

Shackford, in assessing Crockett's political career, comments on his "tendency to pose, like some current demagogues, as being much more ignorant than he really was to attract the votes of the poor, illiterate West Tennessee farmers. Some writers took him at his word and came to the conclusion that he was a nonentity, instead of recognizing his exaggeration."[13] Alexis de Tocqueville, in America to study the ways of a democracy, appears to have gained the same impression. Without being personally acquainted with Crockett, he wrote:

When the right of suffrage is *universal* and when the deputies are paid by the state, its singular how low and how far wrong the people can go. Two years ago the inhabitants of the district of which Memphis is the capital sent to the House of Representatives . . . an individual named David Crockett, who has no education, can read with difficulty, has no property, no fixed residence, but passes his life hunting, selling his game to live, and dwelling continuously in the woods. . . . Full of pride and ignorance, the electors want to be represented by people of their own kind. Moreover to win their votes one has to descend to manoeuvres that disgust distinguished men.[14]

A number of misstatements appear in Tocqueville's comments, based on erroneous information picked up from newspapers and fellow travelers. Already wild tales about Crockett were beginning to appear in scores of papers.

Following his failure to win a fourth term in Congress, Crockett determined to leave Tennessee for far-distant Texas, seeing an opportunity there to recoup his political fortunes. The movement for Texan independence attracted him, and he started for the war front by way of Little Rock. With an area 825 by 745 miles in extent, Texas already had an American population of nearly forty thousand. The adventurous and out-of-luck from the East were flocking in to support Sam Houston, another disappointed Tennessean, who was leading the independence movement. Crockett describes the start of his journey: "I dressed myself in a clean hunting shirt, put on a new fox-skin cap with the tail hanging behind, took hold of my rifle Betsey, which all the world knows was presented to me by the patriotic citizens of Philadelphia, and thus equipped, I started off with a heavy heart for Mill's Point to take a steamboat down the Mississippi, and go ahead to a new world."[15] His triumphal progress westward was marked by many stops.

On 20 December 1835, the Texans issued a declaration of independence from Mexico, and proclaimed a republic. Meanwhile the Mexican general, Antonio López de Santa Anna, with an army of 7,500 men marched northward to put down the revolt. Santa Anna concentrated his drive on an ancient public building called the Alamo in San Antonio, defended by an American force of 153 men, including such redoubtable fighters as David Crockett and Jim Bowie. A siege of several days ended when the invaders stormed the building and killed every American man. Crockett was fifty years old. The fall of the Alamo was avenged about a month later, when Sam Houston's forces met and defeated Santa Anna's Mexican troops at the battle of San Jacinto.

The Crockett of the tall tales, Parrington asserts, "was a deliberate fabrication" and "its immediate purpose was frankly partisan.

It did not spring from the soil of the Tennessee canebrakes; it was created in Washington . . . it was the clever work of politicians."[16] Three successive stages of the myth, Parrington finds, were the exploitation of Davy's canebrake waggery, the exploitation of his dislike of Andrew Jackson, and the exploitation of his dramatic death at the Alamo. Eventually the creations passed into folklore. The Whigs, seeking a weapon to offset Jackson's appeal for the coonskin democracy of the West, played up Davy's picturesque eccentricities, Western honesty, shrewd backwoods intelligence, and frontier humor.

The tall tales began to appear in print as early as 1832, with the *Sketches and Eccentricities of Col. David Crockett, of West Tennessee*, a work which Davy resented and disclaimed having any hand in. The unknown author, he states, had put into his mouth "such language as would disgrace even an outlandish African" and had otherwise done him "much injustice."[17] An early stage of the myth-making process may be observed in the *Sketches*, quoting Crockett when he crossed swords with a partisan of John Quincy Adams: "I'm that same David Crockett, fresh from the backwoods, half-horse, half-alligator, a little touched with the snapping-turtle; can wade the Mississippi, leap the Ohio, ride upon a streak of lightning, and slip without a scratch down a honey locust; can whip my weight in wild-cats—and if any gentleman pleases, for a ten-dollar bill, he may throw in a panther—hug a bear too close for comfort, and eat any man opposed to Jackson."[18]

The Crockett legend underwent further development in the Crockett almanacs, published from 1835 to 1856, first in Nashville, then in New York, Boston, Philadelphia, Albany, Baltimore, and Louisville, as their fame spread. The composers of the almanacs are unknown, as they went about inventing outrageous spellings, comic words, and bizarre phrases. Their principal investigator, Richard Dorson, finds that the most obvious features of the almanacs' humor "are the frontier boast, backwoods invective and imagery, racy dialect, ugly people, earthiness."[19] Though the language is picturesque, it is highly exaggerated and largely unreal.

The almanac yarns relate amazing details of Davy Crockett's life: he was the biggest and smartest infant ever born, he was watered with buffalo milk and weaned on whisky. The family used his baby teeth to build the family fireplace. At eight, he weighed two hundred pounds and fourteen ounces, with his shoes off, his feet clean and his stomach empty. At twelve, he escaped from an Indian by riding on the back of a wolf. His exploits when he grew to manhood were even more fantastic.

The last of the Crockett almanacs appeared shortly before the great North-South conflict. Dorson states that "the literature of frontier humor died with the Civil War. The newspaper sketches changed; the hunting yarns and tall stories of the frontier gave way to the new genre of the professional funny men. Misspellings replaced dialect and the national scene the local; the flavor of the folk disappeared."[20]

Who actually wrote the five works attributed to Crockett: *Sketches and Eccentricities of Col. David Crockett of East Tennessee* (1833), *A Narrative of the Life of David Crockett, of the State of Tennessee* (1834), *An Account of Col. Crockett's Tour to the North and Down East* (1835), *The Life of Martin Van Buren* (1835), and *Col. Crockett's Exploits and Adventures in Texas* (1836)? None was written by Crockett, probably. Biographers have concluded that the *Narrative* is the only reliable and authentic source for learning the truth about Crockett up to 1834. It is believed that the *Narrative* is a work dictated by its subject, but in fact ghostwritten for him by Thomas Chilton, a congressman from Kentucky, even though Crockett in his preface claims that he had merely had the manuscript "hastily run over by a friend or so, and some little alterations have been made in the spelling and grammar."[21]

Despite his denial of having any part in the *Sketches*, it appears likely that Crockett supplied most of the important facts of his life and picturesque episodes for that work; much of the same material was incorporated in the *Narrative*. The *Tour* and *Martin Van Buren* (a satirical campaign document) were claimed by Crockett and were certainly done with his help. The *Exploits* is a complete fabrication, possibly written by Richard Penn Smith, after Davy's death at the Alamo.

A firsthand account of Crockett at the height of his career comes from John Gadsby Chapman, a celebrated historical painter who did a full-length portrait of Crockett at Washington in 1834, about midway in the colonel's last term as congressman from

Tennessee. The portrait now hangs in the Academic Center at the University of Texas. Chapman has also left us a word picture of Crockett, as he knew him:

With all the disadvantages consequent upon deficiency in timely educational training, Col. Crockett's command of verbal expression was very remarkable, say what he might his meaning could never be misinterpreted. He expressed opinions, and told his stories, with unhesitating clearness of diction, often embellished with graphic touches of original wit and humor, sparkling and even startling, yet never out of place or obtrusively ostentatious. As for his back-woods slang—it fell upon the ear meaningly and consistent as might the crack of his rifle or his "halloo" from a harricane or from a cane-brake. It was to him truly a mother-tongue, in which his ideas flowed most naturally and found most emphatic and unrestrained utterance.[22]

Yarns of Frontier Life

AUGUSTUS BALDWIN LONGSTREET'S
Georgia Scenes: Characters, Incidents, &c.,
In the First Half Century of the Republic

In his preface to *Georgia Scenes*, A. B. Longstreet states that the sketches "consist of nothing more than fanciful *combinations* of *real* incidents and characters," and added for the benefit of "those who have taken exception to the coarse, inelegant, and sometimes ungrammatical language, *it is language accommodated to the capacity of the person*" speaking [italics Longstreet's]. Longstreet obviously took delight in observing Georgia rural life, especially in the more primitive districts, and in recounting his experiences. He himself maintained that *Georgia Scenes* had been written to fill a gap in the state's history, revealing "the manners, customs, amusements, wit, dialect, as they appear in all grades of society, to an ear and eye witness of them."

Longstreet was a true child of the Georgia border, born in Augusta in 1790. Vernon Louis Parrington's *Main Currents in American Thought* offers a colorful description of his personality, based on original sources: "A driving, robust, energetic fellow, never squeamish, with a ready wit, he was at home amongst the plain people, the greatest wag in every gathering. He could knock a man down or shoot out a squirrel's eye with any champion of them all; he could enter into a dance or a revival meeting with equal ardor, or take the stump against a seasoned campaigner."[1] Longstreet was highly versatile, at different times serving as a state legislator, lawyer, newspaper editor, writer, minister, politician, and teacher. He filled several college presidencies: Emory College in Georgia, Centenary College in Louisiana, the University of Mississippi, and the University of South Carolina.

The *Georgia Scenes* was written for the most part between 1832 and 1835, and published in two newspapers, the Milledgeville *Southern Recorder* and the Augusta *States Rights Sentinel*. Two pseudonyms, "Baldwin" and "Hall," were employed, and carried over into the book form, when the sketches were collected and printed in 1835. The stories are presented as authentic documents of frontier life in Georgia in the early years of the nineteenth century. The humor of the backwoods contributes to the realistic atmosphere which surrounds them. Longstreet admits to "throwing into those scenes, which would be otherwise dull and insipid, some personal incident or adventure of my own, real or imaginary, as would best suit my purpose. . . . Some of the scenes are as literally true as the frailties of memory would allow them to be."

Georgia Scenes opens with a comic episode worthy of Mark Twain, "Georgia Theatrics." The narrator is riding through the country, in an area called "The Dark Corner" of Lincoln County, when he hears a terrific commotion ahead, apparently a violent and deadly struggle in which the victor has gouged out his opponent's eyes. The traveler forces his way through the underbrush to stop the fight and finds but one combatant, who had simply stopped from his plowing long enough to have rehearsed a fight. Instead of plunging his thumbs into the eyesockets of an antagonist, the eighteen-year-old youth had left his impress on the soft earth. The boy, "with a taunting curl of the nose," said, before he returned to his plow, "There a'nt nobody there, nor ha'nt been nother. I was jist seein' how I could 'a' fout." "Hall" comments that "the youth who had just left me had played all the parts of all the characters in a Courthouse fight." Examining "the ground from which he had risen, there were the prints of his two thumbs, plunged up to the balls in the mellow earth, about the distance of a man's eyes apart; and the ground around was broken up as if two stags had been engaged upon it."

This scene was plagiarized and appears as Chapter 25 of the *Life of Davy Crockett, Written by Himself* (1860).

Of the second scene, "The Dance," Edgar Allan Poe, in a review, wrote, "The oddities of a backwood reel are described with inimitable force, fidelity, and picturesque effect."[2] The old dances are characterized as more modest and moral than those of more sophisticated communities. A comic element is introduced when "Baldwin" has his egotism wounded by the failure of an old sweetheart to remember him.

Poe, writing in the *Southern Literary Messenger*, was also much taken by "The Horse-Swap," the third piece in the *Scenes*, which he characterizes as "a vivid narrative of an encounter between the wits of two Georgian horse-jockies," and adds, "This is most excellent in every respect—but especially so in its delineations of Southern bravado, and the keen sense of the ludicrous evinced in the portraiture of the steeds. We think parts of this free and easy sketch superior, in joint humor and verisimilitude to anything of the kind we have ever seen."[3] In the end, both traders are cheated: one gets a horse with a six-inch saddle sore on its back "that seemed to have defied all medical skill," and the other won a horse that was both blind and deaf.

Practical joking, dear to the frontiersman's heart, is the theme of two pieces in the *Scenes*, "The Character of a Native Georgian" and "A Sage Conversation," in both of which Ned Brace appears as the incorrigible prankster. On a visit to Savannah with "Hall," Ned Brace contrives several elaborate hoaxes involving the dining room of the tavern where they are stopping, "a gay, smirky little Frenchman," disruption of a church service and a funeral, and a fire. The character of Ned Brace is reputed to be based upon two men of Longstreet's acquaintance.

A famous episode in *Georgia Scenes* is "The Fight." "Although involving some horrible and disgusting details of Southern barbarity," as Poe writes, it "is a sketch unsurpassed in dramatic vigor, and in the vivid truth to nature of one or two of the personages introduced."[4] One of the chief actors is a degraded little man named Ransy Sniffle, "who, in his earlier days, had fed copiously upon red clay and blackberries," a diet that had "given to Ransy a complexion that a corpse would have disdained to own," and a misshapen body. Nothing delighted Ransy so much as "witnessing, fomenting, or talking about a fight." Through trickery, he inveigles two backwoods gladiators, previously good friends, into conflict, on the pretext that the wife of one has been insulted. The fight, watched by a large number of spectators, ends in the loss between the combatants of an ear, a nose, and a finger, in addition to many bruises.

"The Song" reflects the musical unsophisticate's lack of appreciation for classical music. Poe calls it "a burlesque somewhat overdone," but concedes that it is "upon the whole a good caricature of Italian bravura singing."[5] Whether or not one enjoys this type of music, the account is often hilarious. The heroine is a young lady who had just returned South from her school in Philadelphia, where "she has been taught to sing by Madam Piggisqueaki, who was a pupil of Ma'm'selle Crokifroggietta, who had sung with Madam Catalani; and she had taken lessons on the piano from Seignor Buzzifussi, who had played with Paganini." Urged on by the assembled company, the coy Miss Aurebia Emma Theodosia Augusta Crump sits down at the piano to play and sing. After what looked to be an acrobatic performance on the piano keys, the song begins with

some very curious sounds, which appeared to proceed from the lips of Miss Augusta; they seemed to be compounded of a dry cough, a hiccough, and a whisper. . . . Miss Crump made a fly-catching grab at half a dozen keys in a row, and at the same instant she fetched a long dung-hill-cock crow, at the conclusion of which she grabbed as many keys with the left. . . . My nerves had not recovered from the shock before Miss Augusta repeated the movement, and accompanied it with the squall of a pinched cat. . . . She now made a third grasp with the right, boxed the faces of six keys in a row with the left, and at the same time raised one of the most unearthly howls that ever issued from the throat of a human being. This seemed the signal for universal uproar and destruction. She now threw away all reserve and charged the piano with her whole force. She boxed it, she clawed it, she raked it, she scraped it. Her neck-vein swelled, her chin flew up, her face flushed, her eye glared, her bosom heaved, she screamed, she howled, she yelled, cackled, and was in the act of dwelling upon the note of a screech-owl, when I took the St. Vitus's dance and rushed out of the room.

Longstreet based "The Song" upon the singing of one of the voice teachers in the Taylor Select Female School of Sparta, Georgia.

"The Turn Out" is a lively account of school boys who have been refused an Easter holiday by their master. When the master arrives at the schoolhouse, in the early morning, he finds every possible entrance fortified and barricaded. He tries to force his way in, but is met by sharp sticks projecting from every crack. The master finally forces an entrance by assaulting the door with a heavy fence rail. Immediately, however, he is swamped by the older boys, and a holiday is granted. Actually, the teacher is not averse to conceding the day off, and his efforts to gain admittance are not very forceful, but he cannot grant the holiday, except under duress, without forfeiting his salary.

"The 'Charming Creature' as a Wife" concerns a rising young attorney, George Baldwin, who falls in love with the spoiled daughter of a wealthy, uneducated merchant. Miss Evelina Caroline Smith, an only child, had just returned home after an absence of three years in Philadelphia completing her education. The new-rich Mr. Smith, the father, is a true snob: "To the poor he was haughty, supercilious, and arrogant, and, not infrequently, insolent; to the rich he was friendly, kind, or obsequious, as their purses equalled or over-measured his own." The mother was "proud, loquacious, silly." As a consequence, pride and vanity became the leading traits of the beautiful daughter's character and "admiration and flattery the only food which she could relish." Her marriage to George Baldwin turns out to be a disaster. She is unable or unwilling to settle down to the homely virtues of thrift and household management. George's attempts to reform her are in vain, his legal practice is ruined, he takes to drink as an escape from a miserable existence, and eventually dies a drunkard's death. Parrington dismisses the story as "a crude sermon on the folly of marrying a lazy woman,"[6] but it contains several excellent character sketches.

"The Gander Pulling" describes a sport condemned by Poe as "a piece of unprincipled barbarity not infrequently practiced in the South and West."[7] The rules of the cruel game are to suspend a greased goose by the legs about ten feet above a roadway, and horseback riders pass under the goose at a dead run, attempting every time they pass to snatch the bird's head off. Each competitor pays twenty-five cents to enter, and the winner takes all. Boys with cowhide whips strike the horses if they slow down beneath the gander. This scene, which Longstreet claims to have witnessed in person, is enlivened by two runaway horses, which refuse participation in the game.

In "The Ball" Longstreet expresses his acute dislike for "modern" dancing. The ladies' dancing, he writes, may be broken down "into the three motions of a turkey-cock strutting, a sparrow-hawk lighting, and a duck walking. . . . The strut prevailed most in balancing; the bobs, when balancing to; and the waddle when going round." The gentlemen's dancing was compared to a man cleaning mud off his shoes on a doormat: "some scraped with a pull of a foot, some with a push, and some with both." A silly quarrel in the course of the dance leads to a duel, an institution for which Longstreet apparently has only disgust.

Another subject for ridicule is found in "The Mother and Her Child," wherein the author makes fun of "the gibberish which is almost invariably used by mothers and nurses to infants." Negro dialect is also introduced into the story, and the mother a coarse, vulgar woman, is harshly critical of an inoffensive little Negro nursemaid because the infant will not stop crying. The problem is resolved when the father discovers a small feather in the child's ear.

Poe rated "The Debating Society" as "the best thing in the book—and indeed one among the best things of the kind we have ever read,"[8] and shows his admiration by reprinting the story in its entirety in his review. The plot concerns two schoolboys who propose a debate and then trick their friends into debating a subject totally lacking in meaning or sense. Parrington calls it "a heavy practical joke" and finds "inexplicable" Poe's enthusiasm for the yarn.[9]

One of the best-known sketches in *Georgia Scenes* is "The Militia Company Drill." The piece was actually written, according to Longstreet, by a friend, revealed later to be Oliver Hillhouse Prince. Many years later, Thomas Hardy was accused of plagiarism when he used a part of the story in his *The Trumpet Major* (1880). As explained by Hardy, however, this satirical account of an American drill was based upon a chapter in Gifford's *History of the Wars Occasioned by the French Revolution* (London, 1817). The British compiler had picked up, perhaps from an American newspaper, the Prince sketch even before Longstreet included it in *Georgia Scenes*.

A favorite pastime of the Georgians of Longstreet's day, horse racing, is the theme for "The Turf," the next sketch. "An Interesting Interview" records the speech, actions, and thoughts of two drunken old men. Longstreet uses the occasion to deliver a moral lecture: "I hope the day is not far distant when drunkenness will be unknown in our highly-favoured country. The moral world is rising in its strength against the all-destroying vice, and though the monster still struggles, and stings, and poisons with deadly effect in many parts of our wide-spread territory, it is perceptibly wounded and weakened."

Longstreet's biographer John Donald Wade called "The Fox Hunt" the most literary of all the sketches in *Georgia Scenes*.[10] There is a long quotation from Somerville's poem "The Chase," and a Latin quote from Horace; the author himself waxes more eloquent than usual. The landscape is described in poetic terms. "The Fox Hunt" is the story of a novice trying to keep up with a group of seasoned hunters and his failure to maintain the pace. In any case, the fox outsmarts the exhausted hounds and escapes.

Practical jokers are the chief characters in "The Wax-Works," a story of several young men from Augusta attending the Waynesboro races who run out of money to pay their bills. Admission is charged to a "wax-works exhibition," in which the boys impersonate George Washington, Sleeping Beauty, and other celebrities. In the midst of the performance, their trick is discovered and they are chased out of town.

Georgia Scenes concludes with "The Shooting Match," depicting another sport common in Longstreet's time. A witty dialogue between "Hall" and a "swarthy, bright-eyed, smirky little fellow," whom he meets on the road, precedes the match—miraculously won by Hall on a lucky shot.

To one who assumes that life in the backwoods and on the frontier was dull and monotonous, *Georgia Scenes* comes as a revelation. The recreational activities were often rough and ready, but scarcely lacking in variety—fox hunting, horse racing, gander pulling, fighting, horse swapping, dancing, debating, music, and practical jokes. The everyday picture of manners and customs discloses in graphic detail much about the popular culture of the early nineteenth century along the Southern border.

Unlike a great majority of later books on the South, *Georgia Scenes* has few Negro characters. The almost total immersion in race problems that characterized the generation immediately preceding the Civil War and after was evidently not yet preoccupying the Southern mind. The blacks who appear in *Georgia Scenes* are musicians, jockeys, and servants, and none figures prominently in the stories.

Franklin J. Meine, historian of American humor and folklore, notes that "with *Georgia Scenes*, Longstreet established a pattern that had a profound influence on all subsequent writers of the South."[11] Bernard De Voto's judgment is that "in some respects, Longstreet's successors never equalled him, in many respects they never surpassed him, and his book remains to-day vital and absorbing—the frontier's first permanent book."[12]

Georgia Scenes within a few years became immensely popular, in both North and South, and imitators proliferated. Close parallels exist in the *Autobiography of Davy Crockett*, Joseph Baldwin's *Flush Times in Alabama and Mississippi*, William Tappan Thompson's "Major Jones," Johnson J. Hooper's "Captain Simon Suggs," George W. Harris's "Sut Lovingood," John B. Lamar's *Polly Peachblossom's Wedding*, and a host of works by lesser writers. In the post–Civil War period, Longstreet's influence was felt by Joel Chandler Harris and probably by Mark Twain and Bret Harte. Several critics have also suggested possible relationships in the novels of William Faulkner.

De Voto concludes that "so far as any man may be credited with the discovery that the realistic humor of the backwoods was the material of literature, the distinction is Longstreet's."[13]

8.

Slave Plantation

FRANCES ANNE KEMBLE'S *Journal of a Residence on a Georgian Plantation in 1838–1839*

Two of the most powerful documents attacking and condemning the institution of slavery in America were written by women—one in fictional and the other in factual form. Of the two, Harriet Beecher Stowe's *Uncle Tom's Cabin* unquestionably had the greater impact, because its moral lesson is wrapped up in an exciting story. Fanny Kemble's *Journal of a Residence on a Georgian Plantation* refused to mix truth and romance; except for an occasional almost poetic description of the Southern landscape, the account is a realistic picture, filled with burning indignation and pity, of slavery in operation. The book's appeal was perforce more limited than Mrs. Stowe's melodramatic tale of cruel aristocrats, stately mansions, and such memorable characters as Simon Legree, blue-eyed Eva, and black-faced Topsy. Nevertheless, the *Journal*'s role in the Civil War and the slavery controversy is of considerable significance.

Fanny Kemble was the last of a great dynasty of English actors and actresses—the daughter, granddaughter, and great-granddaughter of some of the most famous names on the London stage for several generations. Fanny's stage debut came at the age of nineteen, in 1829, at Covent Garden, in the role of Juliet. Her success was phenomenal and theatres were crowded wherever she performed. After three years, however, her father's severe financial reverses as manager of Covent Garden led to a decision to go abroad. In August 1832 Fanny and her father sailed for New York. Again, the Kemble magic fascinated packed houses in New York, Philadelphia, Baltimore, Washington, and elsewhere in the States.

But strangely, Fanny hated acting and yearned to leave the theatre world. Her escape route was marriage in 1834 to Pierce Butler, whereupon, as a historian of the New York theatre commented, "America lost the most intellectual, passionate, and original actress of the age."

Pierce Butler was the grandson of a Southern planter, wealthy from his plantations, high in Philadelphia society, blond, magnetic, with the blood of Irish earls in his veins. Sharply conflicting traditions and ways of life doomed the Butler-Kemble union from the outset. For the preceding fifty years agitation in England against slavery and the slave trade had been constant, and Fanny Kemble had early absorbed British detestation of the hated institution. Butler had apparently told his wife nothing of his slave holdings prior to their marriage; she knew him only as a rich Philadelphian of private means. Revelation of the source of his income, therefore, came as a great shock to her. Writing in 1839, Fanny remarked, "When I married Mr. Butler I knew nothing of these dreadful possessions of his." Henceforth, from the moment that she learned the truth, Fanny felt "a sense of horrible personal responsibility and implication . . . and I felt the weight of an unimagined guilt upon my conscience."[1] In a letter to a friend in 1835 she wrote: "The family into which I married are large slaveholders; our present and future fortune depend greatly upon extensive plantations in Georgia. But the experience of every day, besides our faith in the great justice of God, forbids dependence on the duration of the mighty abuse by which one race of men is held in abject physical and mental slavery by another. As for me, though the toilsome earnings of my bread were to be my lot again tomorrow I should rejoice with unspeakable thankfulness that we had not to answer for what I consider so grievous a sin against humanity."[2]

From this time on, Fanny was almost totally preoccupied with the slavery question, to the alarm and dismay of Pierce Butler and his family. She composed "a long and vehement treatise against

Negro slavery" as part of her *Journal of a Residence in America*, an early work issued by a Philadelphia publisher in 1835. Butler's angry opposition, however, caused her to delete this portion from the published book.

Actually, Fanny knew slavery only in the abstract. Her knowledge was based on extensive reading and her acquaintance with such dedicated antislavery advocates as William Ellery Channing, eminent Boston Unitarian minister, and longtime friends Catharine Maria Sedgwick and her husband Charles. Firsthand observation of slavery in action, Fanny determined, was essential to confirm or to deny Pierce Butler's apologetics for and the abolitionist's condemnation of the institution. Nothing would satisfy Fanny but that she should visit her husband's plantation.

More than two years passed before Butler surrendered to his wife's entreaties that she be allowed to accompany him on his next trip south. The long and arduous journey from Philadelphia to Butler Island, Georgia, began in December 1838. The details of the nine days' exhausting trek by railroad, stagecoach, and steamboat fill two chapters of Fanny's *Journal*. The primitive state of travel in America a century and a half ago is almost inconceivable today. The Butlers were accompanied on their strenuous expedition by their two infant daughters, Sarah and Frances, and an Irish nursemaid.

Fanny had resolved before undertaking the stay in Georgia that she would attempt to maintain an objective view. "I am going to Georgia," she wrote, "prejudiced against slavery, for I am an Englishwoman, in whom the absence of such a prejudice would be disgraceful." Nevertheless, she hoped to find mitigating factors in "the general injustice and cruelty of the system, perhaps much contentment on the part of the slaves and kindness on that of the masters."[3] Accordingly, her report was to be based on careful observation and accurate facts, avoiding malice and noting any extenuating circumstances. Here could be put to an acid test Pierce Butler's claim that "those people are happy—happier than they would be if they were free. They love us and we are fond of them."[4]

As soon as she arrived in Georgia, Fanny began writing her *Journal*, pouring into it her daily experiences and impressions, character sketches, descriptions of the surrounding area, and opinions on slavery. The period covered is from the family's departure from Philadelphia until 17 April 1839, when the Butlers left for the North, altogether a span of approximately four months.

The Butler estate consisted of two plantations. Dominant at the time was Butler Island, swampland devoted to the production of rice, which had become a highly profitable crop. The second plantation, Hampton Point on St. Simon Island, located on higher ground, had earlier been the center of the Butler property. The growing of sea-island cotton, however, had gradually exhausted the land, and by the time of Fanny Kemble's visit, pines and oaks were taking over the abandoned soil. At first, the Butlers stayed on Butler Island, but as the weather in the swamplands grew warmer and the danger of malaria increased they moved to Hampton Point. Fanny's *Journal* is about equally divided between the two sojourns.

In form, the *Journal* is made up of thirty-one letters, each addressed to "Dear Elizabeth." Though never written or mailed as letters, they were intended eventually to be read by Fanny's close friend Elizabeth Dwight Sedgwick. Years later, when the *Journal* was published, it was dedicated to Elizabeth.

Contrary to the romantic notion that the owners of Southern plantations resided in palatial mansions, nowhere on the Butler properties was there a civilized dwelling for Fanny and her family. On Butler Island, they moved into the overseer's shabby five-room cottage and while there lived under the most primitive conditions. The island itself is described by Fanny as "a kind of mud sponge." She adds, "The chief produce of this delectable spot is rice—oranges, negroes, fleas, mosquitoes, various beautiful evergreens, sundry sort of snakes, alligators, and bull rushes enough to have made cradles not for Moses alone but the whole Israelitish host besides." The entire island lay below high-water mark, walled in by dikes; the river water was allowed in through ditches and canals when the rice fields needed flooding. Cabbages were the only vegetable grown on the island. There were three mills for threshing rice, run by steam and tide-water, and four slave villages, where several hundred Negroes were housed in wooden shacks.

The realities of the slave system exceeded Fanny's worst fears. Her *Journal*, which her great-granddaughter, Fanny Kemble Wister, claimed "is the only firsthand account by the wife of a slave holder

of the negroes' lives on a plantation,"[5] is a day-by-day record of
what she saw and did. She immediately gained the confidence of
the black women, and they, hoping for her intercession on their
behalf, told her harrowing stories of the stripping and flogging of
slave women, of hard manual labor being forced on mothers of
infants within three weeks after birth of their children, of families
being divided by the sale of slaves, and of women being forced to
submit to the lusts of owners and overseers.

Most repulsive to Fanny was the lack of sanitation and general
uncleanliness which pervaded everything. Her house servants, for
example, she noted were "perfectly filthy in their persons and
clothes—their faces, hands, and naked feet being literally incrusted
with dirt." But, she pointed out, "this very disagreeable peculiarity
does not prevent Southern women from hanging their infants at
the breasts of Negresses, nor almost every planter's wife and daughter from having one or more little black pets sleeping like puppy
dogs in their very bedchamber, nor almost every planter from
admitting one or several of his female slaves to the still closer
intimacy of his bed." Slavery, Fanny was convinced, was responsible for all such evils, "from lying, thieving, and adultery, to dirty
houses, ragged clothes, and foul smells," since the system led inevitably to a total absence of self-respect.

Fanny's attempts to plead the causes of slaves that she believed
to have been seriously mistreated or to reform some of the worst
aspects of slavery were heard with impatience and resentment on
the part of Pierce Butler, who made a few minor concessions in the
beginning, and then ordered her to bring no further complaints to
him. His attitude was that nothing told to Fanny by the slave
women could be believed. "Why do you listen to such stuff?" he
exclaimed angrily, "don't you know the niggers are all damned
liars?"[6] Her sympathy for the slaves, in Butler's view, only tended
to make them discontented and idle, neglectful of their work, and
therefore more liable to punishment.

Thus began the estrangement between Pierce Butler and his
wife, her loss of respect for him, and later their separation and
divorce.

Frustrated in her desire to alleviate the hardships of the slaves
on the Butler plantation in other ways, Fanny devoted the remain-

der of her stay in Georgia to doing what was possible for their welfare. Ignoring Southern tradition, she went into the slave cabin used as a hospital, where there was no doctor or nurse and the Negroes lay on the earthen floor dying in their filth. There she bathed the infants and ministered to the best of her ability to the sick. She started a campaign to persuade the mothers to bathe their babies, providing soaps, and offering penny bribes. Though forbidden by law, she taught an exceptionally bright young black to read.

Fanny was impressed by the ability of the slaves to learn when given an opportunity. The blacks on the plantation were divided between field hands and mechanics or artisans. A majority, "the more stupid and brutish," were placed in the first category. The others, who were taught trades, performed as coopers, blacksmiths, bricklayers, and carpenters, becoming highly expert and assigned to construct every item of equipment used on the place.

Fanny noted that among the slaves on the Butler plantation there were men who had made considerable sums by boatbuilding in their leisure hours. She observed further that there were "instances of almost lifelong, persevering, stringent labor, by which slaves have at length purchased their own freedom and that of their wives and children." This, she asserts, is "sufficient to prove that they are capable of severe sustained effort of the most patient and heroic kind for that great object, liberty."

At the head of each group or "gang," as they were called, of Negroes was a black driver, who stood over the workers, whip in hand. A driver was allowed to inflict a dozen lashes upon any refractory slave in the field. Even more severe punishment could be meted out by the overseer to individuals considered incorrigible. Slave foremen were notoriously brutal taskmasters and, given the power, might whip more severely than white masters. Fanny Kemble observed the brutalizing effects of slavery in the "unbounded insolence and tyranny" with which the slaves treated each other. An escaped slave, Frederick Douglass, Fanny's contemporary, wrote that "everybody, in the South, wants the privilege of whipping somebody else."[7]

The degrading effects of slavery on the whites also deeply distressed Fanny. At the lowest level were the poor who possessed no land or slaves. These "pinelanders" preferred a life of barbaric sloth and semistarvation to "working like niggers." To Fanny, "these wretched creatures" seemed hardly human, living in rude shelters, squatting on other men's land, and subsisting on wild fowl and venison and stealing from plantation gardens. In the eyes of the poor whites, physical labor was the portion of blacks and slaves alone.

More subtle was the bearing of slavery on the characters of the white masters. From a superficial point of view, Fanny pointed out, "the habit of command gives them a certain self-possession and the enjoyment of leisure a certain ease." On closer acquaintance, however, the social system to which they belonged had infected them with less pleasing traits: "haughty, overbearing irritability, effeminate indolence, reckless extravagance, and a union of profligacy and cruelty, which are the immediate result of their irresponsible power over their dependents."[8]

In considering the condition of the people on the Butler plantations as a whole, Fanny concluded that the principal physical hardships fell on the women. Because slave women could gain favor in the eyes of their master by presenting him with a number of future slaves, some became mothers at the age of thirteen or fourteen. Because of the endless bending and lifting involved in their work, Fanny learned that many slave mothers lost more than half of their babies through miscarriages or stillbirths. After twelve or fifteen births the bodies of slave women were likely to be completely broken. The slaves had to give birth to many more children than white women; the infant mortality rate was such that no more than one out of two or three black babies could expect to grow into an able-bodied adult worker.

After the Butlers' stay in Georgia ended in April 1839, they returned to Philadelphia. Fanny had anticipated a second visit to the slave plantations, but her return was absolutely forbidden by John Butler, Pierce's older brother. She therefore never again saw the sea islands.

From this time on, Fanny began to give serious consideration to publication of her *Journal*. To an intimate friend, Harriet St. Leger, she wrote in 1840: "I have sometimes been haunted with the idea that it was an imperative duty, knowing what I know, and having seen what I have seen, to do all that lies in my power to show the dangers of this frightful institution." Pierce Butler was adamantly opposed to having any part of the document appear in print, and Fanny realized that to proceed against his wishes would mean the end of their marriage, already in a state of disintegration. The divorce came in 1849, but Fanny continued to withhold her manuscript from publication. It was circulated privately, however, among friends in America and England. Meanwhile, the Butler estate in Georgia had ceased to exist. The slaves had been sold to pay Pierce's debts, incurred through reckless stock-market speculations.

Not until the outbreak of the Civil War did Fanny's irresolution vanish. She was no longer a slaveowner's wife nor the mother of future slaveowners. Her decision to publish was directly influenced by the attitude of the British ruling class. The English Tory circles in which Fanny was living at the time were for the most part sympathetic to the Confederacy. As the armies of the South won victory after victory in the early years of the struggle, England began to move toward recognition of the Confederate States. William Ewart Gladstone, chancellor of the exchequer, whose family had made an enormous fortune from slave labor in the West Indies, was speaking favorably of the Southern side. In a letter to a friend, Joshua Francis Fisher, Fanny observed that she was "frequently surprised and pained by the total absence of sympathy with the northern cause."

The issuance of Lincoln's Emancipation Proclamation caused English sentiment to begin swinging in the opposite direction. The working classes, in particular, were antislavery and pro-Northern in their sympathies.

In any event, convinced that the right moment had arrived, Fanny turned over her manuscript to the British publisher Longman, who issued it in May 1863. A New York edition, published by Harper, appeared in July. Fanny's brief preface to the book stated: "The following diary was kept in the winter and spring of 1838–39, on an estate consisting of rice and cotton plantations, in the islands at the entrance of the Altamaha, on the coast of Georgia. The slaves in whom I then had an unfortunate interest were sold some years ago. The islands themselves are at present in the power of the Northern troops. The record contained in the following pages is a picture of conditions of human existence which I hope and believe have passed away."

Fanny herself had modest hopes as to the effects of the book, commenting, "not, certainly that I had in these latter years of my life any fallacious expectation of making converts on the subject, but that I felt constrained at that juncture to bear my testimony to the miserable nature and results of the system, of which so many of my countrymen and women were becoming the sentimental apologists."[9]

What exactly was the impact of the *Journal* on contemporary sentiment and events? Some readers thought the diary the most powerful antislavery book yet written, comparable to *Uncle Tom's Cabin* in its influence. Fanny's story of plantation life under slavery was a best seller in England. It shocked the prudish of the Victorian era by its frankness, and mothers were warned not to permit their daughters to read the book. Supporters of the South were angered, claiming erroneously that the *Journal* had been hastily written for the occasion. One piece of evidence as to the book's popularity is that it was excerpted and circulated in pamphlet form in England and all over the North; because of the demand for the original edition, Harper ordered a second printing early in 1864. The *Atlantic Monthly* described it as "the first ample, lucid, faithful, detailed account from the actual headquarters of a slave plantation in this country, of the workings of the system." Generally, critics praised or condemned the *Journal* according to the policy of their newspaper or magazine. In the North, abolitionists hailed Fanny as a bringer of light and truth, the copperheads called her a liar, and the fastidious were shocked. Some historians then and since argued that the book had little effect, that it came too late, after the tide had already turned in favor of the North.

The *Journal of a Residence on a Georgian Plantation* lacks the romantic atmosphere of *Uncle Tom's Cabin*. It is missing the aristocratic characters, opulent mansions, and beautiful country estates that fascinated the readers of Harriet Beecher Stowe's best-selling novel. Fanny herself explained that her experience had been limited and that life on a remote sea island should not be taken as typical of slave plantations everywhere in the South. Her observations were based on a stay of less than four months on two small islands at the mouth of the Altamaha River, an area about sixteen miles square, but in the center of one of the South's most productive cotton, rice, and sugar areas.

John Anthony Scott, editor of the standard modern edition of the *Journal*, attempts an objective assessment of its influence. He concludes, "There is, in truth, at the present time no way of estimating the impact the *Journal* made at the time it was published."[10] Harper's and Longman's publishing records have been lost. Scott adds, "In the years since publication of the *Journal* scholarly evaluation, as might be expected, has divided along sectional lines. Southern historians have either ignored the *Journal* or have dismissed it as the product of bias. Northern historians have accepted much of Fanny's evidence, in particular where it has been confirmed by similar evidence from other sources."[11]

It is probably an exaggeration to state, as did one writer, that the *Journal* "more than any other book except *Uncle Tom's Cabin* helped to smash the old South, and wipe the plantation civilization out of existence."[12] Other powerful forces were operating to keep England from intervening in the American Civil War. Readers in general recognized the *Journal* as a dreadful indictment of slavery as an institution. The *London Review* conceded that it would have required the imagination of a Dante to have conjured such a vision out of thin air. As the wife of a slavemaster, Fanny had reason to look for the best side of the system, and had hoped before going to Georgia to find ameliorating factors. Her "inside story," from the point of view of a cultured Englishwoman, is unique in the annals of slavery. It fills a place in the history of the "peculiar institution" occupied by no other writer. The historical and literary value of the *Journal* is therefore incontrovertible.

9.

From Slavery to Freedom

FREDERICK DOUGLASS'S *Narrative of the Life of Frederick Douglass, an American Slave Written by Himself*

Accounts of their experiences as slaves were told by numerous black refugees who fled to freedom. At least a hundred such narratives were published and widely read in the antebellum North. Among the early examples are *A Narrative of the Uncommon Sufferings and Surprising Deliverance of Briton Hammon, a Negro Man* (Boston, 1760), and *The Interesting Narrative of the Life of Olaudah Equiano or Gustavus Vassa, the African* (1789); the latter went through various editions. The revelations were filled with the horrors of slavery and generally sensational in style.

The most famous of all autobiographies of ex-slaves was Frederick Douglass's *Narrative*. Unlike most slave accounts, which were ghostwritten by abolitionist hacks, Douglass's work was indeed "Written by Himself," as the title proclaims. As William Lloyd Garrison, author of a preface to the book, states, "Mr. Douglass has very properly chosen to write his own *Narrative*, in his own style, and according to the best of his ability, rather than to employ some one else."[1]

Douglass was born about 1817 in Tuckahoe, on the Eastern Shore of Maryland, and named Frederick Augustus Washington Bailey. He had no exact knowledge of his age, for, like slaves in general, his birth was unrecorded. Neither did he know his father, except that he was a white man and probably his master. Frederick and his slave mother were separated from each other when he was a mere infant, a common custom in that section of Maryland. The mother was hired out to another plantation owner some twelve miles away, and Frederick only saw her three or four times thereafter, until she died when he was age seven.

Due to a strange streak in human psychology, Douglass comments that slave children with white fathers were subjected to more mistreatment than others, because "they are a constant offense to their mistress."[2] She persistently finds fault with them, he observed. They can do almost nothing to please her, she likes to see them whipped, and she is especially resentful if the master shows them special favor. For that reason, the master is often compelled to sell his own children to keep peace at home.

Frederick's first master was a Captain Anthony, whose title was acquired by sailing a craft on the Chesapeake Bay. Anthony owned two or three farms and about thirty slaves, all under the care of an overseer named Plummer, described by Douglass as "a miserable drunkard, a profane swearer, and a savage monster."[3] Plummer always went armed with a cowskin lash and a heavy cudgel, to inflict punishment on the slaves. Anthony was little better: "a cruel man, hardened by a long life of slaveholding," who "would at times seem to take great pleasure in whipping a slave."[4] The "terrible spectacle" of seeing slaves cruelly beaten, and on occasion being whipped himself, was a traumatic experience that haunted Douglass for the rest of his life.

The life of a slave in all its sordid details is recounted by Douglass. The principal products of the plantation where he was owned were tobacco, corn, and wheat. Once each month, the slaves received their allowance of food, consisting of eight pounds of pork or its equivalent in fish of poor quality, a bushel of cornmeal, and salt. Clothing was doled out annually; the standard items were two coarse linen shirts, one pair of linen trousers, one jacket, one pair of trousers for winter, "made of coarse negro cloth," one pair of stockings, and one pair of shoes. Children who did not work in the fields were allowed no clothing except two coarse linen shirts each year; consequently, they went nearly naked in all seasons. The slaves had no beds, but slept on the cold floor covered only by one coarse blanket for each man and woman; there were none for children.

Large plantations as described by Douglass were virtually independent. All mechanical operations—shoemaking and mending, blacksmithing, cartwrighting, coopering, weaving, and grain-grinding—were performed there.

A striking characteristic of the slaves was their singing. Douglass notes that he had "often been utterly astonished, since I came to the North, to find persons who could speak of the singing, among slaves, as evidence of their contentment and happiness. It is impossible to conceive of a greater mistake. Slaves sing most when they are most unhappy." The "rude and apparently incoherent songs told a tale of woe—Every tone was a testimony against slavery, and a prayer to God for deliverance from chains. . . . Crying for joy and singing for joy were alike uncommon to me while in the jaws of slavery."[5]

The contrast between the life of the slaves in their cabins, fed on coarse cornmeal and often tainted meat and clothed in torn linen, and that of their white masters in the "Great House" could hardly have been more marked. The slaveowner and his family lived in regal splendor, dressed in fine clothing; their table groaned with "blood-bought luxuries, gathered with painstaking care at home and abroad."[6] They were served by a small army of servants, who catered to their every whim. A plentiful supply of horses and hounds was maintained for their sport and pleasure.

Extreme caution was the rule among slaves in voicing any complaints against the master and his treatment of them, for dire punishment awaited those who digressed. Douglass remarks "that slaves, when inquired of as to their condition and the character of their masters, almost universally say they are contented, and that their masters are kind. The slaveholders have been known to send in spies among their slaves, to ascertain their views and feelings in regard to their condition. The slaves suppress the truth rather than take the consequence of telling it."[7]

Douglass observed a succession of overseers, nearly uniformly cruel. An especially vicious specimen was an Austin Gore, who interpreted "the slightest look, word, or gesture on the part of the slave, into impudence, and would treat it accordingly."[8] Gore followed to the letter the slaveholders' maxim that "it is better that a dozen slaves suffer under the lash, than that the overseer should be convicted, in the presence of the slaves, of having been at fault."[9]

Southern apologists for the institution of slavery maintained that Southern laws were as stringent against the murder of slaves as of whites, and statutes usually forbade the separation of children below the age of ten from their mothers. Douglass offered evidence to refute both claims. Austin Gore on one occasion undertook to whip a slave named Demby. To escape the scourging, Demby plunged into a nearby creek. When he failed to heed an order to come out, Gore shot and killed him. Douglass's cousin, a girl of about fifteen, was beaten to death by her mistress. Other murders of slaves in the area, known to Douglass at firsthand, were also noted, from which he concludes that "killing a slave, or any colored person, in Talbot County, Maryland, is not treated as a crime, either by the courts or the community."[10] None of the perpetrators of the murders described was ever arrested or punished.

An old Southern plantation custom scathingly criticized by Douglass was the holiday period granted slaves between Christmas and New Year, ostensibly to make them more contented and to mitigate the rigors of slavery. The more industrious and serious-minded slaves would spend the time making brooms, mats, horse-collars, and baskets. Others would hunt for opossums, rabbits, and raccoons. The great majority, however, engaged in playing ball, boxing, wrestling, footracing, fiddling, dancing, and drinking whiskey. A slave who worked during the holidays was regarded as one who rejected the favor of his master. It was a disgrace not to get drunk at Christmas. In Douglass's judgment, "The holidays are part and parcel of the gross fraud, wrong, and inhumanity of slavery—among the most effective means in the hands of the slave-holders in keeping down the spirit of insurrection."[11] After a period of wild dissipation, the slaves found it a relief to return to their labors.

Fortunately, for young Frederick, at the age of about eight, he was sent to Baltimore to be a house servant and companion to little Thomas Auld. Frederick was chosen over a number of other slave children who might have been sent from the plantation to Baltimore. This move, he notes, "laid the foundation, and opened the gateway, to all my subsequent prosperity."[12] At first, his new mistress appeared to be "a woman of the kindest heart and finest feelings."[13] She undertook to teach Frederick his alphabet and to spell simple words. The moment her husband learned of this activity, however, he sternly forbade it, asserting, "A nigger should know nothing but to obey his master—to do as he is told to do. Learning would *spoil* the best nigger in the world. If you teach that nigger how to read, there would be no keeping him. It would forever unfit him to be a slave."[14] From this moment, Frederick realized that the road to freedom was by way of ability to read and to write. Under the influence of slavery, Mrs. Auld's personality changed, and she not only ceased teaching the young slave, but exercised the most severe discipline over him.

Going from the plantation to Baltimore, Frederick immediately observed a marked difference in the treatment of slaves from what he had witnessed in the country. "A city slave is almost a freeman," he writes, "compared with a slave on the plantation. He is much better fed and clothed, and enjoys privileges altogether unknown to the slave on the plantation."[15] In part, the more humane treatment was due to the close proximity of neighbors, who would be shocked by any atrocious cruelties and failure to provide sufficient food for the slaves.

Frederick lived in the Auld household for about seven years, until he was near the age of fifteen. During this time, despite all obstacles, he learned to read and write. To achieve that goal, he resorted to various stratagems to circumvent the opposition of his master and mistress. The most successful plan was to make friends of all the little white boys he met in the street. In exchange for bread which he would carry for the hungry urchins, they would instruct him in reading. When he was sent on an errand he always carried a book, and by going quickly found time for a lesson before his return. At age twelve, Frederick acquired Caleb Bingham's *The Columbian Orator*, the contents of which included a dialogue on the pros and cons of slavery and one of Sheridan's speeches on behalf of

Catholic emancipation, termed by Douglass "a powerful vindi-
cation of human rights."[16]

Learning to write was an equally devious matter, again accomplished mainly through Frederick's young companions. Lacking
paper, his "copy-book was the board fence, brick wall and pave-
ment," his "pen and ink was a lump of chalk." He copied the italics
in *Webster's Spelling Book*. Later, he wrote between the lines in
Tom's copybooks, exactly imitating his young master's handwriting.

In the course of his Baltimore stay, Frederick began to hear of
the activities of the abolitionists and of the abolition movement.
This was the beginning of his resolution to make a break for
freedom and to escape to the North.

A drastic change in Frederick's situation occurred when his old
master Captain Anthony suddenly died. As part of the estate,
Frederick was returned to the plantation. All property—slaves of all
ages, horses, sheep, and swine—was divided between two heirs.
Frederick was fortunate to go to the daughter Lucretia, instead of
her dissolute, brutal brother Andrew. Following the division, he
was sent back to Baltimore to live with the Auld family, but soon
after that Lucretia died and Frederick was transferred to Thomas
Auld's plantation. During his nine months there he was subjected
to a number of severe whippings. Finally, he was turned over to
Edward Covey, who had a notorious reputation for breaking the
spirit of young slaves. Covey was a perfect prototype for Harriet
Beecher Stowe's fictional character Simon Legree.

The sadistic Covey lost no time in trying to whip Douglass into
submission. For the first six months he was beaten every week.
From dawn to dusk, Douglass was kept slaving away in the fields
or in the woods. Covey lurked around his own plantation, spying
on the slaves, sometimes crawling on his hands and knees to
surprise them. One hot summer day, while working in the treading
yard, Douglass collapsed from exhaustion. This so infuriated Covey
that he kicked him several times and gave him a blow on the head
with a heavy hickory slab. The following day, after a new attack,
Douglass ran away and hid in the woods. There seemed no alternative to returning to the plantation. When Covey attempted to tie
him up, however, preparatory to another severe beating, Douglass

resisted, took the whip away from Covey and refused to submit to the lash. "Fighting madness had come upon me," Douglass wrote, "and I found my strong fingers attached to the throat of the tyrant." They fought for nearly two hours before Covey quit, unable to subdue the younger man. During the remaining six months of Douglass's stay on the plantation, Covey never again struck Douglass. The fight with Covey was a turning point in Douglass's career. "I was nothing before; I was a man now," he recalled "with a renewed determination to be a free man."[17]

Douglass's disillusionment with religion as practiced by the slaveholders began early. One of his masters, Captain Auld, was converted at a Methodist camp meeting, but instead of becoming more humane, he was crueler after his conversion than before. According to Douglass, "Prior to his conversion, he relied upon his own depravity to shield and sustain him in his savage barbarity; but after his conversion, he found religious sanction and support for his slaveholding cruelty."[18] Auld prayed morning, noon, and night, was active in religious revivals, and regularly entertained preachers in his home. Edward Covey, too, "was a professor of religion—a pious soul—a member and a class-leader in the Methodist Church,"[19] much addicted to prayer. On the basis of his own experiences and observations, Douglass concludes:

I assert most unhesitatingly, that the religion of the South is a mere covering for the most horrid crimes,—a justifier of the most appalling barbarity,—a sanctifier of the most hateful frauds,—and a dark shelter, under which the darkest, foulest, grossest, and most infernal deeds of slaveholders find the strongest protection. Were I to be again reduced to the chains of slavery, next to that enslavement, I should regard being the slave of a religious master the greatest calamity that could befall me. For of all the slaveholders with whom I have ever met, religious slaveholders are the worst. I have ever found them the meanest and basest, the most cruel and cowardly, of all others.[20]

In an appendix to the *Narrative*, Douglass makes clear that he was not antireligious or an opponent of religion. His denouncements were meant "strictly to apply to the *slaveholding religion* of this land, and with no possible reference to Christianity proper."[21]

After Covey, Douglass worked for two years on the plantation of a neighboring slaveowner, William Freeland. Together with five other slaves, he made plans to seize a canoe, paddle down the Chesapeake, and follow the North Star to freedom. But one of the men turned informer. The conspirators were arrested and jailed on the eve of their planned break. As the leader, Douglass expected to be sold to slave traders and shipped to New Orleans. Instead, Captain Auld sent him back to Baltimore, where for the next two years, 1836–38, he worked in the Baltimore shipyards, first as an apprentice and then as a skilled caulker. All wages earned had to be turned over to Auld.

As a skilled worker, Douglass experienced for the first time "the conflict of slavery with the interests of the white mechanics and laborers of the South." Forced to compete with slaves, the white workers found it impossible to get decent wages. They attempted, therefore, to eliminate all blacks, free and slave, from the trades. On various occasions, Douglass was subjected to physical attack by enraged whites. Later in life, Douglass recognized that the Southern white worker was almost as much a victim of the slave system as was the Negro. He believed that the slaveholders "encouraged the enmity of white laborers against the black and reduced the white to slavery also." The wageless labor of slaves was used to cheapen the wages of white labor.[22]

Meanwhile, Douglass continued to plot his escape from slavery and slave territory. From a seafaring friend he borrowed a sailor's "protection," a paper describing the physical characteristics of its rightful owner, a free American sailor. Douglass waited until the train from Baltimore to Philadelphia was in motion and then jumped aboard. The train conductor was satisfied with the "protection" paper and did not compare Douglass's features with those described. On 4 September 1838, the fugitive rode into New York City. There he was aided by David Ruggles, secretary of the New York Vigilance Committee, an organization to assist runaways and to prevent free Negroes from being kidnapped and returned to slavery. A few days after his arrival, Frederick sent for Anna, a free Negro woman of Baltimore, and the couple were married.

Because of the danger of recapture in New York and inability to find employment there, the Douglasses moved on to New Bedford, Massachusetts. At the same time, a change of name was decided upon, from Frederick Augustus Washington Bailey to Frederick Douglass—the Douglass inspired by reading Sir Walter Scott's *The Lady of the Lake*.

Douglass soon discovered that race prejudice was not sectional. No one would hire him in the New Bedford shipyards as a caulker, because white caulkers refused to work with Negroes. His hand was turned therefore to whatever unskilled or menial work came his way. For the next three years, Douglass sawed wood, shoveled coal, swept chimneys, rolled oil casks, drove a coach, carried a hod, and waited on tables. His earnings averaged one dollar a day. The family income was supplemented by Anna's earnings as a domestic servant, even after her children began to arrive.

Another dramatic turn in Douglass's fortunes began in 1841, when he attended an abolitionist meeting in Nantucket. There he was prevailed upon to talk about his recollections of slavery. His natural talent as an orator was revealed and the Massachusetts Anti-Slavery Society at once engaged him as an itinerant lecturer. For the next four years, Douglass spoke throughout the North, after traveling the reform circuit in company with the two principal leaders of New England abolitionism, William Lloyd Garrison and Wendell Phillips.

Rumors began to circulate that, because of his oratorical ability and lack of a Southern accent, Douglass had actually not been a slave at all. To disprove such charges, he decided to write and publish an autobiography recounting his experiences. The result was the *Narrative of the Life of Frederick Douglass, an American Slave*, printed in Boston in 1845. Friends warned him of the perils of publishing the book. In modern vernacular language, it "blew his cover," thereby making it easy for his Southern slavemaster to trace him and perhaps force his return. The *Narrative* was the first of three autobiographies written by Douglass, the last two considerably more detailed. *My Bondage and My Freedom* appeared in 1855, and the final work, *Life and Times of Frederick Douglass*, came off the press in 1881.

The first edition of the *Narrative*, 5,000 copies, was sold out in four months. Within a year, four more editions, a total of 8,000 copies, were issued. Three editions were brought out in England and two in Ireland. By 1850 a total of 30,000 copies had been distributed in America and the British Isles. Favorable reviews at home and abroad spurred sales. Of all Douglass's prolific writings, the 163-page *Narrative* was undoubtedly the most influential. It was relatively brief, told an absorbing story of slavery experiences, and was well adapted to abolitionist propaganda.

To guard against the potential danger of his being captured and sent back South, Douglass's friends persuaded him to go to England for an eighteen-month stay. He was already being hailed as a rising star among the Negro people. Wendell Phillips wrote to a friend in London, "If you ever see him, remember that *in my opinion*, you see the most remarkable and by far the ablest colored man we have ever had here."[23] While in Britain, Douglass lectured extensively, usually to overflow audiences. He was urged to remain in England, but refused, saying, "America is my home, and there I mean to spend and be spent in the cause of my outraged fellow countrymen." There is solid evidence that Douglass influenced British public opinion and increased the hostility to slavery, a fact that contributed to the British government's later decision not to recognize the Confederacy during the Civil War.

To insure Douglass's safety when he returned to the United States, the Society of Friends raised the purchase price of his freedom and obtained manumission papers, dated 5 December 1846. The step stirred up heated controversy. Many abolitionists contended that the transaction was a recognition of the "right to traffic in human beings," and opposed any payment to a slaveowner. In any event, Douglass was now legally a free man. His English friends also presented him with a purse of about $2,500 to publish a weekly newspaper, the *North Star*; the title was later changed to *Frederick Douglass's Paper*.

Douglass remained in the limelight for nearly half a century, until his death in 1895. His fame derived from a variety of roles: he was an eloquent abolitionist lecturer, newspaper editor, recruiter for black Union troops in the Civil War, a spokesman after the war for the newly freed slaves, and holder of three offices in the federal government. He was an imposing figure, described by a contemporary as "more than six feet in height; and his majestic form, as he rose to speak, straight as an arrow, muscular yet lithe and graceful, his flashing eye, and more than all his voice," rivaling Daniel Webster's in richness, depth, and sonorousness.[24]

The stark realism of Douglass's *Narrative* heightened its impact on the reading public. The work is highly factual, lending credibility to the account. None of the names and places mentioned by the author are ficitious. Recent research has validated all his data. On the other hand, his points of view may occasionally be open to question. Slavery was a more enlightened institution in Maryland than in the Deep South, and, except for a few years of plantation life, Douglass was better fed, clothed, and housed than the great majority of slaves. He made no effort to be charitable to the slaveholding class. There is no mention by him of the problems that would arise with the abolition of slavery. The property rights of the masters and states' rights in his view were of no consequence. As one of Douglass's editors, Benjamin Quarles, commented, "If slavery had a sunny side, it will not be found in the pages of the *Narrative*."[25] Douglass based his unrelenting hatred of and opposition to the "peculiar institution" not so much on his personal experiences as on the sufferings and hardships of three million slaves whose rights were being violated. To him, slavery was "perpetual unpaid toil; no marriage, no husband, no wife, no parent, no child; ignorance, brutality, licentiousness; whips, scourges, chains, auctions, jails, and separations; an embodiment of all the woes the imagination can conceive."[26]

10.

Political Philosopher

JOHN CALDWELL CALHOUN'S
A Disquisition on Government

_____

In the period of violent debates which preceded the Civil War, John C. Calhoun has been called the only notable political thinker. A scholarly analysis by Ralph Lerner states that "Calhoun in effect put his *Disquisition* in a class of which it is almost the sole example: an American political theory."[1] Another critic, Hamilton Basso, rated Calhoun's book as "one of the landmarks of American political theory . . . one of the most brilliant feats of the American intellect, containing perhaps the finest defense of minority rights ever written," but concludes that "it is like a faulty dam trying to hold back the flood-waters of every current of democratic thought and aspiration."[2]

Calhoun's political career stretched over a period of nearly half a century, from the administration of Thomas Jefferson to that of Zachary Taylor. A native of South Carolina, born five years before the drafting of the federal Constitution (which his father, a member of the state legislature, opposed), Calhoun served variously as a member of the South Carolina legislature, of the House of Representatives, and of the United States Senate, as well as holding the offices of secretary of war, secretary of state, and vice-president. For years he ardently sought the presidency, but the office always eluded him, principally because of party machinations and power-ful enemies.

Shortly before the end of his life, Calhoun prepared a manu-script setting forth his views on government in general, a short work of 107 pages, entitled *A Disquisition on Government*, followed by a larger treatise, *A Discourse on the Constitution and Government of the United States*; both were published posthumously. Two basic premises pervade these political credos: the inequality of human beings (especially Negroes) and the supremacy of the individual states within the federal union.

A curious change occurred in Calhoun's thinking in midcareer. Until about 1825, he was a zealous advocate of national unity and national power, including a larger military establishment, an en-larged federal budget, federal roads, higher tariffs, more manufac-tures, and a new national bank. John Quincy Adams wrote of Calhoun: "He is above all sectional and factional prejudices more than any other statesman of this Union with whom I have ever acted." During this period, as a staunch supporter of American nationalism and capitalism, Calhoun worked for all measures that would advance national unity, integration, and prosperity. For ex-ample, in a speech in the House of Representatives in 1817, propos-ing a nationwide transportation network, he urged, "Let us bind the republic together with a perfect system of roads and canals." No "low, sordid, selfish and sectional spirit," he continued, should be permitted "to take possession of this House."[3] When the ques-tion of slavery emerged in the controversy over Missouri, Calhoun stood for moderation, writing to a friend, "We to the South ought not to assent easily to the belief that there is a conspiracy either against our property or just weight in the Union."[4]

Calhoun's conversion from a nationalist to a sectionalist came after his return to South Carolina, following a stay of fourteen years in Washington. He was struck by dramatic differences be-tween the North and the South. The South was virtually un-changed, while the North was increasing in population, building cities, and growing wealthy through industry, trade and commerce, and free enterprise. The Southern economy, in contrast, remained based on agriculture and slavery. At home, Calhoun found strong resentment against Northern economic policies, especially high tariffs, which the Southern farmers were convinced worked to enrich Northern capitalists at the expense of Southern planters. No politician could expect to remain in office who did not take a strong stand for sectional interests. Calhoun, politically a highly ambitious man, thenceforth threw in his lot with his native state and region.

The breaking point came in 1828, with passage of the exorbitant "Tariff of Abominations." Calhoun's first statement on sectional differences, *Exposition and Protest*, denounced the new law in bitter terms. "We are the serfs of the system," he declared. After analyzing the cost of the tariff to the plantation economy, he began to consider possible political solutions, asserting that "no government, based on the naked principle that the majority ought to govern, however true the maxim in its proper sense, and under proper restrictions, can preserve its liberty, even for a single generation." Only those governments which provide checks on power, "which limit and restrain within proper bounds the power of the majority, have had a prolonged existence, and been distinguished for virtue, patriotism, power, and happiness."[5] The answer, Calhoun concluded, was state nullification, the concept that the powers of sovereignty belonged to the states; each state had the right, it was argued, to declare a law null and void within its boundaries and to refuse to permit its enforcement there.

Most divisive, and the prime source of an irreconcilable conflict, was the slavery issue. Calhoun's vigorous defense of state rights had as a chief goal the preservation of the institution of slavery. "Congress," he declared, "has no legitimate jurisdiction over the subject of slavery either here or elsewhere." Abolition could only be voted by the individual states, in his view.

In the years immediately following the Revolution, it had been commonly assumed that slavery was a dying institution and would gradually disappear throughout the country. The assumption ended with the invention of the cotton gin and power-driven textile machinery. Cotton became king and slavery, Southern planters maintained, was essential to cotton production. Economic ruin for the South would result from the abolition of slavery. Calhoun estimated that the property value of slaves was nearly one billion dollars.

Dismissing arguments against the morality of slavery, Calhoun contended that the institution was "good—a positive good" for both races. The basic premise for this conclusion was the assumed natural inferiority of the Negro race. "In the whole history of man," Calhoun states, "there is no instance whatever of any civilized colored race, of any shade, being found equal to the establishment and maintenance of free government."[6] Going back to the ancient Greeks for supporting evidence, he notes that Plato and Aristotle had found no inconsistency between slavery and democracy. Accepting Aristotle's dictum that some men are intended by nature to be slaves, Calhoun extended the idea to the entire African race. The Negro, in his view, was of a servile nature, unfitted for freedom and unable to exist in a civilized society, except as a slave. He held that the blacks in America exhibited a vast improvement, physically, morally, and intellectually, over those of central Africa from whence their ancestors came.

The Jeffersonian theory that all men are born equal was scorned by Calhoun. Only Adam and Eve were "created," he asserts, "and of these one was pronounced subordinate to the other. All others have come into the world by being born, and in no sense either free or equal."[7] Furthermore, he added, it is "a great and dangerous error to suppose that all people are equally entitled to liberty. It is a reward to be earned, not a blessing to be gratuitously lavished on all alike;—a reward reserved for the intelligent, the patriotic, the virtuous and deserving;—and not a boon to be bestowed on a people too ignorant, degraded and vicious, to be capable either of appreciating or of enjoying it."[8]

Jefferson's humanism, the belief that man is innately good, was totally rejected by Calhoun. Following the Calvinistic creed in which he had been reared, he was convinced that man is by nature evil. Only the elect, not the people as a whole, were qualified and had the right to rule—and to hold slaves.

As portrayed by Calhoun, slavery was thus a righteous and beneficent institution, being imperiled by the dominating political and economic power of Northern capitalism. If the principles of Jeffersonian democracy were allowed to prevail, slavery was doomed. It was inevitable that the richer and more populous North would eventually impose its system on the helpless Southern minority. To counteract and to resist this apparently irresistible trend,

Calhoun turned to fundamental political theory. What right, he asked, did majorities have to override minorities?

A philosophic basis for Calhoun's views on government is laid in the opening paragraphs of his *Disquisition*. Government originates, he held, in human nature. Man is a social animal, and he could hardly exist in any other state than in association with his fellows. In no other fashion, Calhoun believed, "could he attain to a full development of his moral and intellectual faculties, or raise himself, in the scale of being, much above the level of the brute creation."[9] Human society cannot exist, however, without government. At the same time, there is a natural tendency for individuals to come into conflict with one another, for it is the nature of each man to pursue his own interests. Without the controlling force of government, the selfishness of individual persons would lead to society's destruction. The problem then becomes one of maintaining control over government, as seen by Calhoun:

But government, although intended to protect and preserve society, has itself a strong tendency to disorder and abuse of its powers, as all experience and almost every page of history testify. The cause is to be found in the same constitution of our nature which makes government indispensable. The powers which it is necessary for government to possess, in order to repress violence and preserve order, cannot execute themselves. They must be administered by men in whom, like others, the individual are stronger than the social feelings. And hence, the powers vested in them to prevent injustice and oppression on the part of others, will, if left unguarded, be by them converted into instruments to oppress the rest of the community.[10]

Calhoun was thus building up a philosophical case for his argument that Northern interests were abusing and oppressing the South through selfish economic policies and attacks on the institution of slavery, the basis of the Southern economy. Unless safeguarded by constitutional means, that is, by the structure of the government itself, the power given to the rulers to prevent injustice and oppression would be used to oppress the ruled.

As a solution to the dilemma, Calhoun proposed an elaborate scheme combining suffrage and what he termed a "concurrent majority." In the establishment of a government, according to Calhoun, there are three possibilities: a government which has too much power, clothed with dictatorial authority; one with too little power, lacking the strength "to protect and preserve society" or "to repel assaults from abroad;" and, third, a government strong enough to carry on its proper functions, but lacking power to abuse the interest of minorities. The last plan, the idea of a concurrent majority, was Calhoun's own preference and is generally recognized as his most original contribution to political theory.

Concurrent majority as conceived by Calhoun was essentially the doctrine of states' rights. He rejected the established practice of majority rule, whereby each vote is counted equal and the largest number of votes decides each issue. He had no faith in the universal democratic belief that mere numbers should always prevail, since majorities usually lacked knowledge, judgment, and wisdom to make sound decisions. "The right of suffrage," wrote Calhoun, "of itself, can do no more than give complete control to those who elect, over the conduct of those they have elected."[11]

The American Constitution had incorporated a system of separation of powers, reinforced by checks and balances, to prevent governmental oppression, but the principle had failed in action, Calhoun claimed, especially when a ruling majority gained control of all three branches of government. A government is not truly democratic if a numerical majority can ignore or disregard minority interests.

Majority rule, according to Calhoun's proposal, would be replaced by government by the whole community, that is, through a constitutional provision for representing both majorities and minorities. Rather than counting heads, society would be governed by the principal economic interests and geographical units of the nation. Minority interests would be guarded by "either a concurrent voice in making and executing the laws or a veto on their execution." This device would insure that "different interests, orders, classes, or portions" of the community were protected, "and all conflict and struggle between them prevented."[12]

An added feature of the concurrent majority scheme, Calhoun thought, should be two presidents, one for the North, the other for the South, each to have veto power over acts of Congress, and no measure could pass without approval of the dual executive. In this way, the South would regain its position of equality with the North and be able to countermand undesirable legislation.

If the idea of the concurrent majority could be made a part of the U.S. Constitution, it would accomplish two purposes, in Calhoun's view. First, it would maintain permanently Southern power within the federal government, and, second, the propertied classes would receive constitutional protection against the excesses of democracy. The North would lose the advantage of its larger population.

Calhoun also hoped for and counted on an alliance between Northern capitalists and Southern conservatives to resist the agitation and demands of Northern radicals, in the belief that their mutual interests were involved. Though such a mutual defense agreement never materialized in Calhoun's time, the twentieth century has witnessed a close working relationship in the United States Congress between Northern and Southern conservatives.

Willard Thorp, editor of *A Southern Reader*, concluded that "when Calhoun propounded his version of the theory of states' rights ('concurrent majority') he was really seeking a device to preserve the authority of the central government without infringing upon the liberty of minorities. His main intention was to help his beloved South Carolina in her refusal to approve the high tariffs insisted upon by the North. But the Southern Democrats preempted his doctrine for quite other ends, and Calhoun was increasingly and disastrously involved with the proslavery cause. Calhoun's 'State Veto,' or Nullification as it was generally called, became the warrant for Secession and, eventually, for civil war."[13] This is a charitable interpretation, for throughout most of his career Calhoun was ardently proslavery and placed sectional ahead of national concerns. In a famous confrontation between President Jackson and Calhoun at a Jefferson Day dinner, Jackson proposed a toast, "Our Federal Union: it must be preserved!" to which Calhoun responded, "The Union—next to our liberty, the most dear."

If the principle of state sovereignty and concurrent majority were constitutionally founded, Calhoun foresaw that the South could always veto national laws considered inimical to its interests, such as tariffs and antislavery acts. "The government of the concurrent majority," stated Calhoun, "excludes the possibility of oppression, by giving to each interest—where there are established classes, the means of protecting itself, by its negative [veto] against all measures calculated to advance the peculiar interests of others at its expense."[14] Federal union, to Calhoun, meant separate sovereign states united through a central agency. He saw the United States not as a nation but as "an assemblage of nations, or peoples . . . united in their sovereign character immediately and directly by their own act, but without losing their separate and independent existence." The federal government had been created by the states for their convenience and it was not superior to the states.

At this point, Calhoun produced his theory of nullification, the essence of which is that each state holds an inherent power of veto over the federal government. It was the duty of each state to "determine definitely, as far as her citizens were concerned, the extent of the obligation which she has contracted; and if, in her opinion the [Federal] act [of Congress or Supreme Court] exercising the power be un-Constitutional, to declare it null and void, which declaration would be obligatory upon her citizens."[15]

Under Calhoun's influence, in 1832 the South Carolina legislature enacted an ordinance of nullification. The tariff act passed by Congress was declared null and void, U.S. customs officers were forbidden to collect any duties in South Carolina ports, and secession from the Union was called for as a last resort. Andrew Jackson as president was unwilling to stand by and watch dismemberment of the Union. "Disunion by armed force is treason," he proclaimed, and threatened to send a force of 35,000 men into South Carolina to stamp out rebellion and to hang Calhoun and other nullification leaders. Calhoun retreated, though never deviating in his stand on states' rights. Congress passed a force bill authorizing the president to use force, if necessary, to avoid any nullification of federal law. South Carolina immediately passed a second ordinance of nullification, to nullify the force bill. Thus the stage was set for civil war.

The failure of nullification, according to Calhoun and his adherents, could lead to a far more drastic step, secession—the withdrawal by a state from the federal union. In any system of federated states, Calhoun insisted, each sovereign state always has the right to secede. Such a radical move could be avoided, however, by adoption of the concurrent majority principle, under which Calhoun believed that any differences between the states and the federal union would be resolved.

The question of where sovereignty resides had been a live issue since the founding of the republic. James Madison, "father of the Constitution," stated that "in the sources from which the ordinary powers of government are drawn, it is partly federal and partly national."[16] Another view comes from John Marshall: "In America, the powers of sovereignty are divided between the government of the Union and those of the states. They are each sovereign, with respect to the objects committed to them."[17] The idea of divided sovereignty to Calhoun seemed absurd: "How sovereignty itself, the supreme power, can be partly sovereign and partly not sovereign, partly supreme and partly *not* supreme—it is impossible to conceive."[18] Furthermore, he argued that sovereignty did not belong to the whole American people, but to the peoples of the several states. In the formation of the United States, according to Calhoun, the individual states delegated governmental powers though never their respective sovereignties.

To his opponents' contention that a government based on a concurrent majority is impracticable or at best weak, Calhoun turned to history for an answer. An extreme application of government by concurrent majority, he noted, was in Poland, where for more than two centuries, during the period of Poland's greatest power and fame, the election of a king required the concurrence of every person in an assembly of 150,000 to 200,000 of the nobility and gentry. Also, in the proceedings of the Polish Diet the unanimous consent of the king, senate, bishops, the deputies of the nobility, and the gentry of the palatinates was required. A classic basis for the theory was found in ancient Rome, where there was separate representation of patricians and plebeians, each of which held veto power over the acts of the government. A more recent illustration was in British parliamentary practice, where there was a balance of classes or estates. Still closer home was an example from Calhoun's home state of South Carolina; in the beginning planters from the low country had dominated both branches of the state legislature. As frontiersmen and farmers in the upcountry increased in number, they demanded fuller representation. By a compromise dating back to 1807, the low country was given control of the senate and the house went to the upcountry. All legislation thereafter required concurrence by both sections of the state. The result,

Calhoun reported, was harmony and concord between the two parts of the state.

Calhoun's theory is easily comprehensible. Its essential element is the absolute sovereignty of the states over the Constitution. His supporting reasons are elaborate, ingenious, and tortuous. In Calhoun's time, many persons, North and South, believed that the states, having voluntarily accepted the Constitution, could rescind their action and withdraw from the Union. From a historical point of view, in the convention which framed the Constitution, the national party had a considerable majority over the state sovereignty party. The compromise by which the states were given equal representation in the Senate was agreed to by the majority to persuade several smaller states against leaving the convention. In general, the statesmen who favored a national government also favored ratification of the Constitution, and the opposition to ratification came from those who were antagonistic to a national government. Prior to adoption of the Constitution, the ineffective confederation of states on several occasions was near dissolution. The Articles of Confederation provided for no executive and only a weak legislature. Congress could not levy taxes or enforce its laws. The founding fathers, whose strenuous efforts saved the Union and succeeded in obtaining ratification of the Constitution, were fully aware that leaders of the forces against acceptance of the Constitution favored splitting the country into a number of separate sovereignties. Calhoun's theory, if made operative, would have effectively undone the work of the early nationalists.

In his *Disquisition on Government* and other writings, Calhoun rejected the basic assumptions on which American democracy was founded. The concept of a united American nation was unacceptable to him, because the idea of equality of people was repugnant. Shortly before his death, he wrote, "I never use the word 'nation' in speaking of the United States. I always use the word 'union' or 'confederacy.' We are not a nation, but a *union*, a *confederacy* of equal and sovereign states."[19]

In his *The American Political Tradition*, Richard Hofstadter offers these discerning comments: "The essence of Calhoun's mistake as a practical statesman was that he tried to achieve a static solution for a dynamic situation. The North, stimulated by invention and industry and strengthened by a tide of immigration, was growing in population and wealth, filling the West, and building railroads that bound East and West together. No concurrent majority, nor any other principle embodied in a parchment, could stem the tide that was measured every ten years in the census returns."[20] Neither was the nation as a whole willing to accept Calhoun's premise that every civilized society must be built upon a submerged and exploited slave class. As an impassioned defender of man's right to enslave man, Calhoun became a tragic figure. In retrospect, his policy for the South, leading as it did to civil war, was suicidal and his defense of slavery at best amoral. In the end, all that he hoped and stood for was rejected. There was no union of Northern and Southern conservatives to defend class rule, the theory of the concurrent majority was met with an increasingly democratic electorate, the people found the idea of human inequality unacceptable, and the principle of nullification went down to defeat in the Civil War.

Hated Helper

HINTON ROWAN HELPER'S *The Impending Crisis
of the South: How to Meet It*

A battle of the books erupted a decade before the firing on Fort
Sumter. The opening fusillade was Harriet Beecher Stowe's *Uncle
Tom's Cabin*; its author was greeted by Abraham Lincoln as "the
little lady who made this big war." The Stowe novel inspired a
flood of "anti-Tom" literature, novels, essays, and poems designed
to counteract its terrific impact on millions of readers. The case
against slavery was powerfully reinforced by Frederick Olmsted's
articles and books on his observations of plantation life during
extensive travels from Maryland to Texas. Olmsted's calm, dispassionate findings demonstrated that economically slavery did not
pay and that it retarded Southern development.

The same theme, though in far more explosive fashion, was
played upon a short time later by Hinton Helper of North Carolina
in his work *The Impending Crisis*. Basing his book upon statistics
from the 1850 census, Helper produced what he believed to be
irrefutable proof that Southern backwardness, especially the de-
pressed state of the poor whites, was due to one factor alone—
slavery. Using numerous statistical tables, Helper showed, as Olmsted had done, that the slave states of the South had long since lost
their early preeminence and fallen behind the North in their prog-

ress because of a system which depleted the soil and depended on inefficient, unwilling workers who could never compete with free labor.

A distinguished Civil War scholar, Earl Schenck Miers, commented, "Although a single book cannot bear the responsibility for beginning the American Civil War, no list of the decisive causes of that tragic conflict would be complete unless it included the publication of *The Impending Crisis of the South: How to Meet It* by Hinton Rowan Helper."[1]

Helper was born on a small farm near Mocksville, North Carolina, in 1829, the son of an illiterate farmer who died early, leaving eleven children and four slaves, and an impoverished household struggling for economic survival. Hinton's limited education was obtained at a local academy, following which he clerked in a bookstore at Salisbury for three years, spent a short period in New York City, and then set off by clipper ship for the gold fields of California. During three years of hand-to-mouth existence there, he failed to strike it rich, and in 1854 he returned to Salisbury, bitter and frustrated.

From early youth Helper was an omnivorous reader. By the light of pine knots he read during long winter nights, resolved to escape what he described as "the prison grounds of those loathsome dungeons of illiteracy in which it has been the constant policy of the oligarchy to keep the masses, the nonslaveholding whites and the negroes, forever confined." His almost rabid hatred of the Southern slaveholding oligarchy came to light in such statements.

As a boy and young man, Helper had often reflected on the evil effects of slavery. His travels in the North and the West had convinced him that the average man in other regions was far better off from an economic standpoint than his Southern counterpart. The situation could be explained in only one way, Helper thought— it was a direct consequence of the institution of slavery. *The Impending Crisis* was the result of his conclusion.

Helper's motive for writing his controversial book was pure. In the preface he states, "An irrepressibly active desire to do something to elevate the South to an honorable and powerful position among the enlightened quarters of the globe has been the leading principle that has actuated me in the preparation of the present volume." Helper had no interest whatever in the moral aspects of slavery. The Negro he regarded as subhuman, incapable of being civilized. His sole concern was to eliminate slave competition and the monopoly held by the large planters, thereby benefitting Anglo-Saxon American workers and farmers.

For two and a half years Helper traveled about the country gathering information and writing. Abundant statistics to support his case were found in the recently published De Bow's census of 1850, which revealed that the Northern rate of material progress was far in excess of that of the Cotton Kingdom. James D. B. De Bow, superintendent of the census, ironically, was a native of Charleston, South Carolina, and a confirmed apologist for slavery.

The Helper manuscript was completed in 1857 and the author carried the bulky document to Baltimore, seeking a publisher. Here Helper encountered a Maryland statute, dating from 1831, which made it a felony with a penalty of not less than ten years in prison knowingly to write or print anything "having a tendency to excite discontent . . . amongst the people of color in this state, or of either of the other states or Territories of the United States." Moving on to New York, Helper found almost as many roadblocks to publication there as in Baltimore. The manuscript was rejected by Harper, Appleton, Scribner, and other established houses, for fear of antagonizing their important Southern clienteles. James Harper estimated that publication of the work would cost his firm twenty percent of its business. Finally, Helper accepted the offer of a book agent, A. B. Burdick, to issue the work on condition that Helper secure him against any loss. The first edition came off the press in June 1857.

In prefatory remarks, Helper assures his countrymen, particularly of the South, "that no narrow and partial doctrines of political or social economy, no prejudices of early education" had induced him to write it. He insists further that his object was not "to cast unmerited opprobrium upon slaveholders, or to display any special friendliness or sympathy for the blacks." Instead, the purpose was to examine the "subject more particularly with reference to its economic aspects as regards the whites—not with reference, except in a very slight degree, to its humanitarian or religious aspects." In an obvious reference to Harriet Beecher Stowe and her *Uncle Tom's*

Cabin, Helper comments, "Yankee wives have written the most popular anti-slavery literature of the day. Against this I have nothing to say; it is all well enough for women to give the fictions of slavery; men should give the facts."

And without further delay, Helper proceeds to marshall the "facts," by presenting detailed statistical comparisons between the free and the slave states. At the time of the first census, 1790, the South was far in the lead. Virginia had 748,308 inhabitants, New York less than half as many. Sixty years later, New York, long without slaves, had a population of 3,097,394; Virginia had less than half as many. In moneymaking ability, New York produced goods to the value of $237,597,249; Virginia produced about one-sixth as much. An equally "humiliating comparison" was made between North Carolina and Massachusetts and between Pennsylvania and South Carolina. Transportation by rail and canal made a worse showing. Further support for Helper's thesis came from contrasts between North and South in agricultural products, exports and imports, manufactures, patents issued, bank capital, post office operations, public schools, and so forth, including public libraries, of which the slave states had 695 containing 649,577 volumes, and the free states 14,911 containing 3,888,234 volumes.

"Less than three quarters of a century ago," Helper declares, "the South, with advantages in soil, climate, rivers, harbors, minerals, forests, and, indeed, almost every other natural resource, began an even race with the North, in all the important pursuits of life; and now, in the brief space of scarce three score years and ten, we find her completely distanced, enervated, dejected and dishonored. Slave-drivers are the sole authors of her disgrace."[2]

Helper next goes on to show that the lack of industrial development in the South had left the region dependent upon the North for virtually every item, both essentials and luxuries. In some of its most telling passages, *The Impending Crisis* deplores this situation:

It is a fact well known to every intelligent Southerner that we are compelled to go to the North for almost every article of utility and adornment, from matches, shoepegs and paintings up to cotton-mills, steamships and statuary. . . . We contribute nothing to the literature, polite arts and inventions of the age. . . . Almost everything produced at the North meets with ready sale, while, at the same time, there is no demand, even among our own citizens, for the productions of Southern industry. . . . We are dependent on Northern capitalists for the means necessary to build our railroads, canals and other public improvements . . . if we want to visit a foreign country, we find no convenient way of getting there except by taking passage through a Northern port.[3]

Helper offers further specifics: "We want Bibles, brooms, buckets and books, and we go to the North; we want pens, ink, paper, wafers and envelopes, and we go to the North; we want shoes, hats, handkerchiefs, umbrellas and pocket knives, and we go to the North; we want furniture, crockery, glassware and pianos, and we go to the North; we want toys, primers, school books, fashionable apparel, machinery, medicines, tombstones, and a thousand other things, and we go to the North for them all."[4] The Southern dependence on the North, from the cradle to the grave, is described by Helper in another bitter diatribe:

In infancy we are swaddled in Northern muslin; in childhood we are humored with Northern gewgaws; in youth we are instructed out of Northern books; at the age of maturity we sow our "wild oats" on Northern soil; in middle-life we exhaust our wealth, energies and talents in the dishonorable vocation of . . . giving aid and succor to every department of Northern power; in the decline of life we remedy our eye-sight with Northern spectacles, and support our infirmities with Northern canes; in old age we are drugged with Northern physic; and, finally, when we die, our inanimate bodies, shrouded in Northern cambric, are stretched upon the bier, borne to the grave in a Northern carriage, entombed with a Northern spade, and memorized with a Northern slab![5]

To the often-repeated boast of Southern politicians that "cotton is King" and their belief, according to Helper, "that the very existence of almost everything in the heaven above, in the earth beneath, and in the water under the earth, depended on it," the author maintains that the cotton crop is of little value to the South. The profits go to old and New England, for cotton "is carried in their ships, spun in their factories, woven in their looms, insured in their offices, returned again in their own vessels, and with double freight and cost of manufacturing added, purchased by the South at a high premium."[6] The South appeared to be losing at every stage of the process.

The Southern planters were accustomed to belittling the importance of agriculture in the Northern states. Detailed statistics were compiled by Helper to refute such misleading statements. In a satirical vein he replies: "The slave-holding oligarchy would whip us into the belief that agriculture is not one of the leading and lucrative pursuits of the free States, that the soil there is an uninterrupted barren waste, and that our Northern brethren, having the advantage in nothing except wealth, population, inland and foreign commerce, manufactures, mechanism, inventions, literature, the arts and sciences, and their concomitant branches of profitable industry,—miserable objects of charity—are dependent on us for the necessities of life."[7]

As Fanny Kemble and Frederick Olmsted had done before him, Helper deplored the reckless exploitation and waste of land under the slavery system. For example, he compares the different treatment, North and South, of the virgin forests:

At the North everything is turned to advantage. When a tree is cut down, the main body is sold or used for lumber, railing or poling, the stump for matches and shoepegs, the knees for shipbuilding, and the branches for fuel. At the South everything is either neglected or mismanaged. Whole forests are felled by the ruthless hand of slavery, the trees are cut into logs, rolled into heaps, covered with the limbs and brush, and then burned on the identical soil that gave them birth. The land itself next falls a prey to the fell destroyer, and that which was once a beautiful, fertile and luxuriant woodland, is soon despoiled of all its treasures, and converted into an eye-offending desert.[8]

Like Olmsted, Helper ridiculed the slaveholders' notion that the Southern climate was too hot and unhealthy for the white man, that only Negroes could endure the extreme heat. Here Helper cited another statistic from the 1850 census: more than a million free white laborers were engaged in agriculture in the South, including many women and children under fifteen. In Helper's own area of North Carolina, white women even hired themselves out during the harvest period, the hottest season of the year, to bind wheat and oats.

Helper's primary concern, constantly reiterated throughout *The Impending Crisis*, is the effect of slavery on the poor whites and other nonslaveholders of the South. In fact, the book is dedicated to "The Non-Slaveholding Whites of the South." Though this element in the population outnumbered the slaveowners five to one, "they have never yet," asserts Helper, "had any part or lot in framing the laws under which they live. There is no legislation except for the benefit of slavery, and slaveholders."[9] In Helper's view, slavery was a greater disaster for the "niggerless" whites than for the Negroes. The institution discouraged free labor and it consumed the capital which would otherwise have been available for the establishment of industry and manufactures, resulting in a lopsided agricultural civilization. As a consequence, the poor white man of the South had no hope of acquiring wealth or education, but was condemned by the plantation system to a life of ignorance and poverty. "Indeed," Helper wrote, "the unprofitableness of slavery is a monstrous evil, when considered in all its bearings; it makes us poor, poverty makes us ignorant, ignorance makes us wretched, wretchedness makes us wicked, and wickedness leads to the devil!"

In another blast, Helper directs his attention to several groups whom he held in utter contempt: "In the Southern States, as in all other slave countries, there are three odious classes of mankind; the slaves themselves, who are cowards; the slaveholders, who are tyrants; and the non-slaveholding slave-hirers, who are lickspittles. The slaves are pitiable; the slaveholders are detestable; the slave-hirers are contemptible."[10]

Helper estimates that the actual number of slaveholders in fifteen Southern states was "certainly less than two hundred thousand," while the total population was reported to be 9,612,979, of whom 6,184,477 were whites. Despite their limited number, the slaveholders had dominated the political life of the nation for decades. "The magistrates in the villages, the constables in the districts, the commissioners of the towns, the mayors of the cities, the sheriffs of the counties, the judges of the various courts, the members of the legislatures, the governors of the States, the representatives and senators in Congress—are all slaveholders."[11] Also, continued Helper, the slavery oligarchy controlled the national government through the diplomatic service, cabinet officers, the Supreme Court, and by a near-monopoly of the presidency of the United States. Since the beginning of the republic, the latter office had been held for forty-eight years by slaveholders from the South and only twenty years by nonslaveholders from the North. "For the last sixty-eight years," Helper noted, "slaveholders have been the sole and constant representatives of the South." It followed then that "the lords of the lash are not only absolute masters of the blacks, who are bought and sold, and driven about like so many cattle, but they are also the oracles and arbiters of all nonslave-holding whites, whose freedom is merely nominal, and whose unparalleled illiteracy and degradation is purposely and fiendishly perpetuated."[12]

A more subtle, but direct effect of slavery was its blight on Southern literature, to which Helper devotes his last chapter. In comparison to the North, he concludes, "the South has no litera-ture." Using his statistical method applied to publishing, Helper shows a great disproportion between Northern and Southern lit-eracy. Nine-tenths of existing publishing houses were in the non-slave states. The Southerners "have their books printed on Northern paper, with Northern types, by Northern artizans, stitched, bound and made ready for the market by Northern industry."[13] Helper's remarks concerning the quality of the published writings are equally scathing: "Southern divines give us elaborate 'Bible arguments,' Southern statists heap treatise upon treatise through which the Federal constitution is tortured into all monstrous shapes; Southern novelists bore us *ad infinitum* with pictures of the beatitudes of plan-tation life and the negro-quarters; Southern verse-wrights drone out their drowsy dactyls or grow ventricous with their turgid heroics all in defense of slavery."[14]

Helper's explanation for the barrenness of Southern literary genius, the "literary pauperism of the South," and the scarcity of publishers inevitably comes back to the same point—the economic impoverishment due to slavery. Further, he felt, the ban on dis-cussion of slavery made freedom of the press impossible.

Helper did not speak solely for himself in denouncing slavery as an institution and urging its abolition. He marshalls an impres-sive array of quotations from a variety of sources to support his arguments. Five of the eleven chapters of *The Impending Crisis* are used to present these statements, beginning with "Southern Testi-mony Against Slavery," noting "what the Fathers of the Republic thought of slavery;" followed by "Northern Testimony," citing the opinions of Franklin, Hamilton, Jay, Adams, Webster, and others; "Testimony of the Nations," quoting writers from ancient to mod-ern times; "Testimony of the Churches," and "Bible Testimony."

The South's missed opportunities to abolish slavery are reviewed by Helper. In Virginia, for instance, "in stubborn disregard of the advice and friendly warnings of Washington, Jefferson, Madison, Henry, and a host of other distinguished patriots who sprang from her soil, and in utter violation of every principle of justice and humanity, *she still persists* in fostering an institution which is so manifestly detrimental to her vital interests."[15]

As early as his second chapter, "How Slavery Can Be Abolished," Helper offers a remedy. Perhaps individual slaveholders would occasionally liberate their slaves, he states, but the planter class as a whole could no more be expected to take that step than one might "expect to hear highway men clamoring for a universal interdict against travelling." Far more drastic measures were necessary. The essence of Helper's solution was a system of taxes and boycotts so stringent as to make slavery impossible. He proposed that the nonslaveholders organize themselves politically in order to take advantage of their numerical superiority and then force slavery out of existence by imposing a tax of sixty dollars on every slaveholder for each slave in his possession, the money so raised to be spent in shipping the freed blacks back to Africa. If any slaveholder insisted on keeping his slaves, he was to pay a tax of forty dollars per year on each slave held. Furthermore, there was to be a complete boycott of slaveholding politicians, merchants, doctors, lawyers, ministers of religion, newspapers which supported slavery, and hotels served by slaves.

In order to make his proposed solutions to the slavery problem more palatable to prospective readers in both North and South, Helper soft-pedaled his strong racial biases. He wished to see every Negro, free and slave, shipped out of the country, and immediately. His prejudiced views on race emerged early, in his book, *The Land of Gold*, on experiences in California, in which he concluded that Chinese immigration was undesirable and that all "inferior races" should become subordinate to the Anglo-Saxon. He included in the inferior people not only the Chinese, but the Irish, the American Indians, Mexicans, Jews, and of course Negroes.

In his attitude toward the Negro, Helper was following in the footsteps of Cassius M. Clay, Henry's cousin, a Kentucky aristocrat turned abolitionist, whose contempt for the slave was shown in such remarks as "I have studied the Negro character. They lack self reliance—we can make nothing of them. God has made them for the sun and the banana!" Clay's point of view, similar to Helper's, was that his home state of Kentucky should encourage manufactures, for which slave labor was unsuitable. Looking on the Negro as the natural economic foe of the poor white, Helper denounced blacks as a menace to the South and to white labor. Two post–Civil War books expressed his virulent race hatred more explicitly than did *The Impending Crisis*: one was *Nojokue* (1867), the stated purpose of which was "to write the Negro out of America and out of existence"; and the other was *Negroes in Negroland*, which has been characterized as "one of the bitterest expressions of racial hatred ever put in print." Helper consistently refused to patronize hotels and restaurants where Negroes were employed.

The Impending Crisis met with an extremely hostile reception in the South, as could have been anticipated. Slaveholders considered it a "deadly attack" upon their "peculiar institution," especially resented because the author was a Southerner. Helper was vilified as a "poor traitor to his native sod and native skies," "one of the most miserable renegades and mendacious miscreants the world has ever seen," and his book as "incendiary, insurrectionary, and hostile to the peace and domestic tranquility of the country." Southern legislatures passed laws forbidding its possession or sale. Three men in Arkansas were hanged for owning copies. Mobs in North Carolina drove several ministers out of the state for defending the book, and there was a public book burning in one town. In other slave states men were mobbed and beaten for having Helper's book in their homes. Soon the author became "the best known and worst hated man in America."

Some 13,000 copies of *The Impending Crisis* were sold during its first year, after which sales languished. Then, two years later, Horace Greeley set about making the book the campaign document for the Republican party in the coming election. Suddenly the book became a center of dissention. After a bitter debate in the House of Representatives, lasting more than two months, the Republican candidate for speaker lost because he endorsed the book, without reading it. An abbreviated version, *Compendium of the Impending Crisis of the South*, was issued for campaign purposes. The number of copies of the original work and of the *Compendium* sold or given away has been estimated at a million or more.

Unfortunately for Helper, he was unable to reach his intended audience: the five or six million nonslaveholding whites in the South. In part because of widespread illiteracy and in part because of severe restrictions on its circulation, few read his book or received his message. Only in the North was it freely available. The historian James Ford Rhodes stated the case: "The reasoning, supported as it was by a mass of figures, could not be gainsaid. Had the poor white been able to read and comprehend such an argument, slavery would have been doomed to destruction, for certainly seven out of ten voters in the slave States were nonslaveholding whites. It was this consideration that made Southern congressmen so furious, for to retain their power they must continue to hoodwink their poorer neighbors."[16]

The publication of *The Impending Crisis* immediately inspired a flood of anti-Helper literature, such as Gilbert Beebe's *A Review and Refutation of Helper's Impending Crisis* (1860) and Samuel Wolfe's *Helper's Impending Crisis Dissected* (1860). These works attacked Helper's alleged misuse of statistics, falsehoods, and twisted logic. Both Beebe and Wolfe also attacked Helper's personal character.

An editor and historian, Earl Schenck Miers, describes Hinton Rowan Helper as an "unhappy victim of circumstance, compulsive genius, irreconcilable bigot, child of an age caught up in a not-too-well-understood struggle with human aspiration," and concedes that he was not an attractive figure. "And yet for one moment in American history," Miers points out, "because he represented the meeting of mind and emotion at the instant the nation was ready to receive both, he became a person of devastating importance. And all because he wrote this book."[17]

12.

Southern Traveler

FREDERICK LAW OLMSTED'S *The Cotton Kingdom:
A Traveller's Observations on Cotton and Slavery
in the American Slave States*

Fanny Kemble's observations on and scathing criticisms of
Negro slavery in the South were based on a limited stay on a single
Georgia plantation. Frederick Olmsted's more dispassionate and
detailed analysis of the "peculiar institution" was drawn from
extensive travels, ranging from Maryland to Texas, during which
visits were paid to a great variety of slaveholding establishments.
Despite their different bases and backgrounds, there are remarkable
similarities in the conclusions of the two writers.

Olmsted was one of the most talented and versatile Americans
of his generation. Born in 1822 in Hartford, Connecticut, his formal education was sketchy. Until about the age of thirty, he appears
to have been without fixed purpose in life. At sixteen, he had
already made four journeys, each over a thousand miles long, in
New England, New York State, and Canada. Later he studied
engineering, was employed by an importer in New York, embarked as a sailor for a year's voyage to China, and operated a farm
on Staten Island.

The experience which led to young Olmsted's subsequent
fame as a travel writer began in 1850 with a walking tour of rural

Britain, out of which came his first book, *Walks and Talks of an American Farmer in England* (1852). Impressed by this work, the editor of the *New York Times*, Henry J. Raymond, commissioned Olmsted to undertake his first Southern journey, for the purpose of writing his unbiased impressions of slavery and of actual economic and social conditions in the South. Two later expeditions followed. The three tours occupied about fourteen months, 1852–54, during which visits were paid to all the states later comprising the Southern Confederacy except Arkansas and Florida, and to Kentucky and Maryland, which did not secede. Every available means of transportation was used, though horseback riding was a favorite conveyance.

Olmsted recorded his experiences, observations, and opinions in three books: *A Journey in the Seaboard Slave States* (1856), *A Journey through Texas* (1857), and *A Journey in the Back Country* (1860). Shortly after the last work appeared, Olmsted's London publisher asked him to revise and abridge the three volumes into a single work for British readers. The condensation was issued also in the United States, shortly after the outbreak of the Civil War, under the title *The Cotton Kingdom: A Traveller's Observations on Cotton and Slavery in the American Slave States* (1861). The dedication was to John Stuart Mill, champion of liberty in England and friend of the Northern cause.

The Olmsted trilogy comprises a thorough, nonpartisan description of Southern life in the antebellum era, especially the social and economic phases, focusing chief attention on the plantation system, the Negro, and the institution of slavery. The author displayed no hint of prejudice against the South, carefully avoided extremes of opinion, and while violent controversy, North and South, raged around him, attempted to play a conciliatory role. As Broadus Mitchell stated, "For passion he sought to substitute thoughtfulness, for raving rationality, and for invective a calm examination of facts and their historical antecedents that should induce tolerance."[1]

Olmsted was omnivorous in his interests and his appetite for detail. He reports on the dress and manner of people that he met, the kinds of homes in which they lived, the quality of the hotels and other public establishments he encountered, the management of plantations, agricultural methods, modes of travel—roads, rail-

THE

COTTON KINGDOM:

A TRAVELLER'S OBSERVATIONS ON COTTON AND SLAVERY
IN THE AMERICAN SLAVE STATES.

BASED UPON THREE FORMER VOLUMES OF JOURNEYS AND INVESTIGATIONS
BY THE SAME AUTHOR.

BY
FREDERICK LAW OLMSTED.

IN TWO VOLUMES.
VOL. II.

NEW YORK:
PUBLISHED BY MASON BROTHERS,
5 and 7 MERCER STREET.
LONDON: SAMPSON LOW, SON & CO., 47 LUDGATE HILL.
1862.

roads, and boats—and the nature of the landscape through which he passed. His open, friendly manner apparently induced everyone to talk with him, including slaves, barroom acquaintances, traveling companions, plantation overseers, farmers, wealthy planters, and housewives. From these conversations, in addition to being a keen observer, he procured information on the subjects which most concerned him, for example, the price, productivity, and use of the land; the character of the poor whites; and such aspects of the slave system as the treatment of slaves, their abilities, their feeding and housing, their religion and morals, amusements, their relationship to their families and to the owners, and the economics of the slave system, such as their efficiency and the actual cost of their labor.

Since the South's economy was based primarily on agriculture, Olmsted had familiarized himself with tobacco, rice, cotton, and sugar culture, lumbering, and turpentine extraction. With this background, he reports on such matters as absentee ownership, the overseer system, the slave trade, the productivity of the labor force, the use of the soil, hiring out of slaves, use of white workers, and trades other than farming carried on on the plantations. Parallel concerns were the social effects of slavery on the whole Southern population: the masters, the nonslaveholding farmers, the landless poor whites, free Negroes, and the slaves themselves.

Economic considerations were uppermost in Olmsted's mind as he investigated the institution of slavery. His considered view, at the conclusion of his tour, was that slave labor was costlier than free, in part because of slow, incompetent workmen; and that slavery was an economic handicap to Southern agricultural and industrial progress. The reasons for these facts, he believed, were not far to seek. Any true estimate of the cost of slave labor had to be based on the purchase price of a slave, the expense of rearing him and keeping him in good health, the tying up of capital, and loss from waste.

The attitude of the slave himself was a key factor in the economic equation. The Negro slave often had no interest in working for or enriching the white man who had enslaved him; many slaves were constantly sabotaging, dawdling, malingering, revolting, or running away. Usually, the slaves worked slowly and carelessly, with as little mental attention to their tasks as mules. Laura

Wood Roper, Olmsted's leading modern biographer, sums up the case thus: "They took two to four times the length of time for a given task as an Irish or German hired man; they broke and neglected implements; they abused and maimed animals; they could not be trusted with complicated tools or on operations requiring skill or judgment; they scamped critical work if any lapse of supervision permitted; they malingered; sometimes they ran away or deliberately hurt themselves, thus obliterating at a stroke not only their owner's anticipated profit but a part of his capital as well."[2] The slaves had to be supervised closely and constantly goaded by "nigger-drivers" with whip in hand.

Even when large plantations using slave labor operated at a profit, especially when cotton, rice, or sugar was bringing high prices, Olmsted concluded that profits would have been larger and with fewer fluctuations from year to year under a system of free labor.

For masters with any considerable number of slaves, the employment of overseers was essential. Overseers were a floating population, rarely remaining on the same plantation more than a year or two, because the slaves learned how to circumvent their efforts to make them work more effectively. The sole mission of overseers was to produce as many bales of cotton or as much other produce as possible. To that end, they drove the slaves mercilessly, with little regard to the quality of the product. Edmund Wilson noted, "Since they are slaves, the master can never treat them like other human beings, whose rights he would have to respect, yet since they are, after all, human beings, he cannot use them up like tools. This is bad for the morale of the master, since he is always obliged to choose between inefficient production and inhuman methods."[3]

Olmsted found a certain amount of support for his economic views among Southerners themselves. For example, he quotes a speech by Representative Charles J. Faulkner in the Virginia legislature of 1832: "Slavery," asserted Faulkner, "is an institution which presses heavily against the best interests of the State. It banishes free white labor—it exterminates the mechanic, the artisan, the manufacturer. It converts the energy of a community into indolence; its power into imbecility; its efficiency into weakness. . . . Must the country languish and die, that the slaveholder may flourish?"[4]

Such persuasive arguments of course did not convince the slaveowners, who were deaf to all debate on the institution. Olmsted contrasts the stifling of public discussion of slavery in the South with the Northern practice of open agitation and debate on social problems. Such outspoken critics of the system as Faulkner were rare in the slave states, though Olmsted reported that he occasionally heard private denunciations of slaveholding.

One of the undesirable economic effects of slavery was to concentrate wealth in the hands of one-thirtieth of the population. "A society so organized," Olmsted's contemporary John E. Cairnes commented, "tends to develop with a peculiar intensity the distinctive vices of an oligarchy. In a country of free labor," he added, "various interests take root, and parties grow up which, regarding national questions from various points of view, become centres of opposition. It is not so in the Slave States. The elements of a political opposition are wanting."[5]

Along with concentration of wealth went monopolization in the ownership of land. Large planters regularly bought out small landholders, because they found white farmers on small tracts to be undesirable neighbors for slave plantations, and the planters' only sources for investment were land and slaves. Olmsted mentioned an important slaveholder in Mississippi who had in the course of a few years purchased the small places of twenty landowners, forcing them to move on.

From the point of view of the ultimate good of the country, a disastrous aspect of the slave system was exhaustion of the land. The planters simply used it up and left whole areas barren and desolate. Olmsted found that the practice of wearing out the soil and removal to new, unexploited land went on in the rich Southwest as well as in the older planting districts. In western Louisiana, for instance, more land had been abandoned to pine woods than remained under cultivation.

The reasons were clear, though dreadfully shortsighted, as Olmsted recognized. Cotton land on the average cost about three dollars per acre. The economics of the matter were analyzed by Olmsted as follows:

Twenty slave laborers cost over twenty thousand dollars. They will cultivate four hundred acres of land, which costs less than a tenth of that sum.

Knowing that he can buy as much more as he wants, at an equally low rate, why, when the production of his land decreases, should the slave owner drain it, or manure it, or "rest" it, or vary his crops, to prevent further exhaustion? It will cost twenty dollars' worth of labor to manure an acre. Why make this expenditure when he can obtain other land at five dollars an acre (fenced and ready for the plow,) which, without manure, will return just as much cotton?[6]

Passing through Mississippi Olmsted saw in one day "four or five large plantations, the hill-sides gullied like icebergs, stables and negro quarters all abandoned, and given up to decay."[7]

Thus on one ground after another, Olmsted maintained that slavery was wrong because it was uneconomic and should be replaced by a free labor system. In good part, this was a matter of the slaves' morale: "A man can work excessively on his own impulse as much easier than he can be driven to by another." Olmsted was impatient with the argument that white men could not work constantly in the Southern summer heat. "The more common and more popular opinion is, that the necessary labor of cotton tillage is too severe for white men in the cotton-growing climate," he wrote, adding, "I do not find the slightest weight of fact to sustain this opinion."

Evidence to support Olmsted's opinion was provided by a settlement of Germans in Texas. Without the use of slave labor, the Germans had created a near Garden of Eden, as viewed by Olmsted. In the area of New Braunfels, Texas, the German families had built simple habitations with "many little conveniences about them, and a care to secure comfort in small ways that was very agreeable to notice." As to farming methods, their "more clean and complete tillage" of their land "contrasted favorably with the patches of corn stubble, overgrown with crab-grass, which are usually the only gardens to be seen adjoining the cabins of the poor whites and slaves."[8]

Careful inquiries were made by Olmsted into the treatment of slaves. Physically, he concluded, they were treated better than he had anticipated, especially considering their inferiority as workmen. As a rule, the slaves were adequately provided with food, clothing, and shelter. "I think the slaves generally (no one denies that there are exceptions) have plenty to eat," he states, "probably are fed better than the proletarian class of any other part of the world."[9] One exception was in Louisiana: "The fact is that ninety-nine in a hundred of our free laborers live, in respect to food, at least four times better than the average of the hardest-worked slaves on the Louisiana sugar-plantations. And for two or three months in the year these are worked with much greater severity than free laborers in the North ever are,"[10] regularly eighteen hours a day during the harvest season.

Olmsted found that slaves were frequently and harshly disciplined, even occasionally killed by savage punishment, though Olmsted felt their treatment on the whole to be less cruel than the treatment he had witnessed of sailors by shipmasters, or the punishment of schoolboys by New England schoolmasters. Most discreditable to the slave system, in Olmsted's eyes, was the deliberate failure to raise the blacks above the level of brutes. They were maintained in ignorance, not permitted to learn to read, nor to form binding family relationships. Such religious instruction as they received was designed to emphasize the duty of submissiveness and to leave them in a state of primitive superstition.

Meanwhile, what was the influence of slavery on the master race, the whites? First, as to the gentry: slaveholders, large and small, constituted a small minority of the population. There were fewer than three thousand owners of considerable numbers of slaves in the South. For the Southern claim that the institution of slavery produced an upper propertied class, highly enlightened and noble, and elevated the status of women, Olmsted was highly skeptical, though he noted occasional exceptions. In the course of his tours, he visited as many large estates as possible. Generalizing on the Southern upper class, he noted marked differences between the Atlantic Seaboard aristocrats and those encountered in the newer Gulf states. The former demonstrated more "refinement and education," but even these, in Olmsted's opinion, had failed to make proper contributions to society's improvement. They had done little "for the advancement of learning and science, and there have been fewer valuable inventions and discoveries, or designs in art, or literary compositions of a high rank than in any community of equal numbers and wealth, probably in the world." Furthermore, on a comparative basis, "there is unquestionably at this time a very much larger number of thoroughly well bred and even high bred people in the free than in the slave states. It is equally certain that the proportion of such people to the whole population of whites is larger at the North than the South."[11] Olmsted does not dismiss the existence of a small Southern aristocracy: "The traditional old family, stately but condescending, haughty but jovial, keeping open house for all comers on the plantations of Virginia or South Carolina," he conceded, "is not wholly a myth." A common characteristic of the Southern gentry was its unmitigated detestation for democracy. There was, according to Olmsted, in "these fine fellows, these otherwise true gentlemen, a devilish, undisguised and recognized contempt for all humbler classes."

In most respects these "humbler classes" of whites were the most pathetic victims of the slave system. Slavery enslaved the white man almost as much as the black. Olmsted was certain that the primitive manner of living which prevailed among a great majority of whites, the lack of conveniences, the slovenly ways, the addiction to violence, and the intellectual destitution were directly attributable to the social system. As he phrased the matter, "Put the best race of men under heaven into a land where all industry is obliged to bear the weight of such a system, and inevitably their ingenuity, enterprise, and skill will be paralyzed, the land will be impoverished, its resources of wealth will remain undeveloped, or will be wasted; and only by the favor of some extraordinary advantage can it compare, in prosperity, with countries adjoining in which a more simple, natural, and healthy system of labor prevails."[12]

Olmsted's sympathy for the poor whites of the South is frequently expressed. The lower level of society lived on the wastelands and pine barrens and in the mountains. Large families barely subsisted in small, dirty cabins where all slept in one room. Beds were filthy and filled with vermin and floors were often of earth covered with trash or straw. The natives lived by hunting, fishing, and stealing from richer neighbors. Their dress was no better than the slaves. "The citizens of the cotton States, as a whole, are poor," observed Olmsted. "They work little, and that little, badly; they earn little, they sell little, they buy little, and they have little—very little—of the comforts and consolations of civilized life."[13] In the backcountry, Olmsted reported that "nine times out of ten at least I slept in a room with others, in a bed which stank, supplied with but one sheet, if with any; I washed with utensils common to the whole household; I found no garden, no flowers, no fruit, no tea, no cream, no sugar, no bread [except corn pone], no curtains, no lifting windows." And these were mainly planters' homes.

Not even in the homes of planters did Olmsted see a thermometer, a book of Shakespeare, a pianoforte, or an engraving. He was appalled by the meager standard of living—the shabby dwellings, the coarse and monotonous fare, the absence of cleanliness and ordinary comforts, the lack of newspapers and other reading matter. The demoralizing effects of slavery on the white man were apparent also in the bad roads, the wretched means of transportation, the poorly cultivated and limited crops, and the dearth of schools, churches, lyceums, and community enterprises and interests.

Even the vaunted Southern hospitality was found wanting by Olmsted. In his *A Journey in the Back Country* he cites a number of examples of inhospitality he encountered in that region of the middle South, during the summer of 1854. "Only twice, in a journey of four thousand miles, made independently of public conveyances," he remarked, "did I receive a night's lodging or a repast from a native southerner, without having the exact price in money which I was expected to pay for it stated to me by those at whose hand I received it."[14] Public inns were few and primitive. Olmsted's stories of rude behavior and wretched fare were much resented by Southern readers. He was denounced by a critic as one of those "lying, sneaking, cowardly knaves" guilty of defaming "the characters of the unsuspecting patrons at whose hospitable boards their miserable carcasses are each day filled with abundance of every species of good cheer." Olmsted was scrupulous, however, in noting the limited number of instances, perhaps a dozen, in which he was delightfully entertained.

Olmsted's travels took him through the highlands of Alabama, Georgia, Tennessee, North Carolina and Virginia. There he found much to commend: "Compared with the slaveholders, these people are more cheerful, more amiable, more sociable, and more liberal. Compared with the nonslaveholders of the slaveholding districts, they are also more hopeful, more ambitious, more intelligent, more provident, and more comfortable."[15] The free areas, however, were so lacking in economic and political power that they could barely hold their own.

Olmsted rejected the Southern contention that Negroes are inherently inferior, destined by fate to be slaves, and unfit for freedom because they were incapable of taking care of themselves when free. The great mass of the race had been poisoned by ignorance, he felt. On occasion, Olmsted noted, when slaves had been encouraged by their masters, they had developed skills that compared favorably with those of free white workmen.

The Southern planters lived in continual fear of a Negro uprising. Many assured Olmsted that there was no danger of a slave insurrection, but underneath he sensed apprehension. In an effort to maintain safety, several states made it a criminal offense to teach Negroes to read and write. "The tranquility of the South," in Olmsted's judgment, was "the tranquility of hopelessness of the subject race. . . . Hence no free press, no free pulpit, no free politics can be permitted in the South."[16] The bloody uprising in Haiti in the late eighteenth century, freeing 400,000 slaves from the French, was always in the back of the Southern consciousness.

Several possible solutions were offered for the slave problem by Olmsted. First, he pleaded for an immediate stop to expansion of slave territory. "Slavery shall, by general consent, be hereafter confined within its present limits."[17] The next step would be gradual emancipation by action of the slaveholders themselves, as Thomas Jefferson had proposed earlier. Features of this scheme would be for the masters to train the slaves in self-reliance and to permit them to buy their liberation by accumulating financial credits as payment for their toil. In any event, Olmsted realized that the sudden abolition of slavery was but a partial answer. The evil consequences of the system would be eliminated from the body politic only slowly, patiently, and painfully.

With the outbreak of the Civil War, Olmsted abandoned his proposal for gradual emancipation of the slaves. The firing on Fort Sumter convinced him that "the one system or the other is to thrive and extend, and eventually possess the whole land," adding that it was essential to "subjugate slavery, or be subjugated by it." Olmsted feared, however, that "the slaves will get emancipated long before we are in a condition to deal with them decently in any other way than as slaves." Accordingly, he urged the federal government to provide constructive employment and otherwise prepare for freedom the slaves in districts occupied by Northern troops.

By the fairness and objectivity of his reports, Olmsted had hoped to win the good will of Southern readers. The hope was vain, except in rare instances. The Southern press was almost unanimously hostile from the time the letters began to appear in print. The *Savannah Republican*, for example, declared editorially that since neither a Northerner nor a Southerner could be unprejudiced about slavery, neither was qualified to discuss it. Actually, Olmsted discovered that there were few newspapers in the South and those had few readers. The press was virtually censored, since no free discussion of slavery was permitted. Willard Thorp comments: "The Southerner, partly out of a subconscious need to find justification for a distinctly feudal social and economic system, read heavily in Scott and in such Southern novels as Caruthers's *Knights of the Golden Horseshoe*, Kennedy's *Horseshoe Robinson*, and Simms's *The Partisan*. In them he found not only a reflection of his way of life but an idealized picture of chivalric warfare."[18]

Olmsted went to some pains to defend his own open-mindedness and unprejudiced point of view. In his *Back Country* he declares that "few men could have been so little inclined to establish previously formed opinions as I was when I began my journey in the South. Looking upon slavery as an unfortunate circumstance, for which the people of the South were in no wise to blame . . . it was with the distinct hope of aiding those disposed to consider the subject of slavery in a rational, philosophical, and conciliatory spirit that I undertook to make a personal study of the ordinary condition and habits of the people of the South."[19]

In their original form, Olmsted's works on the South fill six volumes. Even the condensation, *The Cotton Kingdom*, totals three hundred thousand words. Any further summary is difficult, for Olmsted recounts innumerable incidents and meetings with a great variety of individuals, and describes a number of vastly different cultures. The overall impression—undoubtedly one which considerably influenced Northern and English thinking, if not Southern—is that the antebellum South's economy was basically unsound, slavery degraded both slaves and masters, and its perpetuation directly prevented the region's agricultural and industrial progress.

Following his Southern travels, Olmsted embarked on an entirely different career. During the latter part of the century, he became America's leading landscape architect. Among the monuments to his creativity are Central Park, Riverside Drive, and Morningside Drive in New York City, Prospect Park in Brooklyn, Back Bay Fenway in Boston, the 1893 World's Fair grounds in Chicago, and the creation of Yosemite Park and Niagara Falls as national reservations. Olmsted died in 1903, at the ripe age of eighty-one.

13.

Southern Panorama

The end of the Civil War witnessed an influx of Northern travelers to the Southern states. Dozens of reporters, authors, and artists flocked to the South during the Reconstruction era and sent back reams of copy to satisfy the keen Northern desire for information about the former foe. Among the numerous books and magazine articles produced by the fact-gatherers, Edward King's *The Great South* was by far the most comprehensive and detailed. King's work, written some twenty years later, was comparable in many respects to Frederick Olmsted's *The Cotton Kingdom*. Each man traveled extensively and had an omnivorous curiosity about everything. Olmsted was primarily concerned with economic factors, and King, too, was expected to pay particular attention to agriculture and industry, but he neglected practically no aspect of Southern life and culture as it existed in the mid-1870s.

King, a native of Massachusetts, became a newspaper reporter at the age of sixteen. In 1867 he was sent to the Paris Exposition, then in progress, and gathered material for his first book, an account of Parisian life seen through youthful and romantic eyes. Later, he returned to France, for the *Boston Morning Journal*, to cover the Franco-Prussian War and the events of the Commune. His adventures included being twice arrested by the Germans as a suspected spy, serving as an emergency nurse to the wounded, and caring for the bodies of Americans killed in the street fighting of the Commune. King was thus a seasoned reporter and correspondent by the time of his Southern expedition.

The genesis of King's journeyings through the South was an invitation to him from J. G. Holland, editor of *Scribner's Monthly*, to travel through the Southern states and obtain materials for a series of articles on the effects of the Civil War, economic conditions, and interesting features of the landscape and social life. King appears to have been provided by *Scribner's* with an almost unlimited expense account; on more than one occasion he chartered a special train. For fourteen months, in 1873 and 1874, he covered every section of the South. Accompanied by an excellent artist, J. Wells Champney, he traveled a total of more than twenty-five thousand miles, during which time, he wrote, he "visited nearly every city and town of importance in the South; talked with men of all classes, parties and colors; carefully investigated manufacturing enterprises and sites; studied the course of politics in each State since the advent of reconstruction; explored rivers, and penetrated into mountain regions heretofore rarely visited by Northern men."[1] The fruits of these expeditions appeared in fifteen articles for *Scribner's*, illustrated by more than four hundred of Champney's drawings. Subsequently the articles were rewritten and published in book form under the title of *The Great South: A Record of Journeys in Louisiana, Texas, the Indian Territory, Missouri, Arkansas, Mississippi, Alabama, Georgia, Florida, South Carolina, North Carolina, Kentucky, Tennessee, Virginia, West Virginia, and Maryland*. King noted that the fifteen former slave states covered an area of more than 880,000 square miles and then had fourteen million inhabitants, divided between 9,466,355 whites and 4,538,782 blacks.

A major portion of *The Great South* is an extended travelogue, describing towns and cities, rivers and mountains, natural scenery, architecture, climate, the people's daily activities, and colorful characters encountered en route. King's pages are crowded with black stevedores, white steamboat captains, planters, sharecroppers, mountaineers, politicians, oystermen, and other memorable individuals. A highly readable style brings to life an extraordinary view of Southern life more than a century ago. Champney's drawings add picturesque detail.

King begins his chronicle with Louisiana and New Orleans. Colorful New Orleans, in particular, seems to have fascinated him. The war's effect on the plantations had been drastic; many were entirely deserted because of the Negroes' refusal to work on them; the blacks preferred to flock to the cities or to cultivate their own land. A Negro government had taken over the state. The legislature included fifty-five blacks who could neither read nor write, and, King reported, "The Louisiana white people were in such terror of the negro government that they would rather accept any other despotism."[2] Demoralization was general.

King's picture of the New Orleans blacks was unflattering: "The negroes, taken as a whole, seem somewhat shuffling and disorganized; and apart from the statuesque old house and body servants, they are by no means inviting. They gather in groups at the street corners just at nightfall, and while they chatter like monkeys, even about politics, they gesticulate violently. They live without much work, for their wants are few."[3]

Discussion of Reconstruction governments in *The Great South* reflects changing attitudes in the North. In the years immediately following the war, the Northern press had pictured the South as unrepentant, determined to keep the former slaves in bondage, and plotting to regain national political power. These reports furnished ammunition for the Radicals in Congress, who drafted a policy calling for enfranchisement of the blacks, the disenfranchisement of the leading Confederates, and installing Republicans in power throughout the South. By the time of Edward King's travels, however, horror stories about the depredations committed on a prostrate, impoverished region by carpetbaggers, scalawags, and illiterate Negroes were penetrating northward, creating sympathy for Southern whites. The North, in any case, was becoming disillusioned with Radical Reconstruction and its consequences. By 1877, when Rutherford B. Hayes became president, therefore, general sentiment approved withdrawal of the last federal troops from the South.

King deals only in part with political questions, but discussions of Republican state governments and of the Negro in politics crop up frequently, as he moves from state to state. There was wide variance in the competence and integrity of the governments set up under Reconstruction. In Louisiana, for example, King found that the ruling party was "composed of ignorant and immoral negroes, led on by reckless and greedy white adventurers,"[4] as a result of which "the state has been broken down by taxation and debt; the negro has been demoralized; the principal cities and towns are impoverished."[5] In Georgia, all blacks had been expelled from the state legislature by dominant white forces and then readmitted by act of Congress. Under the Reconstruction government in Georgia, King notes that "some good laws were passed" and "a system of internal improvements was inaugurated," but bonds to provide state aid to new railroads were overissued, and the governor "was surrounded by an atmosphere of corruption."

Moving, farther south, King concluded that "Florida accepted reconstruction peacefully, and the new Constitution is, on the whole, a good one. It makes proper provision for schools, and the management of the courts and the provisions with regard to the distribution of lands are wise."[6] The balance of power in the state was held by the blacks, led by a few white men, though a conservative element was gaining strength. "A great deal of fraud and plundering on the part of county officers" was reported to King.

Far worse troubles were observed in the state where the Civil War's first shot had been fired. In his chapter "The Spoliation of South Carolina," King dwells at length on the political problems of the Palmetto State. South Carolina towns were pervaded by "complete prostration, dejection, stagnation." Planters' land was confiscated after the war by the blacks, and "hundreds of white families were left homeless, moneyless, and driven into cities where they were friendless."[7] The two houses of the legislature, predominantly black, soon ran the state's bonded indebtedness into millions of dollars. The Conservatives, "as the white natives style themselves, alarmed at the riot of corruption and the total disregard of decency manifested by the governing powers, rallied and made a decided effort to get the State into their own hands" in 1870, but failed to win the governorship.

Conditions were little better in neighboring North Carolina, King discovered. "The evils of universal suffrage have been very great in this State," he writes. "The great mass of densely ignorant and ambitious blacks suddenly hurled upon the field created the wildest confusion and crushed the commonwealth under irredeemable debt. The villainy and robbery to which the white population of the State was compelled to submit, at the hands of the plunderers maintained in power by the negro, did much to destroy all possibility of a speedy reconciliation between the two races."[8] The whites were inclined, however, to place more blame for the situation on a native son, Governor Holden, than upon the blacks. With Holden's impeachment, the white population recovered its power and influence.

The happiest state, from a political point of view, was Virginia. King thought that "the present government of the State is in good hands. The officers of the State Government are allied to the Conservative party, but seem determined to do equal and exact justice to all classes of citizens." The governor, a former Confederate general, made a conscious effort "to avoid the narrow and mean-spirited policy which has latterly characterized some of the other Southern States. He has thus far done everything that he could to develop goodwill and confidence between the races."[9]

In King's opinion, slavery was mainly responsible for the Negro's shortcomings and he was convinced that if the blacks were educated and given equal opportunity, their achievements could equal those of the white race. The long road ahead for the blacks was indicated by scattered references throughout *The Great South*. In Texas, "the negro seems to do well in his free state, although indulging in all kinds of queer freaks with his money; he saves nothing."[10] The Negro's improvidence was remarked upon again as applied "to the majority of the negroes engaged in agriculture throughout the cotton region of the Mississippi valley. Still there are praiseworthy exceptions to this general rule."[11] In some Alabama towns and smaller communities, King learned that "the negroes seem to be absolutely dependent upon the charity of the white folks. Their lives are grossly immoral, and the women especially have but little conception of the true dignity of womanhood. . . . It often struck me that the thousands of idle negroes I saw were in the attitude of waiting. Their expectant air was almost pathetic to witness."[12]

A point of friction between the races was the belief, implanted in them by their own leaders, that emancipation and suffrage would automatically endow them with property. When their expectations were unrealized, they felt defrauded. "They have also been told by so many legislators of their own race, that all the property once their masters' now properly belongs to them, that they literally believe it, in many cases," King comments, "while in others, they consider the whole thing a muddle entirely beyond their comprehension."[13] To gain their favor, the Negroes were told by some unscrupulous white politicians that they ought to take possession of the planters' land. A more favorable view, on the other hand, emerges in King's statement that "the negro along the Mississippi works better than ever before since freedom came to him, because he is obliged to toil or starve, and because being the main stay of the planters, they accord to him very favorable conditions."[14]

King pays tribute to the work of the American Missionary Society in its successful efforts to educate and uplift the black race. He disagreed with the notion that the Negro's mental ability is innately inferior to that of the white Caucasian and was convinced that the freedmen's schools had proved "a negro can go as far in mental processes as the white child. The blacks have wonderful memories and strong imitative propensities; eloquence, passionate and natural; a strange and subtle sense of rhythm and poetry; and it is now pretty well settled that there are no special race limitations."[15] The solution, in King's opinion, lay in good teachers and better education for the Negro. "Everywhere that the Union armies went in the South," he remarks, "they found the negro anxious for knowledge. The wretched slave was like a blind man who heard around him tumult and struggle, and who constantly cried aloud for light, for the power of vision. He was weighted down with the crushing burden of his past life; he saw the great chance slipping away from him, and in his intense desire to become intelligent and independent, he fairly laid hold upon the soldiery for help."[16]

The entire subject of education is of primary concern to King, and references to its problems, limitations, and needs appear in the account of practically every state visited. A typical case was Texas, where it was estimated that some 71,000 whites and 150,000 colored persons over the age of ten were unable to read or write. A system of free public schools was established by the legislature in 1871, despite the objections of many citizens to being taxed for the purpose, and especially to being taxed for the education of their neighbors' children and for the education of the children of former slaves. There was also strong objection to the compulsory feature of the new system, with "parents furiously defending their right to leave their children in ignorance."

In Alabama, King reported that "the commonwealth labors under a dreadful burden of ignorance; the illiteracy in some sections is appalling."[17] With a population of approximately one million, 380,000 persons were unable to read or write, nearly 100,000 of them white. During 1873, when King visited the state, the schools were closed, except in the cities, because there were no funds to pay teachers. South Carolina's situation was similar. An appropriation of $300,000 for educational purposes was approved, but no money reached the schools and many were closed. A shortage of good teachers existed. For the state as a whole, King estimated that school facilities were available for only 75,000 of a school population of 200,000.

An equally pessimistic picture is painted of North Carolina, where illiterates numbered 350,000, and only 150,000 of 300,000 school-age children were actually in school. Taxes for school support could not be levied except with the approval of the qualified voters of each county. Few counties rejected such levies outright, although, King observes, "nearly all the people in the back country have a most unaccountable aversion to paying 'school taxes.'"

Summing up his findings on the state of education, King states, "Taking the statistics of the Southern public schools, as given in 1871 and 1872, it will be seen that seven years after the close of the war the impoverished Southern States had managed to bring under the operation of a school system proportionately four-sevenths as many children as are at school in the North, and to keep them at school three-fourths as long. In view of the fact that great numbers of the Southern people (*i.e.*, the negroes) own little or no property, it must be asserted that the Southern property holder is paying a much heavier school tax than is his Northern brother." The proper answer, King suggested, was federal support "to foster and protect education in all the Southern States."[18]

The "peculiarities" of the Southern people could be best judged, King states, if two classes, under the old order, were recognized:

"the high up and the low down"—the gentleman planter and the poor white, the latter "brawling, ill-educated, and generally miserable." Actually, there was a third class, the Negro, who did not count, for he was a mere commodity, an article of barter, and had no identity. King found a middle class gradually emerging, including "some of the more intelligent and respectable negroes." Industry was drawing poor whites, "once utterly useless and degraded," into the large towns. A disgusting habit to King, even among pretty young girls, in this class was dipping snuff. He observed that the poor whites always had large families: "It was not at all uncommon to see lean fathers and lank and scrawny mothers entering railroad cars, followed by a brood of ten or more children of all sizes."[19] An immense exodus in progress from the old cotton states to the far Southwest was witnessed by King, as the poor white race sought greener pastures. "The flood of emigration from South Carolina, Alabama and Georgia is formidable, and turned the tide of politics in Texas," he writes. "Old men and little children, youths and maidens, clad in homespun, crowd the railway cars, looking forward eagerly to the land of promise."[20]

King was enthusiastic about the future of Texas, pointing out its tremendous mineral resources, millions of acres of fertile land, vast size, outlet on the Gulf, equable climate, and rapidly expanding population. The cattle business had already grown to large proportions. In 1872 alone, 450,000 cattle were driven overland from western Texas to Kansas, up the famous Chisholm Trail. The estimated profits of cattle raising were enormous.

The addiction of Southerners to violence was commented upon by King, in several connections. "There exists in all of the extreme Southern States," he states, "a class of so-called gentlemen who employ the revolver rather suddenly when they fancy themselves offended, sometimes killing, now and then only frightening an opponent. These people are not, as yet, treated with sufficient rigor in Texas society. There are even instances of men who have killed a number of persons and are still considered respectable. The courts do not mete out punishment in such cases with proper severity, sometimes readily acquitting men who have wantonly and willfully shot their fellow-creatures on the slightest provocation."[21] One of the last chapters in *The Great South*, entitled "The Carrying of Weapons," indicates that tales of violence may have been exaggerated. "In our journeys," King writes, "we traveled not infrequently in regions remote from the railroads, or along rivers, where the people were somewhat rough, but never on any occasion did we see pistol or knife drawn or displayed during our fourteen months' stay in the South. While, however, we never saw weapons displayed, we heard plenty of stories to confirm the impression that large classes carried them and used them freely."[22]

Another subject of interest to King was Southern food. Northern travelers returning from the South almost invariably complained of the poor food, even in prosperous regions. Exceptions were noted by King: "Nowhere in the world is there better cookery or a richer bill of fare than that offered in Baltimore, in Charleston, in Savannah, and in New Orleans." Yet, within a few miles of those cities "coarse bread, coarser pork, and a few stunted vegetables are the only articles of diet upon the farmers' tables." Worst of all were the mountain areas, where, except in hotels and the homes of the well-to-do, "we were usually invited to partake of hot and indigestible corn bread, fried and greasy ham, or bacon." If, rarely, a beefsteak was served, "it had been remorselessly fried until not a particle of juice remained in its substance."[23]

Epidemic diseases were a plague in certain areas of the South. Perhaps most devastating was yellow fever, the "fearful ravages" of which had frequently stricken New Orleans. The fever came to Memphis in 1855, 1867, and 1873, apparently brought on Mississippi steamers. Thousands died, but the terrible visitation did not, according to King, "prevent Memphis from holding her annual carnival, and repeating, in the streets so lately filled with funerals, the gorgeous pageants of the mysterious Memphis."[24]

King found much to admire in Southern women. The trying years of the war, he thought, had developed many noble qualities in them, and he was particularly attracted by "the frankness and earnestness with which these ladies accepted a changed order of things," and by "their beauty, their wit, their vivacity." The burdens of war had fallen as heavily upon them as upon the men who had survived the conflict, and they "toiled unceasingly and uncomplainingly."[25]

In concluding his wide-sweeping chronicle of the South, King states that he found much that was discouraging in the condition of the region, but he was optimistic about the prospects for "its thorough redemption." In his opinion, "The South can never be cast in the same mould as the North. Its origin was too different, it will not be thoroughly emancipated from the influence of the old system for several generations." King went on to prophesy that the South would become increasingly progressive and liberal, its provincialisms would gradually fade away, its educational system would increase and flourish, and that the Negro would get justice, as liberalizing influences prevailed.[26]

The Great South played an important role in influencing Northern public opinion, helping to shape Northern attitudes and policies toward Reconstruction issues. Tens of thousands read the articles as they appeared in *Scribner's Monthly* and later in book form. A critical judgment stated by one historian, James M. McPherson, in an introduction to a 1969 reprint of the book, is that King considered Reconstruction a failure and felt it should be abandoned; he "did not want it overthrown completely; he hoped it would be reformed by education, economic progress, increased wisdom and restraint on the part of both races." The end result, however, was that Reconstruction was overturned by a white counterrevolution in the South, and the blacks and their Republican allies were abandoned by the North. "King had not intended this result," McPherson says, "but he must bear partial responsibility for it."[27]

Romantic New Orleans

GEORGE W. CABLE'S *Old Creole Days*

It was George W. Cable's great good fortune to have been born in the midst of a literary gold mine—nineteenth-century New Orleans, the most exotic of American cities. Edward Laroque Tinker graphically describes the New Orleans of Cable's boyhood: "The city then was as unbridled a port as any on the continent. Bull-baiting, cock-fighting, and gambling in every form were rampant. Slavery was considered sanctioned by Holy Writ, and pretty cream-colored quadroons, tricked out in ribbons, were exposed for sale as 'fancy girls' in the windows of slave marts. . . . The Creoles, enriched by slave labor and nourished by French culture, had developed a life of great luxury—their houses filled with tapestries and fine French furniture. Pride of possession added to pride of race had made of them a haughty, high-strung tribe."[1] It was this colorful city and its people that Cable was destined to present to the world, at the same time building his own literary reputation.

Cable was born and bred in New Orleans; his father was a native of Virginia, his mother of New England descent. The son was seventeen years old at the outbreak of the Civil War; he volunteered, and saw active service with the Fourth Mississippi

Cavalry. His writing career began a few years later when he became a reporter and columnist for the *New Orleans Picayune*. A marked leaning toward history and themes dealing with social criticism and reform characterized his newspaper contributions, forecasting life-long interests.

Cable was discovered in 1873 by *Scribner's Monthly Magazine*. The initial introduction to Scribner came through Edward King, who was in New Orleans gathering material for his *The Great South*. King was impressed by Cable's stories and sent them on to the editor of *Scribner's Monthly*. Publication of these romantic, local-color tales began soon afterward. Seven of the stories centering on the Creoles of New Orleans and Louisiana were collected and published in book form by Scribner in 1879, under the title *Old Creole Days*. By then, Cable had accumulated a rich store of New Orleans lore and history.

Old Creole Days became the most famous and most successful of Cable's voluminous writings. The fancy of Northern readers was immediately caught by the bizarre settings and equally strange characters. There was instant and unanimous recognition of the work as an American classic.

It was ironic that Cable should have been chosen by fate to chronicle Creole culture, for the ways of the Creoles were utterly alien to his own life-style. He had been dropped from the *Picayune* staff for refusing to see and review a theatrical performance. As Tinker comments, "He was as much of a misfit in French New Orleans as a turtle hatched in a peacock's nest."[2] His mother had brought him up in the strictest Presbyterianism, teaching him that idleness was a vice, drink a curse, and dancing and the theatre traps set by the devil. Evidently it was the complete dissimilarity between his own manner of living and that of the gay, extravagant, pleasure-loving, hedonistic Creoles which attracted Cable to them in the first place.

The opening paragraph of "'Sieur George," the first story in *Old Creole Days*, sets the scene and the atmosphere: "In the heart of New Orleans stands a large four-story brick building, that has so stood for about three-quarters of a century. Its rooms are rented to a class of persons occupying them simply for lack of activity to find better and cheaper quarters elsewhere. With its gray stucco peeling off in broad patches, it has a solemn look of gentility in rags, and stands, or, as it were, hangs, about the corner of two ancient streets, like a faded fop who pretends to be looking for employment."[3] This is the Vieux Carré, the ancient district that had been laid out when Jean Baptiste Le Moyne, Sieur de Bienville, founded New Orleans in 1718. In mid-nineteenth century, the French and Spanish Creoles were still the principal inhabitants of the old area, maintaining their separation as far as possible from the bustling American city across Canal Street.

"'Sieur George" is the tale of an American gentleman whose gambling fever has caused him to spend his life and fortune buying Cuban lottery tickets, always on the losing end. The landlord of the building in which 'Sieur George has dwelt for fifty years in two rooms is Kookoo, "an ancient Creole of doubtful purity of blood." Kookoo has an avid curiosity to know the contents of an old hair trunk which 'Sieur George keeps locked in his apartment, but the latter never relaxes his close guardianship of the trunk. 'Sieur George's way of earning a living is mysterious, he drinks a good deal, and he reveals nothing of his past. When he departs to fight in the Mexican War, his rooms are occupied by a handsome woman and her mulatto maid, a slave. Upon his return from the war, 'Sieur George is accompanied by a friend, a "tall lank iron-gray man," who courts and wins the handsome woman. The marriage is a disaster; the drinking companion is drowned and "poor, robbed, spirit-broken and now dead Madame" is gone, leaving an infant daughter to be cared for by 'Sieur George. When she comes of age, the proprieties require that the girl must live with her guardian no longer. The thought of separation is painful to them both, and to avoid it, 'Sieur George proposes that the girl become his wife. She recognizes that such a solution is totally unsuitable, flees to her room, and locks the door. That night, Kookoo finds 'Sieur George in a drunken stupor, and at last has an opportunity to satisfy his curiosity. He steals into the apartment, opens the trunk, and finds it "full, full, crowded down and running over full of the tickets of the Havana Lottery" instead of the treasure Kookoo had anticipated. Early the next morning, the girl slips out of the house, and departs to take comfortable refuge in a nearby convent. Neither Kookoo or 'Sieur George ever sees her again. 'Sieur George searches for her, however, hoping to borrow ten dollars to place another bet, convinced he has a winning "combination" that would bring him the fortune he has for so long vainly pursued.

'Sieur George is portrayed variously as hero, villain, and victim of an incurable disease—gambling. Louis D. Rubin, Jr., a perceptive critic, sees in the tale such characteristics as a "sense of decadence, of moral ruin," and "sensual indulgence and moral squalor."[4] Another commentator, Philip Butcher, considers the plot "banal," the characters as "drawn from stock," and the social criticism "insipid," but concludes that "despite its weaknesses, the story is an arresting one because it is so adroitly told."[5]

The second of the seven *Old Creole Days* stories, "'Tite Pulette," involves slavery and caste, both major factors in the Louisiana society of Cable's youth. The chief characters are a young Dutch hero, Kristian Koppig, a recent immigrant; an octoroon woman, Zalli, called Madame John; and her beautiful daughter, "white like a waterlily! White—like a magnolia!" The humble quarters occupied by the two women are across the street from Koppig's rented room. Monsieur John had tried to provide security for his mistress and Poulette before his death, but they are now destitute because of a bank failure, unable to support themselves by embroidery and music lessons or by Madame John's occasional employment as a nurse. To earn money, Zalli dances at one of the quadroon balls. Poulette accompanies her mother to the ball, and the manager, catching sight of her, tries to force his attentions on her. When Kristian Koppig comes to her rescue and slaps the roué's face, the manager and two of his hired ruffians set upon him and beat and stab him. Koppig is nursed back to health by Madame John and Poulette, after which he declares his love for the daughter. But he is reminded that the law forbids their marriage because of Poulette's colored lineage. The problem is resolved by Madame John's producing "sworn papers" to prove that Poulette is not her daughter, but the child of a Spanish couple who died of the fever. The finish is of course contrived to provide a happy ending, without suggesting any answer to the question of racial discrimination.

The theme of miscegenation appears again in "Belles Demoiselles Plantation." The characters are two branches of the proud Creole family of De Charleu. The legitimate side of the family "rose straight up, up, up, generation after generation, tall, branch-less, slender, palm-like." There are now seven beautiful daughters and their father, whose home is aptly named "Belles Demoiselles." The nonaristocratic branch was descended from a union of the original De Charleu and a Choctaw Indian wife. Only one member, Ingin Charlie, whose family name had been corrupted to De Carlos, survives. "With this single exception, the narrow, thread-like line of descent from the Indian wife, diminished to a mere strand by injudicious alliances, and deaths in the gutters of old New Orleans, was extinct."[6]

The De Charleu mansion was situated perilously near the Mississippi River. Nine miles of river could be seen from the veranda, a shady garden was full of rare and beautiful flowers, and farther away were broad fields of cane and rice, the distant slave quarters, and a dark belt of cypress forest. The master was a "hoary-headed old patriarch," proud, penurious, and loving "nothing but himself, his name, and his motherless children."

Injin Charlie and Colonel De Charleu communicate with each other occasionally, since blood ties are always recognized among Creoles, "no matter what sort of knots those ties may be." The main point of the story is the colonel's attempts to persuade Injin Charlie to sell him his town property, a run-down business block, where the colonel proposes to build a summer home to give his daughters an opportunity to enjoy the delights of the New Orleans social season. At first, Charlie refuses, because of his own family pride, but finally consents when the colonel agrees to exchange "Belles Demoiselles" for the town property—though only after the colonel discovers that the point on which the plantation house is located is rapidly eroding and will soon collapse into the Missis-sippi. The two men go out to inspect the mansion. As they watch, the river breaks through, and "Belles Demoiselles, the realm of maiden beauty, the home of merriment, the house of dancing, all in the tremor and glow of pleasure, suddenly sunk, with one short, wild wail of terror—sunk, sunk, down, down, into the merciless, unfathomable flood of the Mississippi,"[7] drowning the seven daugh-ters. A sentimental deathbed scene ends the tale, with Injin Charlie nursing the colonel in his last hours, the latter repenting of his scheme to cheat a kinsman, and dreaming of being reunited with his beautiful daughters.

For "Jean-ah Poquelin," the scene of action shifts to an old colonial plantation house half in ruins, set in "one of the horridest marshes within a circuit of fifty miles." This was the home of old Jean Marie Poquelin, once a wealthy indigo planter, now a hermit. All other members of the family, including a favorite younger brother, were reported deceased. Former friends died off "and the name of Jean Marie Poquelin became a symbol of witchery, devilish crime, and hideous nursery fictions." The house itself was "the object of a thousand superstitions," among both blacks and whites.

The old Creole society, as portrayed in "Jean-ah Poquelin," is gradually having to give way to the hard-driving, more enterprising Americans. New Orleans is growing outside the old city, and streets are laid out beyond the Poquelin house. Old Jean tries in vain to persuade the American authorities to ban the draining and filling in of the swamp near his home. The secretary of the board of a building and improvement company, Little White, is sympathetic with the old man and makes ineffectual efforts to prevent his persecution. Spurred on by the Americans, a mob of Creoles goes out to the Poquelin place one night to shivaree its owner: "Dogs and boys were howling and barking; men were laughing, shouting, groaning, and blowing horns, whooping, and clanking cow-bells, whinnying, and howling, and rattling pots and pans."[8] When this disorderly crowd reached the old mansion, they saw coming from it a deaf-mute slave with the coffin of Jean-ah Poquelin, followed by a figure as white as snow—the long-hidden brother, a leper. The secret of the Poquelin place is finally revealed. For a moment, the mute and the leper were seen by the rabble; then they disappeared into the depths of the swamp known as Leper's Land, and were never seen again.

Offering a change from the somber tone of "Jean-ah Poquelin," the fifth story in *Old Creole Days*, "Madame Délicieuse," is a romance. The characters are pureblooded Creole aristocrats, three in number: a young woman, Madame Délicieuse, General Hercule Mossy de Villivicencio, a martial-minded old veteran of the War of 1812, and his son Dr. Mossy, physician and scientist, beloved by Madame Délicieuse. The father and son are estranged and have not spoken in years, because Dr. Mossy has no interest in military affairs and has failed to challenge a newspaper editor to a duel for derogatory comments about the general. Madame Délicieuse manages to reject the general's marriage proposal without losing his friendship, brings about a reconciliation between father and son, and marries Dr. Mossy. The story is slight and deals with no significant issues, but reveals, incidentally, various facets of Creole manners and customs.

"Café des Exilés" deals with a group of Spanish Creoles from Barbados, Martinique, San Domingo, and Cuba, living in New Orleans as exiles, who are plotting an expedition to Cuba and the smuggling of weapons out of New Orleans. The hero of the tale is an Irish adventurer, who marries the café owner's daughter, a beautiful Creole girl, and the villain is one of the refugees, Manuel Mazaro, whose treachery sabotages the smuggling scheme, and who ends up floating in the canal, the victim of multiple stabbings.

Old Creole Days concludes with "Posson Jone'." The central character is a Baptist clergyman from West Florida. Cable had a problem getting the story published. *Scribner's, Harper's,* and other magazines rejected it because, as the editor of *Harper's* commented, "The disagreeable aspects of human nature are made prominent, and the story leaves an unpleasant impression on the mind of the reader."[9] The tale—a comedy rather than a tragedy—concerns the intrigues of Jules St.-Ange, an irresponsible young Creole gambler, to defraud a hulking drunken backwoods minister of a large roll of bills belonging to the latter's church. The pair come upon a circus where a fight between a tiger and a buffalo is to be staged. The man of God from the Florida parishes begins to preach to the jeering multitude, and then single-handedly carries the tiger out of its cage and places it on the buffalo's back. Jules St.-Ange is so overcome with admiration that he later rescues the preacher from the confinement of the calaboose, and offers to make good the lost money. Posson Jone' refuses, but when he boards a schooner to return home, he finds that his Negro slave has been protecting his money all along. So impressed is Jules St.-Ange by these events that he resolves to pay his debts and henceforth lead an honest life.

When it was finally published, "Posson Jone'" became one of the most popular and widely commended of Cable's stories, despite its somewhat ribald, irreverent plot.

The Creoles of New Orleans were outraged by Cable's stories, especially by his quadroon ball scenes and references to miscegenation. Writing many years later, Edward Laroque Tinker notes the "vindictive rancor engendered in the Creoles" by *Old Creole Days* and other tales, "an animosity that persists today as fierce and malevolent as ever."[10] To the Creoles, Cable was worse than a carpetbagger. They called him a "renegade scalawag," and refined families would not permit his books in their homes. Instead of parading quadroon women across his pages as heroines and dishing up the dregs of society, the Creoles felt that he should have written of Southern ladies and gentlemen, as did other Southern novelists. In addition to their strong resentment against implications of mixed blood, the Creoles protested vehemently against Creole speech as reported in Cable stories—dialect French or broken English which in their view held them up to the world as an ignorant, illiterate people. It was claimed also that Cable drew his characters from the lowest level of the Creole population, leaving the reader to make the inference that there was no more cultured or refined grade.

As time went on, Cable became increasingly a reformer and propagandist and less the literary man and creative artist. He left New Orleans in 1886 to reside in Northampton, Massachusetts, and thereafter devoted himself to crusades for Negro rights, changed election laws, and moral reform. Out of this period came such books as *The Silent South* and *The Negro Question*, rated by Edmund Wilson as "among his most valuable writings."[11]

Cable was the first to break the Southern taboo against writing objectively and realistically about Negroes and to portray truthfully the social conditions around him. This was accomplished at the cost of social ostracism among his own people. Tinker suggests, therefore, that Cable "may well be called the first martyr to the cause of literary freedom in the South."[12]

A summary of Cable's literary career, showing insight and understanding, comes from the pen of Fred Lewis Pattee, American literary historian: "More and more it is evident that his ultimate literary fame will depend upon a few of his earlier romantic creations. There is a vivacity, a Gallic brilliance, and exotic atmosphere about these creations that make them stand alone among American works of fiction. Coming as they did at the moment that new literary forces were gathering for the new literary period following the Civil War, they were widely influential."[13]

Black Folktales

JOEL CHANDLER HARRIS'S *Uncle Remus:*
His Songs and His Sayings

Some years ago, a leading Southern literary scholar, C. Alphonso Smith, commented that Joel Chandler Harris's *Uncle Remus: His Songs and His Sayings* was "the most important single contribution to American literature before 1880."[1] Four reasons were offered to justify such a sweeping statement: the character of Uncle Remus added a new figure to literature, typifying a race and perpetuating a civilization; the folktales of the Negro were brought into literature, laying the foundation for the scientific study of Negro folklore; the dialect, reproduced so completely and accurately, is valuable for the study of primitive English; and the sympathetic approach to the principal character is a contribution to improved race relations.

Harris himself remarked that he had two purposes in writing the stories. The first was his desire "to preserve in permanent shape those curious mementoes of a period that will no doubt be sadly misrepresented by historians of the future"; the second was to preserve the dialect through which the folktales had been transmitted. "If the language in which the legends have been framed," he writes, "has given vivid hints of the really poetic imagination of the Negro; if it has embodied the quaint and rugged humor which was the most characteristic; if it has made clear a certain picturesque

UNCLE REMUS

HIS SONGS AND HIS SAYINGS

THE FOLK-LORE OF THE OLD PLANTATION

By JOEL CHANDLER HARRIS

WITH ILLUSTRATIONS BY FREDERICK S. CHURCH AND
JAMES H. MOSER

NEW YORK
D. APPLETON AND COMPANY
1, 3, AND 5 BOND STREET
1881

sensitiveness—a curious exaltation of mind and temperament—if this has been done, then the attempt to reproduce plantation dialect has been measurably successful."[2]

Joel Chandler Harris was born in 1848 in the little town of Eatonton, Georgia, the illegitimate son of a Georgia girl, Mary Harris, and an Irish day laborer. The red-haired, freckle-faced, undersized, painfully shy boy was given a few years' education in the Eatonton Academy, with tuition paid by generous friends. His real, though less formal, education began, however, when at age thirteen he went to live on the plantation of Joseph Addison Turner. There he was employed on a country weekly newspaper, *The Countryman*, reputed to have been the only newspaper ever edited and published on a plantation. Young Harris learned to set type and began to contribute articles for the paper. Turner's 4,000-volume library was a gold mine for the youth, who started to read widely in English classics. Time for recreation was not lacking, and Harris hunted foxes, raccoons, opossums, and rabbits. More important for his future career, he spent spare hours listening to the Negro folk-tales told by two of Turner's slaves, Old Herbert and Uncle George Terrell.

With the end of the Civil War, *The Countryman* ceased publication. For several years following, Harris held various newspaper jobs, in Macon, New Orleans, and Savannah. He moved to Atlanta in 1876, where he soon became one of the leading writers on the *Constitution*, then acquiring an outstanding reputation among American newspapers. From 1886 until his retirement in 1906, Harris was the *Constitution*'s chief editorial writer.

In addition, Harris began to produce for the paper sketches, stories, poems, news notes, and commentaries. The idea of Uncle Remus evolved slowly. Apparently the original impetus came from reading an article, "Folk-lore of Southern Negroes," in *Lippincott's Magazine*, which Harris thought showed a lack of understanding of Negro speech. Harris decided to try his hand at setting down in Negro dialect the tales with which Turner's slaves had entertained him years before. The first Uncle Remus tale, "The Story of Mr. Rabbit and Mr. Fox," appeared in the *Constitution* on 20 July 1879. There followed next the famous tar baby story, and others came along in rapid succession. The series became popular immediately in both the North and the South, and by 1880 enough material had accumulated for D. Appleton and Company in New York to bring out the first volume of the stories under the title *Uncle Remus: His Songs and His Sayings, the Folk-Lore of the Old Plantation.* The collection contained thirty-four plantation legends or Negro folk-tales, a few plantation proverbs, a story of the war, and twenty-one sayings or opinions of Uncle Remus—all narrated by Uncle Remus himself. Nine more Uncle Remus collections were to follow. Among the later works were *Nights with Uncle Remus: Myths and Legends of the Old Plantation* (1883), *Uncle Remus and His Friends* (1892), *Mr. Rabbit at Home* (1895), *The Tar-Baby and Other Rhymes of Uncle Remus* (1904), *Told by Uncle Remus: New Stories of the Old Plantation* (1905), and *Uncle Remus and Brer Rabbit* (1906).

Jay Hubbell, American literary historian, points out that "until after the Civil War, American writers almost wholly neglected the rich treasury of the Negro's folk songs and legends."[3] William Cullen Bryant, on a visit to the South in 1843, was intrigued by the singing of Negro workers in a Richmond tobacco factory. Harriet Beecher Stowe's *Uncle Tom's Cabin* and *Dred* featured Negro characters but made little use of songs and folktales. The chief writers who preceded Harris in the attempt to portray Negro character, other than Stowe, were William Gilmore Simms, Edgar Allan Poe, Stephen C. Foster, and Irwin Russell. The man to whom Harris and Thomas Nelson Page gave major credit for discovering the literary material buried in Negro character and Negro dialect was Irwin Russell of Mississippi, whose most famous work was *Christmas Night in the Quarters* (1878). Harris's tales began to appear just at the moment when interest in the Negroes was rapidly rising.

The character of Uncle Remus was modeled after that of an old Negro whom Harris had known intimately on the Turner plantation. The Uncle Remus of the stories is eighty years old but still vigorous in movement and speech. "He had always exercised authority over his fellow servants. He had been the captain of the corn-pile, the stoutest at the log-rolling, the swiftest with the hoe, the neatest with the plough, and the plantation hands still looked upon him as their leader."[4]

In the introduction to his first book, Harris describes the familiar setting in which the Uncle Remus stories are invariably presented:

If the reader not familiar with plantation life will imagine that the myth-stories of Uncle Remus are told night after night to a little boy by an old Negro who appears to be venerable enough to have lived during the period which he describes . . . he will find little difficulty in appreciating and sympathizing with the air of affectionate superiority which Uncle Remus assumes as he proceeds to unfold the mysteries of plantation lore to a little child who is the product of that practical reconstruction which has been going on to some extent since the war in spite of the politicians.[5]

Uncle Remus's characters are speaking animals and the central figure is Brer Rabbit, always the hero of the tales. His quick mind is always a jump ahead of his enemies. When traps are laid for him, those who laid them are caught. He is smart, full of tricks, and adept at fooling others and playing them against one another. Brer Rabbit "smokin' his seegyar" or "chawin' his terbacker" moves from one adventure to another, and wriggles out of every situation, no matter how perilous.

When asked why the rabbit and not the fox, as in European folklore, is the star of his tales, Harris explained, "It needs no scientific investigation to show why the Negro selects as his hero the weakest and most harmless of all animals, and brings him out victorious in contests with the bear, the wolf, and the fox. It is not *virtue* that triumphs, but *helplessness*; it is not *malice*, but *mischievousness*." "Brer Rabbit was the Negro Hercules," suggests Van Wyck Brooks, "and indeed the rabbit had always been in African mythology the great central figure and wonder-worker. The weaker creatures, in every case, discomfited the stronger, as the Negroes wished, by their mischievous arts and cunning."[6]

Brer Rabbit is a thoroughly amoral creature. He willingly cheats and lies, and he has cruel, savage traits in his character. He scalds the Wolf to death, makes the innocent Possum die in a fire to cover his own crimes, tortures the Bear by setting a swarm of bees on him, and after causing the fatal beating of the Fox, carries his victim's head to Mrs. Fox and her children, trying to trick them into eating it in their soup. Uncle Remus's reply to the little boy, when questions are raised about such behavior, was that creatures should not be judged by human moral standards. Perhaps these are the reasons why Harris is said to have never read or told the stories to his own children.

The general interpretation today of Harris's fables is that they were the Negroes' method of getting even with cruel overseers and masters. Harris himself was shrewd enough to realize that behind the tricks of Brer Rabbit and the defeats of Brer Fox lay the Negroes' desire to triumph over the white man, at least in their imagination.

A controversial article by Bernard Wolfe in *Commentary* magazine, "Uncle Remus and the Malevolent Rabbit," carries this thesis to extremes. In what amounts to a psychoanalytic study of the Uncle Remus stories, Wolfe argues that, taking Brer Rabbit as a symbol, the stories reflect "the Negro slave's festering hatred of the white man." Wolfe also sees an overt sexual aspect: "In sex, Brer Rabbit is at his most aggressive—and his most invincible. . . . In their sexual competition the Rabbit never fails to humiliate the Fox viciously." Another point of tension is communal meals. Traditionally, the South forbids Negroes to eat at the same table with whites. "But Brer Rabbit," Wolfe notes, "through an act of murder, *forces* Brer Fox and all his associates to share their food with him." Harris is accused of taking over "the hate-imbued folk materials" and fitting them into a white man's framework of love to a point where "the genuine folk was almost emasculated into the cute folksy."[7]

The Uncle Remus tales teem with "creeturs" in addition to Brer Rabbit. They include the fox, the opossum, the bull, the cow, the billy-goat, the wolf, the lion, the frog, the bear, the deer, the alligator, the snake, the wildcat, the mink, the weasel, the pig, the ram, the dog, the terrapin, the polecat, and the turtle. The birds and fowls are the partridge, the hawk, the sparrow, the goose, the chickens, the buzzard, and the guinea-fowls. The most frequent trickster after Brer Rabbit is Brer Terrapin, the winner in eight of the tales. Stella Brewer Brookes, in her *Joel Chandler Harris–Folklorist*, expresses the belief that the terrapin plays so conspicuous a part because of "his shell, which no animal could penetrate; his ability to live for a long time without food; his silence; the extreme slowness and caution of his movements; his peculiar air of 'dogged determination' with which he sets about overcoming or circumventing obstacles."[8]

Uncle Remus has antecedents going back into the remote past. The fables appear to be as old as the earliest folktales of the most primitive peoples. Adolf Gerber traced fifty of the stories to direct sources in Africa. "The resemblances among the stories," Gerber states, "are so close that Harris might be accused of having manufactured his on the African patterns, were he not supposed to be a reliable and honest man." A leading characteristic of animal tales examined by Gerber is the triumph of cunning and craft over brute force. Thus, in India the jackal and the hare rate first among sly, clever animals; in European medieval epics, the fox is the hero; in Africa, the jackal, fox, hare, and tortoise; and in Brazil the cotia, a species of tortoise.[9]

A recent Harris editor, John Tumlin, concludes that "the folklore that Harris undertook to record had its roots in an African oral tradition much richer generally than its Western counterparts. The richness of the tradition arises in part from the nature of the languages which gave it birth . . . much of the African narrative genius was channeled into the oral tales, evolving large vocabularies and startingly opulent poetic expressions. For the same reason, these tales often show a complexity and sophistication which the Western reader ordinarily associates only with written literature."[10] Similar versions of the fables told by Southern Negro slaves have been discovered in Siam, India, Egypt, the Arab countries, and South America.

Even in the United States, the tales appear to have been universally known in the South long before they were recorded by Harris. John James Audubon heard them in the Louisiana bayous; Opie Read, American novelist, claimed to have heard them from an old Negro shoemaker in Tennessee; Mark Twain recalled them from his boyhood in Missouri; and Theodore Roosevelt, one of Harris's warmest admirers, reported that they had reached him by way of his Georgia-born mother and aunt.

Harris was unaware, when they were first published, of the almost universal distribution of Uncle Remus–type stories. He was unprepared, therefore, for the excitement created among folklorists, at home and abroad, as they read the tales. Any notion of being an eminent folklore specialist or an authority in the general field of folklore was immediately disclaimed by Harris. Having been apprised by professional folklorists of the ethnological and scientific value of his work, however, he undertook to acquaint himself with the field by extensive reading of folklore magazines and books by specialists in the field. An introduction to *Nights with Uncle Remus*

(1883) reports his findings and views on comparative folklore. In any event, Harris insisted that no matter how many parallels or analogues the folklorists might discover, they could rely on the authenticity of the Uncle Remus stories. They had not been invented or polished by him in any way.

A factor which might militate against permanent significance in American literature for the Uncle Remus stories is the dialect in which they are written. Harris consciously tried to avoid what he called the "intolerable misrepresentations of the minstrel stage" and aimed for a "phonetically genuine" dialect. As a rule, he carefully refrained from using the black folk speech to ridicule or to belittle and, as far as it could be done in printed form, he tried to present the full richness of the Afro-American language which he had heard from childhood. In a letter to the editor of the *Folk-Lore Journal* of London, written three years after the first volume of Uncle Remus tales was published, Harris commented:

It is a misfortune, perhaps, from an English point of view, that the stories in that volume are rendered in the American Negro dialect, but it was my desire to preserve the stories as far as I might be able in the form in which I heard them, and to preserve also if possible the quaint humor of the Negro. It is his humor that gives the collection its popularity in the United States, but I think you will find the stories more important than humorous should you take the trouble to examine them. Not one of them is cooked, and not one nor any part of one is an invention of mine. They are all genuine folklore tales.[11]

A scholarly analysis of American Negro speech was undertaken a number of years ago by C. Alphonso Smith, who found four distinct varieties: the Eastern or Tidewater Virginia (used in Thomas Nelson Page's writings), the Gullah dialect of the South Carolina and Georgia rice plantations, the French-English dialect spoken by the Southern Louisiana Creole Negroes, and finally "the dialect spoken by the great majority of the uneducated Negroes of the United States, that of the Uncle Remus stories. . . . The language used by Uncle Remus still embodies the characteristic qualities of Negro speech as heard especially in the country districts of the South."[12]

Some skepticism about the long-range endurance of the Uncle Remus stories is expressed by another literary critic and historian, Jay Hubbell, who wondered how long Harris would be remembered. "The folklorists will always find his work important," Hubbell writes, "but few persons at the present time, even in the South, can read the Negro dialect with any facility." Further handicaps pointed out by Hubbell are the lack of enthusiasm for the stories among Negroes themselves, who see Uncle Remus as an Uncle Tom- type of character; and the ignorance of rural life and customs among urban-bred children. "In spite of the difficult dialect," Hubbell concedes, "the Uncle Remus tales are still a classic in children's literature."[13]

Certainly, Uncle Remus has qualities that have caused him to endure far beyond American dialect literature in general. Quite unreadable today are the writings of Josh Billings, Artemus Ward, Finley Peter Dunne (Mr. Dooley), and a multitude of other authors who specialized in misspellings and outdated slang.

The contemporary reception of the Uncle Remus stories amazed Harris. It was recognized at once that they represented a new kind of Southern literature—a complete departure from the chivalric gentlemen, charming belles, white-columned mansions, and lordly manor houses with retinues of servants characterizing the overdrawn romances of the past. There was no trace in the Harris tales of racial tensions, partisan politics, or sectional prejudices. Their appeal was to all ages and all classes, without regard to race or geographical boundaries. Abroad, the Uncle Remus stories were translated into Swedish, French, Bengali, Dutch, Spanish, Japanese, and a number of African dialects.

A perceptive critic, John Tumlin, notes certain limitations in Harris's knowledge of black folklore: "For instance, his collections omit altogether the sometimes comic and often powerful sexual overtones of much Afro-American folklore. He was probably unaware of this aspect of the tales, for he was always the white outsider no matter how fully he was able to penetrate the Negro's reluctance to tell his tales to a stranger. . . . Recognizing such limitations, no one should conclude that the Uncle Remus tales capture the full sweep of the Afro-American folktale. The bulk of the old man's narratives are animal tales, which constitute only a fraction of the whole spectrum. Still these, along with the ghost, devil and witch tales, which are also plentiful, are among the most popular, especially with children."[14]

Father of Waters

Whether or not Mark Twain was a Southerner has been an ongoing debate among biographers, historians, and literary critics. A leading literary historian, Jay B. Hubbell, offers a number of persuasive reasons for so classifying him: Twain served for several weeks as a Confederate soldier; his three best books—*Tom Sawyer, Life on the Mississippi,* and *Huckleberry Finn*—dealt with life in the Old South; his first literary efforts occurred while he was living in the South; he learned the art of storytelling from accomplished Southern raconteurs; he was influenced by the writings of the old Southern humorists; and he never lost his Southern drawl.[1] Furthermore, Twain's father was a Virginian and his mother a Kentuckian; Missouri, his native state, was a slave state, and many of its professional and political leaders came from Virginia, Kentucky, and Tennessee; Hannibal, where Twain grew up, was distinctly a Southern town.

The Mississippi River was unquestionably the most significant single factor in Mark Twain's early years. The river was his university, the boundary between East and West and a connecting link between North and South. Hannibal was a river town, and a microcosm of the frontier personalities of every variety was to be found passing through in the westward surge of migration. Here were river adventurers, gamblers, fleeing criminals, runaway slaves, and other human castoffs and riffraff. A river pilot, such as Mark Twain became, had the broadening experience of daily contact with Northern, Southern, Eastern, and Western men. "In that brief, sharp schooling," Twain recalled later, "I got personally and familiarly acquainted with about all the different types of human nature that are to be found in fiction, biography, or history. . . . When I find a well-drawn character in fiction or biography I generally take a warm personal interest in him, for the reason that I have known him before—met him on the river."[2]

Incidentally, Samuel Clemens claims that the river gave him his pen name, Mark Twain. Previously, he states, the name had been signed in communications to New Orleans newspapers by a veteran pilot, Isaiah Sellers. "It is an old river term," he explains, "a leadsman's call, signifying two fathoms—twelve feet. It has a richness about it; it was always a pleasant sound for a pilot to hear on a dark night; it meant safe water." This account appears to be a pure fabrication on Twain's part; research has found no communications in New Orleans papers signed by Sellers, and there is no record of a river pilot named Isaiah Sellers.

The initial impulse for *Life on the Mississippi* came from William Dean Howells, editor of the *Atlantic Monthly*. Though the subject was so clearly a natural for him, it had never occurred to Twain to write his reminiscences of his years as a riverman. In a letter to Howells in the fall of 1874, from Hartford, he wrote: "Twichell [the Rev. Joseph H. Twichell, a longtime friend] and I have had a long walk in the woods, and I got to telling him of the old Mississippi days of steamboating glory and grandeur as I saw them (during four years) *from the pilot-house*. He said 'What a virgin subject to hurl into a magazine!' I hadn't thought of that before. Would you like a series of papers to run through three months or six or nine—or about four months, say?"[3]

A series of articles, Chapters 4 through 17 of the book published eight years later, appeared in the *Atlantic* from January through June and August 1875, under the title *Old Times on the Mississippi*. Not until 1882 did Mark return to renew his impressions of "Old Man River," and to complete the work for *Life on the Mississippi* in book form. Chapters 1 to 3 and 18 to 60 were added.

In the opening sentence of his river epic, Mark Twain com-

LIFE ON THE MISSISSIPPI

BY

MARK TWAIN

AUTHOR OF 'A TRAMP ABROAD' 'THE INNOCENTS ABROAD'
'THE PRINCE AND THE PAUPER' ETC.

Mississippi Steamboat of Fifty Years Ago

WITH OVER 300 ILLUSTRATIONS

London

CHATTO & WINDUS, PICCADILLY

1883

ments, "The Mississippi is well worth reading about. It is not a commonplace river, but on the contrary is in all ways remarkable."[4] On the mind of the imaginative youth, the magnitude of the Father of Waters, the beauty of its rugged bluffs and heavily wooded banks, and its irresistible might in spring and summer floods left an indelible impression. In the eyes of Sam Clemens and other young lads living in river towns, steamboats and rivermen—especially river pilots—were the ultimate in glamor. "When I was a boy," Twain reminisces, "there was but one permanent ambition among my comrades in our village. That was, to be a steamboatman."[5] The ambition became a reality for many. The minister's son grew up to be an engineer, the doctor's and the postmaster's sons became "mud clerks," the wholesale liquor dealer's son became a barkeeper on a boat, four sons of the chief merchant and two sons of the county judge became pilots. Mark Twain's first attempts to break into the charmed circle failed.

In the summer of 1856 Twain discovered a book describing a recent exploration of the upper Amazon River. He was immediately fired with the desire to go to South America, gather coca and get rich. Leaving Cincinnati, where he was working as a printer, he "took passage on an ancient tub called the *Paul Jones*, for New Orleans," where he hoped to pick up a steamer for South America. But as the *Paul Jones* reached Louisville, it "stuck hard and fast on the rocks in the middle of the river, and lay there four days."[6]

The event was a turning point in Mark Twain's life. During the two weeks' voyage from Cincinnati to New Orleans, he used all his powers of persuasion to induce Horace Bixby, pilot of the *Paul Jones*, to employ him as a "cub-pilot." Bixby finally capitulated and agreed to teach him the Mississippi River from New Orleans to St. Louis for five hundred dollars, payable out of his first wages. In any case, Twain discovered that "a vessel would not be likely to sail for the mouth of the Amazon under ten or twelve years," and he was down to his last ten dollars.

Twain began his pilot training with all the confidence of youth. "If I had really known what I was about to require of my faculties," he remarks, "I should not have had the courage to begin. I supposed that all a pilot had to do was to keep his boat in the river, and I did not consider that that could be much of a trick, since it was so wide."[7]

The infinite detail associated with piloting comes alive under Mark Twain's descriptive powers. As he writes, "Piloting becomes another matter when you apply it to vast streams like the Mississippi and the Missouri, whose alluvial banks cave and change constantly, whose snags are always hunting up new quarters, whose sand-bars are never at rest, whose channels are forever dodging and shirking and whose obstructions must be confronted in all nights and all weathers without the aid of a single light-house or a single buoy."[8]

The remarkable skill possessed by a super-pilot like Bixby is shown on one occasion, when his boat is about to run aground on an island:

Fully to realize the marvelous precision required in laying the great steamer in her marks in that murky waste of water, one should know that not only must she pick her intricate way through snags and blind reefs, and then shave the head of the island so closely as to brush the overhanging foliage with her stern, but at one place she must pass almost within arm's reach of a sunken and invisible wreck that would snatch the hull timbers from under her if she should strike it, and destroy a quarter of a million dollars' worth of steamboat and cargo in five minutes, and maybe a hundred and fifty human lives into the bargain.[9]

After a time Twain felt that he had packed his "head full of islands, towns, bars, 'points,' and bends," but gaps in his knowledge continued to trouble him. Piloting conditions at night were particularly fearsome: a clear starlight night throws heavy shadows; the river is a very different shape on a pitch-dark night from what it is on a starlight night; on nights when there are "grisly, drizzly gray mists, there isn't *any* particular shape to a shore"; and "different kinds of *moonlight* change the shape of the river in different ways."[10]

As Twain's rigorous training proceeded, he found that "the face of the water, in time, became a wonderful book—a book that was a dead language to the uneducated passenger, but which told its mind to me without reserve, delivering its most cherished secrets as clearly as if it uttered them with a voice. And it was not a book to be read once and thrown aside, for it had a new story to tell every day. Throughout the long twelve hundred miles there was never a page that was void of interest, never one that you could leave unread without loss, never one that you would want to skip." Where the passenger saw only "pretty pictures painted by the sun and shaded by the clouds," the trained pilot saw "not pictures at all, but the grimmest and most dead-earnest of reading matter." In gaining such realistic knowledge, Mark Twain observes that he "had lost something which could never be restored to me while I lived. All the grace, the beauty, the poetry, had gone out of the majestic river!"[11]

Following Bixby's advice, Twain concentrated all his thought on learning the shape of the river, studying sharp, wooded points, conspicuous dead trees, and prominent hills. But tangible objects seemed to be constantly changing. "It was plain," Twain found, "that I had got to learn the shape of the river in all the different ways that could be thought of—upside down, wrong end first, inside out, fore-and-aft, and 'thort-ships'—and then know what to do on gray nights when it hadn't any shape at all."[12]

One quality above all must be possessed by the skillful pilot, and that is memory. Every trivial detail of twelve hundred miles of river had to be known with absolute exactness. "I think a pilot's memory is about the most wonderful thing in the world," Twain observed. The well-trained pilot's memory functions effortlessly and subconsciously, hour after hour and day after day. As Twain points out, "Astonishing things can be done with the human memory if you will devote it faithfully to one particular line of business."[13]

The pilots were indisputably the aristocracy of the rivermen. They formed a powerful association which dictated wages and pensions and controlled the granting of pilots' licenses. According to Twain, "It was the tightest monopoly in the world" and seemed indestructible. "And yet the days of its glory were numbered." New railroads began to divert the passenger travel from the steamers; the steamboating industry came to a complete halt during the Civil War; the association's funds were embezzled; after the war the steamers were largely limited to carrying freight; and then "some genius from the Atlantic coast introduced the plan of towing a dozen steamer cargoes down to New Orleans at the tail of a vulgar little tug-boat." Thereafter, "the association and the noble science of piloting were things of the dead and pathetic past."[14]

Mark Twain's observations on riverbank inhabitants are graphic. The natives were often the most miserable of human derelicts. During a period of flood, he writes:

Behind other islands were found wretched little farms, and wretched little log cabins; there were crazy rail fences sticking a foot or two above the water, with one or two jeans-clad, chills-racked, yellow-faced male miserables roosting on the top rail, elbows on knees, jaws in hand, grinding tobacco and discharging the result at floating chips through crevices left by lost teeth; while the rest of the family and the few farm animals were huddled together in an empty wood-flat riding at her moorings close at hand. In this flatboat the family would have to cook and eat and sleep for a lesser or greater number of days (or possibly weeks), until the river should fall two or three feet and let them get back to their log cabin and their chills again.[15]

The river's behavior was quite unpredictable. In flood seasons, prosperous towns would be cut off from the mainland, left on an island, and reduced to insignificance. Towns and islands in one state would be moved into another state.

Twain was not quite twenty-three when he received his pilot's license. Thereafter, he reports, "intermittent work gave place to steady and protracted engagements. Time drifted smoothly and prosperously on, and I supposed—and hoped—that I was going to follow the river the rest of my days, and die at the wheel when my mission was ended. But by and by the war came, commerce was suspended, my occupation was gone."[16] Twain's last ascent of the river was not as a pilot, but as a passenger on the *Uncle Sam*. Preparations for war were in evidence all the way. There were blockades at Memphis and St. Louis, but the boat was allowed to go through. It was the last boat from New Orleans to St. Louis.

Mark Twain's ability as a pilot has been the subject of controversy. An expert witness is his trainer, Captain Horace Bixby, one of the great river pilots. Bixby's testimony is contradictory. On one occasion, he stated, "Not only was he a pilot, but a good one. Sam was a fine pilot, and in a day when piloting on the Mississippi required a great deal more brains and skill and application than it does now." In his old age, however, Bixby seems to have revised his judgment. While praising Twain's ability as a student and master of detail, he went on to say, "But Sam was never a good pilot. He knew the Mississippi like a book, but he lacked confidence."[17]

A Mark Twain biographer and literary executor, Bernard De Voto, charges that *Life on the Mississippi* omits important aspects of river life, possibly because of prevailing Victorian prudery. Significant gaps are noted by De Voto: "Harlots of all degree, New Orleans courtesans in the grand manner as well as broken-down yaller gals no longer useful to riverside dives, were habituées of the boats. They and their pimps and all the machinery of bought protection, of display and sale, of robbery and murder were a constant in the trade. . . . There is no mention, either, of the parasitism that was also constant in the trade. The skin games, the frauds, the robberies, the gambling, the cozenage, the systematic organization of the sucker trade are wholly absent from its pages."[18] Neither the river's cruelties nor its indulgences are revealed, there is no materialism, and sex never "raises its ugly head."

Twenty-one years after his career as a pilot on the Mississippi ended, Mark Twain returned to the river. The year was 1882. He traveled down from St. Louis to New Orleans and up again to St. Paul. "I felt a very strong desire to see the river again and the steamboats, and such of the boys as might be left," he said, "so I resolved to go out there." The matters that interested him most on the trip, after the river itself and his old acquaintances, were the striking changes in river traffic due to competition with railroads and towing fleets; the changes in steamboat tradition and custom, particularly the diminished glory of the pilots; the changes in navigation due to beacons and other safety devices; and the growth and decay of river towns. These impressions and reminiscences constituted the second part, about three-fifths of the whole, of *Life on the Mississippi* when it was published the following year.

On the return trip, Twain saw Hannibal again, then a town of about 15,000 inhabitants. He explored and gossiped with old friends in Quincy, Keokuk, St. Paul, Minneapolis, Muscatine, Winona, Moline, Rock Island, La Crosse, Burlington, Dubuque, and Davenport.

The magic and fascination of the mighty Mississippi continued to grip Mark Twain's imagination even after all the years that had passed. Here is his almost poetical picture of the vast river at sunrise:

I had myself called with the four-o'clock watch, mornings, for one cannot see too many summer sunrises on the Mississippi. They are enchanting. First, there is the eloquence of silence; for a deep hush broods everywhere. Next, there is the haunting sense of loneliness, isolation, remoteness from the worry and bustle of the world. The dawn creeps in stealthily; the solid walls of black forest soften to gray, and vast stretches of the river open up and reveal themselves; the water is glass-smooth, gives off spectral little wreaths of white mist, there is not the faintest breath of wind, nor stir of leaf; the tranquillity is profound and infinitely satisfying. Then a bird pipes up, another follows, and soon the pipings develop into a jubilant riot of music. You see none of the birds; you simply move through an atmosphere of song which seems to sing itself. When the light has become a little stronger, you have one of the fairest and softest pictures imaginable. You have the intense green of the massed and crowded foliage near by; you see it paling shade by shade in front of you; upon the next projecting cape, a mile off or more, the tint has lightened to the tender young green of spring; the cape beyond that one has almost lost color, and the furthest one, miles away under the horizon, sleeps upon the water a mere dim vapor, and hardly separable from the sky above it and about it.[19]

Twain's voyage down the Mississippi of course also took him to the lower South, which he had not seen in twenty years. He talked to the inhabitants of Vicksburg, who described their life during the bombardment of the town by Union forces. He visited Louisiana and expressed horror at the sham castles considered by their owners to be the ultimate in architectural style. He was critical of much that he saw throughout the Mississippi Valley. The South was unprogressive, and Twain urged it to emulate Yankee business methods and New England thrift. He was impatient with the Southern newspapers and the "wordy, windy, flowery 'eloquence,' romanticism, sentimentality" of Southern journalistic writing. He was skeptical of the vaunted civilization of the South, citing as one example an advertisement of a Southern school which boasted that its president was Southern born, its teachers Southern in sentiment, and its people represented the "highest type of civilization." The young ladies who attended the school were "trained according to the Southern ideas of delicacy, refinement, religion and propriety."[20]

Twain was inclined to attribute the South's excessive sentimentalism and backwardness, its "maudlin Middle-Age romanticism" to the continuing influence of Sir Walter Scott's novels. He argued that the ideals derived by Southerners from their addiction to Scott kept the South "in love with dreams and phantoms . . . decayed and swinish forms of religion . . . decayed and degraded systems of government," and were perhaps "in great measure" responsible for the Civil War—though Twain concedes that the last point was a "wild proposition."[21]

On the other hand, Twain thought that certain aspects of Southern life and culture were attractive and commendable. He praised such writers as George W. Cable and Joel Chandler Harris: "But when a Southerner of genius writes modern English, his book goes upon crutches no longer, but upon wings, and they carry it swiftly all about America and England—as witness the experience of Mr. Cable and 'Uncle Remus,' two of the very few Southern authors who do not write in the Southern style."[22] Twain also found "the half-forgotten Southern intonations and elisions as pleasing to my ear as they had formerly been. A Southerner talks music. At least it is music to me, but then I was born in the South."[23]

Critical comments on the South were responsible for the suppression of a portion of the original manuscript of *Life on the Mississippi*. The complete work was not published until 1944. The publisher became worried about the possibility of offending potential readers. Caroline Ticknor, daughter of a member of the Boston firm which issued the 1883 edition, told the story of the censorship in an article for *The Bookman*: "While *Life on the Mississippi* was going through the press, it was decided to omit Chapter 48, in which the author has drawn some rather lively comparisons between the North and South, not essential to the interest of the book, and which it was thought might have a detrimental effect upon the Southern buyer. This chapter was set up and then cancelled in the proofs, and its existence was from that time forgotten until after the writer's death."[24]

From a literary point of view, some of the most entertaining material in *Life on the Mississippi* is the yarns. "The Professor's Yarn" in Chapter 36 tells the story of a naive Ohio cattleman who is about to lose $10,000 to professional gamblers, but the cattleman turns out to be a professional gambler in disguise and fleeces the schemers. "A Dying Man's Confession," in Chapter 31, has Poe-like qualities of revenge and terror. The tall tale is represented in the feats of Louisiana mosquitoes, Chapter 34, and "deceiving the yokel" tales in Chapters 30 and 34. Other anecdotes scattered through the *Life* are numerous.

Among numerous critics who have commented on, and assessed the place of *Life on the Mississippi* in American literature, the three following judgments are highly relevant. An early editor, J. W. Rankin, concludes, "*Life on the Mississippi* shows us clearly the plasmic forces which did much toward molding the character of Mark Twain and training him for his career; it is an epic of the Father of Waters and a living record of an age in its habit as it lived; it is full of graphic pictures, humorous tales, and valuable information about not only the author but also the life and traffic of the river."[25] Twain's principal biographer, Albert Bigelow Paine, characterizes the book as an "absolutely unique story of Mississippi life which to-day constitutes one of Mark Twain's chief claims to immortality."[26] And Edgar Lee Masters concludes that "*Life on the Mississippi* comes as near being the American epic as anything we have."[27]

17.

Moonlight and Magnolia

THOMAS NELSON PAGE'S *In Ole Virginia*

An eminent *Baltimore Sun* editor, Gerald W. Johnson, a native Tar Heel, declares that "the greatest enemy of the late confederacy was certainly not Ulysses S. Grant, or even William T. Sherman. . . . Far more lasting damage was done it by men whom the South adores: at the head of the list Stephen Collins Foster. . . . Deceivers of the same kind were orators of Henry Grady's school and a long procession of literary gents, beginning with John Pendleton Kennedy and culminating in Thomas Nelson Page."[1]

Johnson goes on to comment that these men "meant no harm and, to do them justice, they told no lies." Instead, they created a legend, "informing and irradiating the landscape but distorting the vision and paralyzing the will." The myth, Johnson believes "is, in fact, a recrudescence of the Arthurian legend, of loyalty, love and derring-do all compact—in short, romance." It is no more substantial than the "dream stuff that composed the walls and towers of Camelot."[2] Out of these traditions grew certain typically Southern characteristics, according to some caustic critics: ancestor worship, an exaggerated gallantry toward women, over-emphasis on honor, and a glorification of war.

Thomas Nelson Page was a Virginia aristocrat, counting among his kinsmen Randolphs, Pendletons, Wickhams, Carters, Lees, and members of other distinguished families. He was only nine years of age when the Civil War erupted. His youth was spent amid scenes of war and reconstruction. Though too young to have experienced actual battlefield situations, his later life and career were permanently shaped by accounts he heard of the golden age before the war and of Civil War combat. A further influence may have been his acquaintance, as a student, with General Robert E. Lee, then president of Washington College, in Lexington, Virginia. From childhood, Page was devoted to literature and writing. An early start as a professional author was made in 1884 with publication in *Century Magazine* of a dialect story, "Marse Chan."

Despite Page's voluminous literary output, he never again surpassed or equaled in popularity his first book, *In Ole Virginia*, a collection of short stories issued in 1887, mainly written in a Negro dialect almost impenetrable today, and, like the bulk of Page's work, dealing with life in the South before, during, or just after the Civil War.

As will be noted later, Page was not the first writer to extol the virtues of the Old South and to help create a romantic plantation tradition, but he was by all odds the most successful. A contemporary, Grace King, a Louisiana novelist, described the impact of *In Ole Virginia* on her generation of aspiring Southern writers: "It is hard to explain in simple terms what Thomas Nelson Page meant to us in the South at that time. He was the first Southern writer to appear in print as a Southerner, and his stories, short and simple, written in Negro dialect, and, I may say, Southern pronunciation, showed us with ineffable grace that although we were sore bereft politically, we had now a chance in literature at least."[3]

The times were propitious for Page: local-color writers were at the height of their popularity, there was a widespread desire for reconciliation of the sections, and there was avid interest for rediscovering a unique region of the nation. In the introduction to a recent addition of *In Ole Virginia*, Kimball King observes that "Even Northern authors found attractive qualities in ante-bellum Southern life, which they attempted to portray as romantically as any native might do." King adds that Page's "idealized view of the

Old South reassured a nation that was weary of disharmony."[4]

The initial inspiration for Page's first short story, "Marse Chan," the lead story for *In Ole Virginia*, was a letter he had read, found in the pocket of a dead soldier from Georgia. The letter written by a young girl in Georgia to her sweetheart told him that if he would get a furlough and come home, she would marry him. But the soldier dies in battle. "Marse Chan" incorporates all the basic ideas of the letter: honor, loyalty, love, the dangers of battle, death, and a past shared by the hero and heroine. The story is told by Sam, a Negro, to a white man. The romantic, superstitious, and nostalgic black, an ex-slave, now the only survivor of a wasted plantation, recalls the past in every detail. When Chan, later a Confederate hero, was born, his father assigned the Negro boy Sam to him as a body servant. Thus, the two, growing up together, developed a lifelong close relationship. Sam is a happy slave, never rebellious or discontented, completely content to share his master's life. The antebellum past is remembered and described in ecstatic terms in Sam's account.

As Chan grows up, he not only receives a formal school education, but learns how to act as a Southern gentleman, to know the true meaning of such concepts as chivalry, loyalty, honor, and heroism. His early romance with Anne Chamberlain, the daughter of his father's political rival, inevitably travels a rough road. Chan's father is blinded in rescuing a Negro who was trying to save the horses in a burning barn. The feud with Chamberlain eventually leads to a duel, for both Chan and Chamberlain are Southern firebrands, fiercely aware of the code of honor. Both men escape unscathed, since Chamberlain misses and Chan fires into the air. The two lovers, Anne and Chan, however, remain unreconciled. The former is, of course, a perfect symbol of Southern purity and innocence. Chan and Sam go off to war; Anne Chamberlain sends Chan a letter confessing her love; and Chan dies on the battlefield. His body is brought home by the grieving Sam, Anne dies of a broken heart, and the story concludes with the lovers being buried together.

The literary device used by Page in "Marse Chan" and two other stories *In Ole Virginia*, "Meh Lady" and "Unc' Edinburg's Drowndin'" is simple: an old Negro, sentimental in praise of the old days, tells a tale of handsome cavaliers and lovely ladies, stressing the love between master and slave. Page's biographer, Theodore L. Gross, suggests that the only credible person in "Marse Chan" and in the stories that follow is the Negro. "The other characters belong to a mythical past that cannot be realistically created because it is not real; it is the author's evocation," in Page's words, the "picture of a civilization which once having sweetened the life of the South has since then well-nigh perished from the earth."[5]

"Unc' Edinburg's Drowndin': A Plantation Echo," again seen through the eyes of a slave, also centers its action on an unconsummated love affair. As in "Marse Chan," the lovers, Charlotte and George, are separated by their families' political differences. George's political opponent is Charlotte's stepbrother, and the two men stage public debates, a contrivance used by Page to dramatize political conditions in prewar Virginia. The lovers are doomed never to be united, because the hero is fatally injured in saving Uncle Edinburg, narrator of the tale, from drowning. Charlotte comes to stand over George's deathbed as he expires; thus in death the two are spiritually joined. Among the striking features of the story are the description of the rural landscape, the celebration of Christmas, the loyalty and devotion of Negro and white toward each other, and insights into Southern social and political attitudes before the war. Page attempts to recreate plantation life as he imagined that it existed. Arlin Turner, in his *Southern Stories*, remarks, "The portrayal here employs double reflecting surfaces: the Negroes as the whites imagine them look at the whites as the whites want to appear and as they appear to the Negroes. The result in Page is a fascinating portrayal of both whites and blacks of the plantation era, however unreal they may be."[6] The main characters, as in "Marse Chan," are the Southern hero, his beloved, and a Negro slave.

"Meh Lady: A Story of the War," the third tale in *In Ole Virginia*, is narrated by another Negro slave, Billy, and again builds up into an epic tragedy. The central theme is reconciliation, with nostalgic glimpses of the South before, during, and after the Civil War. Paul H. Buck, in *The Road to Reunion*, concludes that "'Meh Lady' was a fresh creation in which the baser metals of sectional strife were transmuted into pure gold. A later generation may deem it insignificant but in the eighties it was one of the brightest ornaments of reconciliation."[7] Page himself states in the introduction to the collected edition of his writings that he "feels that he may without impropriety claim that with his devotion for the South, whose life he has tried faithfully to portray, and his pride in the Union, which he has rejoiced to see fully restored in his time, he has never wittingly written a line which he did not hope might tend to bring about a better understanding between the North and South, and finally lead to a more perfect Union."[8]

Marse Phil, the hero of "Meh Lady," grows up on a wealthy plantation with his sister Meh Lady, otherwise nameless. The brother goes to war and is killed. The sister, possessing the traits ascribed to Southern women—courage, stoicism, dignity, and loyalty—claims his body and returns it to the plantation. Only the sister and her mother are left to maintain the home, which is ravaged by Northern soldiers; the women are defenseless. Their salvation comes by way of an heroic Northern officer, Captain Wilton (who has one Virginian parent), who reprimands the men and takes personal responsibility for protection of the house. The brave captain is wounded in defense of the home and Meh Lady nurses him back to health. Meh Lady makes every effort to preserve the plantation from ruin, but eventually she is forced to sell her personal possessions and at last the plantation itself. With the end of the war, Captain Wilton returns, and after much importuning, Meh Lady accepts his marriage proposal. Amid surroundings of pathos, sentimentality, and plantation traditions (as Page imagined them) the Northern man and the Southern lady are wedded. As the ceremony is performed in the Southern mansion, portraits of Phil and his mother look down on the assembled company. The reader is never permitted to forget the central importance of the Southern past and way of life.

In "Ole Stracted," the fourth story in *In Ole Virginia*, Page abandons the device of telling the tale through a black slave's dialect and reverts to his own language. The story revolves around a demented old man who had been sold to a new master, and at the same time separated from his wife and son. With the coming of emancipation, the ex-slave is under the illusion that his former master is coming for him and he will be reunited with his wife and child. The deranged old man is incapable of adjusting to a Reconstruction period without his master to guide and protect him. Gross's judgment is that "one may dispute the historical validity of the author's creation, one may accuse him of perpetrating the notion of Negro infantilism, but there is a fictional validity that transcends the real world: the Negro's loneliness and nostalgia and loss and ultimate madness are thoroughly convincing, especially as seen by the white narrator and the other Negroes in the story."[9]

Two minor tales of a quite different character complete *In Ole Virginia*. "No Haid Pawn" is a ghost story, with haunted house and a gigantic ghost, calling to mind Edgar Allan Poe in its evocation of the macabre and grotesque, a vivid tale of the supernatural, set in a quiet rural community. In the end, the haunted house is struck by lightning during a thunderstorm, burned to the water's edge, "and the spot with all its secrets lay buried under its dark waters."

"Polly: A Christmas Recollection," the final tale, returns to a depiction of the antebellum plantation life. Page repeats himself by keeping two young lovers apart because their families belong to different political factions. The story, generally agreed to be the weakest of those collected in *In Ole Virginia*, has been described as banal, sentimental, and maudlin. The lovers finally revolt, elope, and marry. From a reader's point of view, two characters are of moderate interest: a Negro, Torm Drinkwater, a chronic drunk, and an uncle, a stiff-necked bigot, who had opposed the marriage.

Critics are in general agreement that there was no growth in Page's work. His first story, "Marse Chan," was his best, containing all the elements that made his writings celebrated. After this minor stroke of genius, Page could only repeat himself endlessly. The dramatic action in four of the six stories in *In Ole Virginia* centers around the theme of young lovers being separated by feuding families. Running through the stories, like a Greek tragedy, are unrequited love, the untimely death of the young and brave, and chaste sexual relationships consummated only in spirit. Page's chief characters belong to two classes—the masters of the great plantations and the faithful house servants, the latter contemptuous of field-hand blacks and poor white "trash." Sam in "Marse Chan" and Billy in "Meh Lady," his two best known and most believable

Negroes, are ex-slaves. The masses of people, the black field hands and Negro women, freed blacks, the small farmers, and poorer whites scarcely exist for Page.

Page's black heroes become stereotypes. Old Sam, for example, is an object of sympathy—dispossessed, lacking any identity of his own, and finding no alternative to the paternalism of the slave system. In effect—though the fact is never acknowledged by Page—Sam is a victim of the old order, unable to adjust to the new. Sam, in short, is a bewildered, disoriented ex-slave suffering the horrors of Reconstruction.

The heroic code appears again and again in Page's writings. In numerous short stories he shows how the code is manifested in a variety of situations how it has been the sustaining force in Southern civilization. The idyllic lives of the plantation owners are revealed in sentimental memory, mainly remote from historical fact, and white supremacy is always to the fore. Gross declares that "Page was so committed to certain political and social attitudes—and to the defense of the entire Southern way of life—that he was incapable of writing realistically. The code of Southern heroism stifled his imagination." In Page's later novels, when he aimed at realistic portrayals, Gross states that "the code was anachronistic and completely incompatible with the tensions of an industrial society."[10]

A leading literary historian, Jay B. Hubbell, concludes that the kind of life depicted by Page belonged to a "Southern literary legend which pictures a Golden Age in the slaveholding South. Now the remarkable thing about this legend is that apart from the poor-whites it plays up the very same classes as the Northern legend: the great planters and the Negro slaves. Like the Northern legend, it practically ignores some four million yeomen farmers. They did not belong to the First Families. . . . In Virginia in 1860 in a population of over one million whites there were only 52,128 men who owned any slaves. There were only 114 who owned as many as one hundred. At least nineteen out of every twenty slave-holders was a yeoman, who held two or three slaves and worked in the tobacco fields beside them. The great planters were few in numbers, but it was from their class that as a rule the people chose their representatives in Congress and the General Assembly."[11] Viewed in the light of hard facts, therefore, Page's picture of the Old South was extremely limited, partial, one-sided, and sentimental.

Nevertheless, Page's panegyric descriptions would credit the Old South with virtually every advance in American culture and civilization: the leadership of its armies and navies, the establishment of a strong federal government, the opening up of the West, the christianizing of the Negro race, and the maintenance of white supremacy—"upon which all civilization seems now to depend." The South's "heroic fight" during the Civil War had "enriched the annals of the human race," Page continues, producing "a people whose fortitude in defeat has been even more splendid than their valor in war. It made men noble, gentle, and brave and women tender and pure and true."[12] It was upon such fantasy that Page drew to picture a prewar Garden of Eden in the South and the postwar loss of that paradise.

Like a later Southern writer, the historian Ulrich B. Phillips, Page was convinced that the South had been misrepresented and misunderstood, especially by Northern historians, which may be cited as part of the reason for Page's chauvinism and elaborate defense of the South. His bitterness and extreme sensitivity are reflected in an essay entitled "The Want of a History of the Southern People," in which Page maintains that "there is no true history of the South. . . . By the world at large we are held to have been an ignorant, illiterate, cruel, semi-barbarous section of the American people, sunk in brutality and vice, who have contributed nothing to the advancement of mankind: a race of slave-drivers, who, to perpetuate human slavery, conspired to destroy the Union, and plunged the country into war."[13] Persuaded that a conspiracy existed and a grave injustice had been done to his beloved section, Page became the South's champion, with the avowed purpose of setting the record straight. Unfortunately, Page did not possess the proper qualities to succeed in that aim. Hubbell notes that his conception of the Old South was "so idealized that he cannot see it in any other way even when he assumes the role of historian."[14]

The plantation literary legend was not created by Page, as noted earlier. Before the Civil War, John Pendleton Kennedy, William Alexander Caruthers, Beverly Tucker, John Esten Cooke,

William M. Thackeray, and G. P. R. James adopted the plantation as a locale for their romantic fiction. The popular conception pictured the South as one great plantation "open as an inn and rich as a castle," where gaiety, hospitality, and prosperity abounded. One American novelist, Mrs. E. D. E. N. Southworth, writes: "In the South, houses are almost palatial; social activity is ceaseless, cultured, idyllic; men are gallant, courtly—princely is the favorite adjective—prodigal in the uncalculating Southern fashion; the heroines are beyond description in beauty, sentimentality, and the ineffable sickliness from which the maid of romance often languishes."[15]

Page's views on the Southern Negro and race problems in general have been a topic for considerable critical comment. His beliefs are set forth most explicitly in an essay, "The Race Question." Therein, Page discusses racial differences between the Anglo-Saxon and the African Negro; contends that the master-slave relationship as it existed under slavery was not necessarily immoral, and had advantages for both whites and blacks; and insists that history demonstrates the Negro's innate inferiority. At the same time, Page claims that he has great affection for the Negro: "What has been stated has been said in no feeling of personal hostility, or even unfriendliness to the Negro, for I have no unfriendliness toward any Negro on earth; on the contrary, I have a feeling of real friendliness toward many of that race and am the well-wisher of the whole people."[16] Page was especially resentful of the new, aggressive, freed Negroes who were insisting upon equality. His affections appear to have been limited to what he called the "old-time Negro," an ex-slave, content with his servile state, and demonstrating undying loyalty to his white master.

At the height of his career, Page received much critical acclaim in both North and South. An instance is Arthur Hobson Quinn's tribute, written in 1909: "In the renaissance of the South, Thomas Nelson Page played a most prominent part, not only in his poems, his novels, and his short stories, but also in the addresses he had made throughout the country, in which he deals directly with Southern life and character. . . . The quality which makes these short stories great is the surety with which the effect is reached."[17]

But some years before Page's death in 1922, literary tastes had begun to change. Romance and sentiment were out, realism was in.

Even in Virginia, such writers as James Branch Cabell, Ellen Glasgow, and Mary Johnston rejected, early in the present century, excessive claims for Southern heroism, manners, social customs, military accomplishments, and womanhood. Cabell went so far as to satirize Page's "Meh Lady" in *The Rivet in Grandfather's Neck* (1915), and later expressed regret that "the ghost of Thomas Nelson Page still haunted everybody's conception of the South, keening in Negro dialect over the Confederacy's fallen glories."[18] On the other hand, a revival of Page's attitude and style may be observed in Stark Young's romantic *So Red the Rose* and Margaret Mitchell's phenomenally popular *Gone with the Wind*. Kimball King points out, too, that William Faulkner, Katherine Anne Porter, Robert Penn Warren, "and a multitude of very recent Southern artists absorbed certain aspects of Page's code—the emphasis on honor, the importance of land, the concern with racial attitudes—even while reacting violently against certain injustices in the system that the elegant Virginian had defended."[19]

Page has few readers today, and, as Hubbell remarks, "not many will care to read or reread Page's novels." Nonetheless, Thomas Nelson Page has continued significance for the literary historian, as the creator of memorable stories evoking Southern plantation legends prior to the Civil War and of heroic myths of the Southern gentleman, the Southern lady, and the Southern way of life. These traditions persist nearly a century after Page wrote his first short story.

The Great Compromiser

BOOKER TALIAFERRO WASHINGTON'S
Up From Slavery

When Frederick Douglass died in Washington, D.C., on 2 February 1895, he had been for fifty years the accepted leader and champion of American Negroes. In the same year of Douglass's death, the black leadership was assumed by Booker T. Washington. Like Douglass, Washington was born a slave, though he was barely ten years old when the Civil War brought freedom. The two men had something else in common: both were reputed to be sons of white men, and neither ever saw or knew his father.

Almost every conceivable handicap was overcome by Booker T. Washington in his climb upward. The name Washington was adopted. As a child, Booker slept on filthy rags and foraged for his food. Shortly after the Civil War ended, the Washington family moved from Franklin County, Virginia, to Malden, West Virginia, where Booker worked as a child in salt furnaces and coal mines. The entire family endured dire poverty, and Booker's school attendance was limited to no more than two or three months out of the year. Meantime, rumors began to reach him of a new school for colored people in Virginia, Hampton Institute, founded by General

Samuel C. Armstrong to train Negroes as "skilled farmers, mechanics, and teachers in the manual and liberal arts." The seventeen-year-old Booker Washington, driven by ambition and a burning zeal for education, in some way managed to travel the five hundred miles to Hampton, and, despite his meager educational background, was admitted.

General Armstrong, the son of a missionary and a remarkable personality in his own right, was convinced that the South's hope for the future depended upon "a vigorous attempt to lift the colored race by a practical education that shall fit them for life." At Hampton he trained selected colored youth to go out and lead their people by showing them how to acquire land and homes, by teaching vocations and skills, by teaching respect for labor, especially skilled labor, and through the molding of character. This educational philosophy was absorbed by young Washington as a student and later as an instructor under General Armstrong; he subsequently applied it as head of the newly founded Tuskegee Institute in Alabama. Washington acknowledged that his general approach to education and to the race question was permanently influenced by the general's teachings.

The era in which Booker T. Washington reached maturity was in some respects more difficult for Negroes than pre–Civil War slavery had been. The position of the blacks in the last quarter of the nineteenth century was steadily deteriorating. By a series of repressive measures, the Southern whites were avenging their defeat in the war, the pain of Reconstruction years, and the brief time of Negro dominance in Southern state governments. After the end of Reconstruction, the blacks were unprotected against the Ku Klux Klan and other terrorist groups who whipped up fear of Negro rule as an excuse for lawlessness. A system of peonage grew up, under which the newly freed slaves were arrested for vagrancy and on other pretexts and their convict labor leased to farmers and businessmen. Under the sharecropping system, both white and black tenant farmers were effectively tied to the land. Lynching became a common practice, as is shown by the fact that some thirty-five hundred persons, nearly all Southern black men, were hanged or burned to death between 1885 and 1915. Direct legislation in the Southern states disfranchised a great majority of black voters; a few

Negroes continued to vote, but they did so at grave physical risk. The Negro was also severely discriminated against in travel accommodations, education, public facilities, and police protection. Educational opportunities for blacks were limited; segregated schools were shortchanged in the allocation of public funds, and denominational schools were inadequately supported by Northern benefactors. From an economic viewpoint, the South was in virtual bankruptcy, and such new industries as were being developed were generally closed to black labor.

When Negroes moved from rural to urban communities, they were confronted by new problems, the most terrifying of which were race riots. In dozens of towns and cities in both North and South riots destructive of lives and property, ugly evidences of white hostility, erupted. Books and leading magazines and newspapers portrayed the Negro as innately inferior—ignorant, lazy, improvident, clownish, irresponsible, childish, and criminal.

This was the dismal picture faced by Booker T. Washington when in 1881, at the age of twenty-five, he was invited to become the principal of a school for Negroes in Tuskegee, Alabama. The school's prospects were bleak. The Alabama legislature had appropriated two thousand dollars for teachers' salaries, but nothing for land or buildings. Undismayed, young Washington opened the school in an old church and a shanty, with thirty students on hand. In the years that followed, Washington was remarkably effective in persuading wealthy philanthropists, mainly Northern, to contribute generous support. Subsidies were received from the Peabody and Slater funds, from the great railroad magnate Collis P. Huntington, and from such industrialists as John D. Rockefeller, Andrew Carnegie, H. H. Rogers of the Standard Oil Company, William H. Baldwin, and Robert Ogden. Washington traveled widely to solicit support. Almost entirely the result of his missionary zeal and genius as a fund raiser, by the time of Washington's death thirty-five years later, Tuskegee had more than a hundred buildings—for the most part erected by the students themselves—owned two thousand acres of local land and had been granted by Congress an additional twenty-five thousand acres in northern Alabama; possessed an endowment of two million dollars; enrolled fifteen hundred students, taught by two hundred faculty members (all Negroes); and was offering training in thirty-eight trades and professions.

From the outset Tuskegee stressed practical training, the guiding principle with which Washington had been so thoroughly indoctrinated at Hampton Institute. As described in Washington's autobiography, *Up From Slavery*:

We found that most of our students came from the country districts, where agriculture in some form or other was the main dependence of the people. We learned that about eighty-five per cent of the coloured people in the Gulf states depended upon agriculture for their living. Since this was true, we wanted to be careful not to educate our students out of sympathy with agricultural life, so that they would be attracted from the country to the cities, and yield to the temptation of trying to live by their wits. We wanted to give them such an education as would fit a large proportion of them to be teachers, and at the same time cause them to return to the plantation districts and show the people there how to put new energy and new ideas into farming, as well as into the intellectual and moral and religious life of the people.[1]

Washington's pragmatic approach to Negro education, reflecting General Armstrong's contention that the race would advance in a competitive, capitalist civilization by working hard, buying land, saving money, raising Christian families, and learning trades, was nothing new. As August Meier traced the history of the movement, in a chapter called "The Rise of Industrial Education in Negro Schools," it has antecedents back to the early nineteenth century.[2] Washington's approach bears a close resemblance also to the teachings of Benjamin Franklin.

Nevertheless, the philosophy of education enunciated by Washington was opposed or at best accepted with reluctance by many Negro students and their elders. Hard physical labor under slavery had turned them against work with their hands. They believed that the mystic power of education, especially acquiring the ability to read and write, would lift the hated burden of physical toil from their backs. One of Washington's tasks was to dispel the fetish that book learning alone would provide salvation for the race. His travels through the Southern states had convinced him that practice as well as theory were indispensable to a race whose opportunities in the foreseeable future would be mainly in agriculture or other forms of manual labor.

The Tuskegee plan was simple. The student worked to pay part of his expenses; he learned how to work most effectively, and was taught the dignity of labor. Negro youth was trained to be teachers, nurses, mechanics, and dietitians, and to become skilled in many other practical fields. "We must admit the stern fact," Washington stated, "that at present the Negro, through no choice of his own, is living among another race which is far ahead of him in education, property, experience, and favorable condition; further, that the Negro's present condition makes him dependent upon white people for most of the things necessary to sustain life, as well as for his common school education." It was Washington's belief that through practical education, the Negro could make himself such a valuable factor in the economic life of the South "that he would not have to seek privileges, they will be freely conferred upon him."

Washington saw the emphasis on practical education as a way not only of achieving real progress for the blacks, but of helping to break down racial prejudice. In short, the dominant whites had to be persuaded that the education of the former slaves was in the true interest of the South. Washington warned the white race that if it kept blacks in the gutter, they themselves would have to remain in the gutter, also. The Negro could not be neglected or degraded without depressing both races. Washington was fully aware that the cooperation and good will of the white leaders were essential to obtaining funds for Negro schools, justice in the courts, and solutions to a multitude of other problems vitally affecting the blacks. In his efforts to show that the whole community would profit by what was done for the Negro, Washington was surprisingly successful. His insistence that the great majority of his race did not expect or desire social equality further disarmed and placated the whites.

A controversial feature of the Tuskegee program was the intentional downgrading of liberal education. Washington conceded that the educational system should eventually produce black teachers, ministers, doctors, lawyers, and statesmen, and not be restricted to agriculture, mechanics, and domestic arts; but he saw the latter areas as offering the most immediate opportunities for the race's advancement. In *Up From Slavery*, he derides the popular picture of "an educated Negro, with a high hat, imitation gold eye-glasses, a showy walking-stick, kid gloves, fancy boots, and what not—in a word, a man who was determined to live by his wits."[3] Among the first students at Tuskegee were a number of former schoolteachers. "Some had studied Latin and one or two Greek," Washington wrote; "this they thought entitled them to special distinction"[4]— which Washington did not.

A leading Negro literary figure, Louis Lomax, comments that "Washington did not condemn the arts outright. But he never hesitated to speak scornfully of Negroes trained in the arts, and this work [*Up From Slavery*] reeks with citations of Negroes who were trained in the arts and classics and then went on to develop tastes and habits their incomes and home lives could not support. Without exception, the Washington morality play has these Negroes falling into sin and disgrace."[5]

Robert Factor, in his book *Black Response to America*, describes Washington's commencement address in 1895 at Fisk University, a liberal arts college: "The tenor of the speech as a whole," he notes, "went further in the total emasculation of liberal education than at any previous time."[6] The graduates were told that "the educated colored man must more and more go to the farms, into the trades, start brickyards, sawmills, factories, open coal mines."[7]

Lomax maintains that Washington's philosophy of Negro education was based on his desire and determination to please white people, because the latter believed that the whites would object to and "not support a school where Negroes were being taught to be other than sophisticated menials."[8] The Negro sociologist E. Franklin Frazier, who taught at Tuskegee in his early years, was reprimanded by Washington for walking across the campus with books under his arm. As reported by Frazier, Washington said, "After all, we don't want our white friends to feel we are teaching our students to think!"[9]

As the fame of the Tuskegee experiment spread, Washington realized that in a sense the eyes of the nation were upon him. "I know," he wrote in his autobiography, "that, in a large degree, we were trying an experiment—that of testing whether or not it was possible for Negroes to build up and control the affairs of a large educational institution. I knew that if we failed it would injure the whole race. I knew that the presumption was against us. I knew that in the case of white people beginning such an enterprise it would be taken for granted that they were going to succeed, but in our case I felt that people would be surprised if we succeeded. All this made a burden which pressed down on us, sometimes, it seemed, at the rate of a thousand pounds to the square inch."[10] Years later, John Dewey was to popularize the concept of fusing practical and intellectual training, teaching his doctrine of the educational value of learning by doing useful and cooperative tasks, but when Booker T. Washington began, Hampton was the only institution with a comparable program.

An invitation to speak to the National Education Association, meeting at Madison, Wisconsin, on 16 July 1884, provided Washington with a nationwide audience to whom he could express his views on race relations. In his well-received speech, he declared, "Any movement for the elevation of the Southern Negro, in order to be successful, must have to a certain extent the cooperation of the Southern whites," adding "whatever benefits the black man benefits the white man." Washington insisted that the whole future of the Negro rested on the question of whether or not he could, through his skill, intelligence, and character, make himself of such value to his community that he would become indispensable.

The most famous of Booker T. Washington's many speeches was delivered at the Cotton States and International Exposition at Atlanta in 1895, when he was asked to speak as a representative of the Negro people. Echoes of that controversial speech continue to be heard down to the present day. Washington was deeply moved by the invitation, recalling that he had been born a slave, that his early years had been spent in poverty and ignorance, and this was the first time in history that a member of his race had been asked to speak from the same platform with Southern white leaders on any important national occasion.

Washington began his celebrated Atlanta speech with a statement of fact: "One-third of the population of the South is of the Negro race." He made it plain that nothing affecting the material or moral welfare of the region could afford to overlook such a large element of the population. In remarks addressed to his own people, he used the metaphor of the ship lost at sea, with its phrase, "Cast down your buckets where you are," urging the blacks to "make friends in every manly way of the people of all races by whom we are surrounded." Washington continued, "No race can prosper till it learns that there is as much dignity in tilling a field as in writing a poem. It is at the bottom of life we must begin, and not at the top. Nor should we permit our grievances to overshadow our opportunities." Washington pleaded with the whites to appreciate the abilities and loyalty of his race and to intertwine the industrial, commercial, and religious life of the two races.

In one important aspect of race relations, Washington retreated, by declaring, "In all things that are purely social we can be as separate as the fingers, yet one as the hand in all things essential to mutual progress. . . . The wisest among my race understand that the agitation of questions of social equality is the extremest folly, and that progress in the enjoyment of all the privileges that will come to us must be the result of severe and constant struggle rather than of artificial feeding. . . . The opportunity to earn a dollar in a factory just now is worth infinitely more than the opportunity to spend a dollar in an opera-house."[11]

The Atlanta speech was received with tremendous enthusiasm by Southern white leaders, who thereafter viewed Washington as the chief spokesman for the Negro people. In effect, he was willing to accept the status quo, which was exactly what the whites wanted to hear. A severe critic, Louis R. Harlan, commented, "Booker Washington's incorrigible humility made him the kind of symbolic black figure that whites accepted. His self-help advice to blacks shifted from whites the responsibility for racial problems they were thoroughly tired of. His economic emphasis took the question of Negro progress out of politics. His materialism was thoroughly American and attuned to the industrial age. His proposals of racial compromise promised peace not only between the races but between the sections."[12]

Other less conservative and less patient Negro leaders likewise reacted with dismay to the Atlanta speech. They felt that in the "Atlanta Compromise," as it came to be called, Washington had conceded too much. It was apparent that he was willing to forego political and social rights in exchange for economic opportunity. The critics held that Washington's doctrine would reduce Negroes as a whole to the status of laborers, barred from the higher walks of life; his emphasis on industrial training, they asserted, would keep the Negro in virtual bondage. A group of Boston intellectuals took the position that the upper ten percent of the graduating class of every Negro high school should be given a chance to pursue advanced studies.

Among the most outspoken and influential black leaders who condemned Booker T. Washington for meekly submitting to injustice and committing treason against his race was W. E. B. Du Bois, a graduate of Fisk and Harvard and a sociologist at Atlanta University. "There is among educated and thoughtful colored men in all parts of the nation," Du Bois wrote, "a feeling of deep regret, sorrow, and apprehension at the wide currency and ascendancy which some of Mr. Washington's theories have gained." He challenged Washington's equivocal attitude on political rights, his willingness to submit to race discrimination in the South, his failure to speak out in the face of injustice, and his narrowly materialistic conception of Negro education. Du Bois especially resented Washington's almost exclusive emphasis on industrial education, because he saw it as standing in the way of Negro ambitions for professional, literary, and artistic distinction. He believed that Washington was asking black people to give up political power, civil rights, and higher education. Du Bois concluded with a declaration that "so far as Mr. Washington apologizes for injustice, North or South, does not rightly value the privilege and duty of voting, belittles the emasculating effects of caste distinctions, and opposes the higher training of our brighter minds,—so far as he, the South, or the Nation, does this,—we must unceasingly and firmly oppose them."[13]

Much evidence points toward the failure of many of Washington's ideas. Critics have pointed out that stopping the agitation for civil liberties did not change the attitude of the Southern whites toward the Negro; lynchings reached their peak during the period of Washington's leadership; the modern race riot was born when he was at the height of his power and influence; segregation on the basis of race and color increased; occupational opportunities in skilled trades diminished; farm ownership declined and farm tenancy grew; and the Southern press, by and large, remained racist in its policies. It soon became apparent, too, that the kind of education advocated by Washington was already obsolescent. Merle Curti observed in his *Social Ideas of American Education* "that at the very time when the crusade for industrial training was being launched, the technological basis of industry was rapidly shifting from that of the skilled artisan to machine production. They failed to see that the machine, by invading the farm, was already beginning to push even the established farmer to the wall."[14]

The criticism of Washington by Du Bois and others appeared not to weaken his role as chief spokesman for the Negro race, especially among his powerful white friends. When he died in 1915, Washington was still firmly entrenched in the position of leading black educator and leading racial adviser to presidents, Congress, and at many other levels.

Certainly, Booker T. Washington was not unaware of the injustices and restrictions which severely handicapped his people. "I do not overlook," he said, "the wrongs that often perplex us in this country." Curti suggests that "Washington's position is better understood when it is remembered that he began his work when race hatred was at its height and when emotions were strained and tense."[15] Another commentator, August Meier, offers further clarification: "Although overtly Washington minimized the importance of the franchise and civil rights, covertly he was deeply involved in political affairs and in efforts to prevent disfranchisement and other forms of discrimination."[16] Washington was particularly irked by discrimination in public education, arguing that no color line should be drawn in the operation of the legal system or in the opportunity to get an education in the public schools.

An objective opinion comes from the Swedish economist and sociologist Gunnar Myrdal, a keen observer of the American scene: "It is wrong to characterize Washington as an all-out accommodating leader. He never relinquished the right to full equality in all respects as the ultimate goal. But for the time being he was prepared to give up social and political equality, even to soft-pedal the protest against inequalities in justice."[17]

Booker T. Washington's story was effectively told in his autobiography, *Up From Slavery* (1901), a simple but dramatic account of his varied career. The book first appeared in serial form in *Outlook*. The author's preface notes that "much of what I have said has been written on board trains, or at hotels or railroad stations while I have been waiting for trains, or during the moments that I could spare from my work while at Tuskegee." The reception of the work far exceeded Washington's expectations. Hundreds of thousands of copies were sold in all parts of the English-speaking world, and numerous translations were issued in Western and Eastern languages. The style was obviously influenced by constant reading of the Bible and of Shakespeare, and the narrative bears some resemblance to *Pilgrim's Progress*. Unfortunately, there is a gap in the record; the last fifteen years of Washington's life were unrecorded.

Samuel R. Spencer, Jr., author of *Booker T. Washington and the Negro's Place in American Life*, sums up Washington's principles and philosophy: "That Washington looked forward to the day of liberty and justice for all cannot be doubted. He accepted half a loaf, not as a permanent settlement, but as a means to a whole loaf later. He did what was possible, given the time and place in which he lived, and did it to the utmost." Washington's approach to race problems was realistic rather than heroic. As a consequence, the luster of his name and fame has diminished with time. The folk heroes of American Negroes today are such militants as W. E. B. Du Bois, William Monroe Trotter, and Martin Luther King, Jr.

Howard Brotz, in his work *Negro Social and Political Thought* suggests, however, that Washington was fifty years ahead of his time, because the fundamental problems of the Negro are "beyond civil rights." That is, the Negro may have achieved full legal equality, but he remains unequal in a number of important economic and social aspects. Without the ability to earn a good living, legal equality falls far short of meeting the Negro's needs.[18] This is the essence of Booker T. Washington's teachings.

19.

Black Protestant

In his review, *Negro Thought in America, 1880–1915*, August Meier concludes that of the great trio of Negro leaders, Frederick Douglass best expressed the aspirations toward full citizenship and assimilation, Booker T. Washington the interest in economic advancement, and W. E. B. Du Bois "most explicitly revealed the impact of oppression and of the American creed in creating ambivalent loyalties toward race and nation in the minds of American Negroes." Meier adds that of the three, "Douglass was the orator, Du Bois the polished writer, and Washington the practical man of affairs."[1]

A noted Negro poet and educator, James Weldon Johnson, expressed the view that W. E. B. Du Bois's *The Souls of Black Folk* is "a work which, I think, has had a greater effect upon and within the Negro race in America than any other single book published in this country since *Uncle Tom's Cabin*." The immense popularity of the book is demonstrated by the fact that since its publication in 1903 *The Souls of Black Folk* has been issued in more than thirty English-language editions.

Du Bois was born in Great Barrington, Massachusetts, in the year that Ulysses S. Grant was elected president of the United States. The backgrounds of Booker T. Washington, born to slavery on a Virginia plantation, and the man destined to contest his leadership of the Negro race, W. E. B. Du Bois, could hardly have been more dissimilar. Du Bois conceived of himself as an aristocrat, and his personal history is atypical for a black man. Western Massachusetts had been a center of abolitionist sentiment; the twenty-five colored families in the valley from which Du Bois came dated back to the War of 1812. As old residents, they mingled freely with farmers and townspeople, attended the same churches, went to town meetings, and otherwise participated fully in community affairs. On his mother's side, Du Bois was descended from Tom Burghardt, who was brought by Dutch slave traders to the Hudson Valley about 1740 and whose service in the Army during the Revolutionary War won freedom for himself and his family. On his father's side, Du Bois was a descendant of French Huguenots who migrated to America three centuries earlier. Du Bois himself described his mixed ethnic origins as "a flood of Negro blood, a strain of French, a bit of Dutch, but, thank God, no 'Anglo-Saxon.'"

As a young man, Du Bois showed brilliance. He graduated with distinction from the Great Barrington public schools in 1884 and was the class orator, speaking on the great abolitionist Wendell Phillips. Since he lacked financial means to attend Harvard College, which was his chief ambition, his family decided that he should enter Fisk University in Nashville, Tennessee, an experience that permanently changed his life. At Fisk, Du Bois came to know other eager and ambitious students like himself, met inspiring teachers, and came face to face with the plight of some typically poverty-stricken blacks by teaching in an East Tennessee rural school. "Henceforward I was a Negro," Du Bois declared later. After Fisk, he received a scholarship at Harvard, where he earned a bachelor's and a doctoral degree, and studied history, economics, and sociology. Another scholarship took him to Germany—the intellectual mecca for Americans in the 1890s—where he enrolled in the University of Berlin for two years. In brief, Du Bois received the best education available to an American, and he always considered himself as belonging to the "Talented Tenth" (Du Bois's phrase), the small group of intellectual and hard-working Negroes who were to serve as examples to the Negro mass and to uplift it.

Du Bois's first teaching opportunity when he returned to the

United States, at the age of twenty-six, was at Wilberforce College in Ohio, where he was assigned classes in Latin, Greek, German, English, and a new subject, sociology. After a two-year stay, he was offered a one-year appointment at the University of Pennsylvania for a study of Negro life in the city of Philadelphia. His final academic appointment was a professorship of economics and history at Atlanta University, from 1896 to 1910; later, from 1932 to 1944, he was head of the same institution's department of sociology.

Du Bois's first notable contribution to the scholarly study of the American Negro was his doctoral dissertation at Harvard, entitled *The Suppression of the African Slave Trade to the United States of America, 1638–1870*, issued in 1896 as the first number of the Harvard Historical Series. By then, he had reached the conclusion that the most important work he could undertake to improve the Negro's position in the United States was a series of studies of the blacks, which Du Bois intended should be "primarily scientific—a careful search for Truth conducted as thoroughly, broadly, and honestly as the material resources and mental equipment will allow."

To further this aim, Du Bois wrote *The Philadelphia Negro: a Social Study*, which was published in 1899 by the University of Pennsylvania. The completed report offered convincing statistical evidence that the life of the Negro in Philadelphia was a direct consequence of the Negro's treatment by that city. Du Bois described what it meant to be snubbed in employment and in social intercourse. The Negro's participation in politics, he found, had benefitted both the city and the race. The necessity for the blacks to help themselves was stressed, especially through enterprises that would provide employment and training in business and trades. Negroes must resist prejudice and injustice, Du Bois contended, and at the same time work to reduce crime and to uphold such virtues as self-respect, truth, honesty, and charity. *The Philadelphia Negro* is reputed to be the first work in urban sociology to be produced in the United States.

After reaching Atlanta University, Du Bois set up a program of studies of the American Negro; a series of sixteen monographs was published from 1898 to 1914. Basic research, according to his premise, was essential prior to any program of action. "The sole aim of any society," Du Bois stated, "is to settle its problems in accordance with the highest ideals, and the only rational method of accomplishing this is to study those problems in the light of the best scientific research." Among subjects investigated, in what has been called the first real sociological research in the South, were Africa, education, crime, family life, the black businessman, artisan, farmer, and college student, social betterment, health, the Negro common school, and the Negro church.

As time went on, however, Du Bois became increasingly disillusioned about the effectiveness of his research and the resulting publications. More information about blacks in America had been assembled than ever before, yet few people, black or white, read the findings or appeared to be influenced by them. Scientific inquiry seemed to prove nothing to the American people regarding the Negro. Even more distressing, in complete disregard of published facts, the oppression of blacks in the United States continued, and in many ways grew more unbearable. Dissatisfaction with the usefulness of his scholarly work caused Du Bois to turn gradually to advocacy of programs of direct action, and to find a wider audience for his writings.

One manifestation was the publication of Du Bois's volume of essays, *The Souls of Black Folk*, in 1903, intended partly as open propaganda for his race, to rouse a common consciousness among blacks and in part to educate whites, perhaps shocking them into positive action. Some chapters had appeared previously in mass-circulation magazines: the *Atlantic*, *World's Work*, *Dial*, and *New World*. Henceforth, Du Bois, while not abandoning scholarly research and writing, aimed to reach a general public. Furthermore, he became a political activist, campaigning for the civil rights of all minority groups in the nation.

The initial chapter of *The Souls of Black Folk* describes the spiritual strivings of the Negro—how to be a Negro and at the same time an American—"to be a co-worker in the kingdom of culture, to escape both death and isolation; to husband and use his best powers and his latent genius,"[2] up to now so wasted, dispersed, and ignored. Du Bois describes how he became aware of a veil between the white and black races while still a public-school pupil in Massachusetts. "Then it dawned upon me with a certain suddenness," he writes, "that I was different from the others; or like, mayhap, in heart and life and longing, but shut out from their world by a vast veil."³ Du Bois describes the Negro's condition as "double consciousness," a "sense of always looking at one's self through the eyes of others. . . . One ever feels his two-ness,—an American, a Negro; two souls, two thoughts, two unreconciled strivings; two warring ideals in one dark body."⁴

What freedom meant to the American slave is related by Du Bois in graphic terms: "Few men ever worshipped Freedom with half such unquestioning faith as did the American Negro for two centuries."⁵ Slavery was the sum of all evils, while "emancipation was the key to a promised land of sweeter beauty than ever stretched before the eyes of wearied Israelites."⁶ But now, forty years later, the high hopes had faded: "The bright ideals of the past,—physical freedom, political power, the training of brains and the training of hands" had "waxed and waned."⁷

The second chapter of *The Souls of Black Folk*, "Of the Dawn of Freedom," tells the story of emancipation, what it meant to the blacks, and reviews the events of the carpetbagger and Reconstruction period. The emphasis is on the Freedmen's Bureau, its strength and failings. Du Bois pays eloquent tribute to "the crusade of the New England schoolma'ams" in the South, which in one year gave instruction to more than 100,000 blacks.

The work of the Freedmen's Bureau, under which the United States government officially assumed charge of the emancipated Negro as the ward of the nation, is sympathetically viewed by Du Bois. As he notes, "It was a tremendous undertaking . . . at a stroke of the pen was erected a government of millions of men," all black men.⁸ An act passed by Congress in 1866, over President Johnson's veto, established the organization, charged largely with the government of the unreconstructed South, granting it authority to make and enforce laws, levy and collect taxes, punish crime, maintain a military force, and to exercise such other powers as might seem necessary for the social regeneration of four million slaves. The bureau's agents, Du Bois points out, "varied all the way from unselfish philanthropists to narrow-minded busybodies and thieves. Amid all crouched the freed slave, bewildered between friend and foe." On one side were arrayed the North, the government, the carpetbaggers, and the ex-slave. On the other stood the solid South, "whether gentleman or vagabond, honest man or rascal, lawless murderer or martyr to duty." Upon the bureau fell the responsibility for the relief of physical suffering, overseeing the beginnings of free labor, the buying and selling of land, the establishment of schools, the paying of bounties, the administration of justice, and the financing of all these activities.

Such an institution as the bureau, Du Bois comments, "from its wide powers, great responsibilities, large control of moneys, and generally conspicuous position, was naturally open to repeated and bitter attack."[9] The crowning blow was the bankruptcy of the Freedmen's Bank, carrying down with it the hard-earned dollars of the freedmen. Officially the bureau ended in 1872, leaving, according to Du Bois, much of its task unfinished, including Negro suffrage. As a consequence, when Du Bois was writing in 1903, "despite compromise, war, and struggle, the Negro is not free." He adds: "In the backwoods of the Gulf States, for miles and miles, he may not leave the plantation of his birth; in well-nigh the whole rural South the black farmers are peons, bound by law and custom to an economic slavery, from which the only escape is death or the penitentiary. In the most cultured sections and cities of the South the Negroes are a segregated servile caste, with restricted rights and privileges. Before the courts, both in law and custom, they stand on a different and peculiar basis. Taxation without representation is the rule of their political life."[10]

The third chapter of *The Souls of Black Folk*, entitled "Of Mr. Booker T. Washington and Others," created much controversy. No small degree of courage was required to attack Washington, described by William M. Tuttle, Jr., as "the nation's most prominent black, an extremely influential Republican politician, the controller of large sums of white philanthropic money for black institutions, the leading spokesman for black capitalism and for 'practical' rather than liberal arts education, the exerciser of almost dictatorial powers in black education, and a manipulator of other black leaders, newspapers, and organizations."[11] Washington's rise to power, states Du Bois, is "easily the most striking thing in the history of the American Negro since 1876." The Tuskegee Institute head's "program of industrial education, conciliation of the South, and submission and silence as to civil and political rights . . . startled and won the applause of the South, it interested and won the admiration of the North; and after a confused murmur of protest, it silenced if it did not convert the Negroes themselves."[12]

Du Bois conceded that Washington had often used his power to benefit his race, but the gains had come at a high price. Washington was seen as offering to the white world contented Negro workers who would raise no claim to social and political equality. By following his policies, the Negro was giving up political power, civil rights, and the higher education of Negro youth. Du Bois accused Washington of stifling dissent by urging blacks to accommodate themselves to segregation and second-class citizenship. The consequences of Washington's ideas, which had been actively promoted for ten or fifteen years prior to publication of *The Souls of Black Folk*, are summarized by Du Bois: "(1) The disfranchisement of the Negro. (2) The legal creation of a distinct status of civil inferiority for the Negro. (3) The steady withdrawal of aid from institutions for the higher training of the Negro."[13]

Concerning the third point, Du Bois insisted that good common-school and industrial training could not exist without institutions of higher learning: "Tuskegee itself could not remain open a day were it not for teachers trained in Negro colleges, or trained by their graduates."[14] In a telling rebuttal to Washington's contempt for classical education, Du Bois noted that the Tuskegee faculty included "the son of a Negro Senator, trained in Greek and the humanities, the son of a Negro Congressman and lawyer, trained in Latin and mathematics," and the third Mrs. Washington was "a woman who read Virgil and Homer in the same classroom with me."

James Weldon Johnson's opinion was that the chief significance of Du Bois's essay on Washington lay "in the effect wrought by it within the race. It brought about a coalescence of the more radical elements and made them articulate, thereby creating a split of the race into two contending camps." A Washington biographer, Basil Mathews, agreed that the article supplied "the anti-Washington movement, for the first time with a coherent argument." Anti–Du Bois sentiment was also stirred up. *Outlook* magazine, which had serialized Washington's *Up from Slavery*, attacked Du Bois as a whining, impractical racial renegade who was "half ashamed of

being a Negro."[15] The press in general, under Washington's influence, embarked upon a campaign to vilify and intimidate Du Bois.
The *Nashville Banner* warned, "This book is dangerous for the
Negro to read, for it will only excite discontent and fill his imagination with things that do not exist, or things that should not bear
upon his mind." The Washington *Colored American* urged President
Burnstead of Atlanta University to silence Professor Du Bois.[16]

In an interview with Ralph McGill of the Atlanta *Constitution* a
few months before Du Bois's death, the latter looked back on the
extended debate with Washington and his supporters: "As I came
to see it, Washington bartered away much that was not his to barter.
Certainly I did not believe that the skills of an artisan bricklayer,
plasterer, or shoemaker, and the good farmer would cause the white
South, grimly busy with disfranchisement and separation, to change
the direction of things. I realized the need for what Washington was
doing. Yet it seemed to me that he was giving up essential ground
that would be hard to win back."

Du Bois was a brilliant intellectual who insisted that enlightened Negroes should accept only unconditional equality, and held
that there was an immediate need for the training of a Negro elite
he called "The Talented Tenth," who would lead the black masses.
He was a believer in political action and that the black world should
fight for equality with "the weapons of Truth, with the sword of
the intrepid, uncompromising Spirit." In contrast, the politically
passive Washington was a compromiser and gradualist, who believed that his economic program would yield more immediate and
visible benefits to his race than constant agitation for equal rights.

Closely related to the differences with Booker T. Washington
on the proper nature of Negro education is Du Bois's sixth chapter,
"On the Training of Black Men." Education is regarded by the
author as a panacea for many of the problems troubling race relations: "Such human training as will best use the labor of all men
without enslaving or brutalizing; such training as will give us poise
to encourage the prejudices that bulwark society, and to stamp out
those that in sheer barbarity deafen us to the wail of prisoned souls
within the veil, and the mounting fury of shackled men."[17]

The key question, however, was, what kind of education?
Following the Civil War, there were army schools, mission schools,

and Freedmen's Bureau schools, the whole lacking systematic planning and cooperation. There next came a decade of constructive effort toward building complete school systems in the South. Meanwhile, starting about 1885, the Southern industrial revolution was beginning, and industrial schools sprang up. While recognizing the value and importance of such schools for the training of the Negro race, Du Bois raised "the broader question of the permanent uplifting and civilization of black men in America" and wondered "if after all the industrial school is the final and sufficient answer in the training of the Negro race."[18] The greatest need as seen by Du Bois was for schools to train teachers, and it was in response to the urgent demand that such institutions as Fisk, Hampton, Howard, Atlanta, Shaw, Spelman, Wilberforce, and Lincoln University were established. "In a single generation," Du Bois noted, "they put thirty thousand black teachers in the South; they wiped out the illiteracy of the majority of the black people of the land, and they made Tuskegee possible." The primary aim of the Negro colleges was to give "teachers and leaders the best practicable training; and above all, to furnish the black world with adequate standards of human culture and lofty ideals of life." In addition, several hundred Negroes had graduated from Harvard, Yale, Oberlin, and other leading Northern colleges, thus demonstrating their ability and talent for higher education in institutions with the highest standards. Du Bois saw the Negro college as having four functions: to maintain standards of popular education, to seek the social regeneration of the Negro, to aid in the solution of problems of race relations and cooperation, and "finally, beyond all this, it must develop men."

"Of the Sons of Master and Man," Chapter 9 of *The Souls of Black Folk*, is a powerful indictment of the evils of racial discrimination and prejudice in the Southern states, a society marked by segregated housing, economic hardship for the Negro, imposed by custom and law; a ban on political activity, including disfranchisement of the Negro; inferior public schools for the black race; and the effectual elimination of social contacts between the races. "There is almost no community of intellectual life or point of transference," Du Bois asserts, "where the thoughts and feelings of one race can come into direct contact and sympathy with the thoughts and feelings of the other." He continues, "It is not enough for the Negroes to declare that color-prejudice is the sole cause of their social condition, nor for the white South to reply that their social condition is the main cause of prejudice. They both act as reciprocal cause and effect. Both must change, or neither can improve to any great extent."[19]

The changing nature of the Negro church and of Negro religious attitudes is reviewed by Du Bois in his discussion "Of the Faith of the Fathers." In the early days, slavemasters encouraged religious activity, for nothing suited the slaves' condition better than "the doctrines of passive submission embodied in the newly learned Christianity." At the turn of the century, when Du Bois was writing, the Negro church was still the social center of Negro life in the United States, "and the most characteristic expression of African character." But the Negro faced a dilemma: "Conscious of his impotence, and pessimistic, he often becomes bitter and vindictive; and his religion, instead of a worship, is a complaint and a curse, a wail rather than a hope, a sneer rather than a faith."[20] Du Bois observed two "divergent ethical tendencies" among Negroes. In the North the trend was toward radicalism, in the South toward "hypocritical compromise." Between the two extreme types of ethical attitudes wavered millions of Negroes, North and South, while their religious life and activity reflected the social conflict within their ranks.

Other chapters of The Souls of Black Folk help to make the work a classic. "Of the Passing of the First Born" is a poignant account of the death of Du Bois's son. "Of Alexander Crummell" is a touching story of a black Episcopal priest, one of the most learned men of the nineteenth century, and his long struggle against racial discrimination within the church. "Of the Sorrow Songs" is one of the first treatments of Negro spirituals and their meaning.

Du Bois was one of the leaders in the Niagara Movement, a group of young Negro intellectuals pledged to seek complete equality in American life. After a few years, these individuals joined with other Negroes and their white supporters to found the National Association for the Advancement of Colored People. After Du Bois left Atlanta University, under pressure, he became director of research for the NAACP and editor of a militant new monthly periodical, *The Crisis*, from 1910 to 1932. From 1952 on, he was a full-time worker for world peace, socialism, and Pan-Africanism. Du Bois died in Ghana, at the age of ninety-five, after renouncing his American citizenship.

Several of his biographers have commented on Du Bois's striking personal appearance. One noted that "with his VanDyke beard and haughty eyes, he resembled a Spanish grandee." He also affected a high silk hat, gloves and a cane—a basis perhaps for Booker T. Washington's caricature of the "educated Negro."

Essentially, *The Souls of Black Folk* is an impassioned black nationalist document, consciously directed toward the Negro people, and identifying with Africa, blackness, and the rural Negro. In that work and other writings, Du Bois prefigured recent directions of American thought: the need for racial solidarity, an identification with Africa, a stress on the distinctive qualities and achievements of Negro culture, and the Negro's need to maintain his racial integrity in order that he might fulfill his special mission to humanity. For fifty years, Du Bois was a passionate fighter for full civil rights and equality of citizenship for the Negro. By the time of his passing in 1963, his concept of the Negro's proper status in America had gone far toward realization.

20.

Hymn of Hate

THOMAS DIXON'S *The Clansman:*
An Historical Romance of the Ku Klux Klan

The enormous popularity of Thomas Dixon's *The Clansman* and other novels relating to the Civil War and Reconstruction era in the South can best be understood by an examination of their historical background.

By the time *The Clansman* had been published, in 1905, the South had thrown off the bonds of the Reconstruction governments, which the Irish historian, W. E. H. Lecky, in his *Democracy and Liberty*, had extravagantly characterized as "a grotesque parady of government, a hideous orgy of anarchy, violence, unrestrained corruption, undisguised, ostentatious, insulting robbery, such as the world had scarcely ever seen."[1] Unrestricted by military occupation or congressional or judicial control, Southern legislatures redrafted their constitutions, effectively disfranchising Negro voters. White supremacy as an official policy was firmly planted throughout the former Confederacy. Jim Crowism, separate educational systems, and other discriminatory practices received Supreme Court approval through the "separate but equal" doctrine. A rising number of racially inspired riots and lynchings were occurring, manifestations of virulent race hatreds. At the same time, the South's economic plight was worsening, with a gradual decline in the cotton industry. A ruinous system of credit and production victimized white and black farmers. Demagogic leaders were on the rise by way of a widespread populist revolt. As a youth, Thomas Dixon realized that his kind of people in the Piedmont South were sinking into poverty, economic defeat, and, indeed, economic chaos.

Dixon was born the year prior to the Civil War's end, the son of a poor farmer, near Shelby, North Carolina. Somehow, the poverty-stricken family managed to hold together during the Reconstruction years. Young Thomas received scarcely any schooling before the age of thirteen, but by a strenuous regimen of study, he prepared himself for admission to Wake Forest College at the age of fifteen, earned B.A. and M.A. degrees, with high honors, and received a scholarship to Johns Hopkins University. At Hopkins, he formed a close friendship with Woodrow Wilson, a fellow student. Dixon's ambition for a stage career, for which he left Hopkins, ended in failure. He returned to North Carolina, therefore, entered a private law school, received a license to practice law in 1885, and was elected to the legislature before he was old enough to vote. Disillusioned by legislative corruption after a brief time, he turned to the Baptist ministry, first in Raleigh and subsequently in Boston and New York. Still restless and dissatisfied with his career, Dixon became a popular public lecturer. The desire to reach a still larger audience induced him, at the age of thirty-eight, to begin writing novels.

A trilogy of novels, *The Leopard's Spots*, *The Clansman*, and *The Traitor* (1902–07), all centering on the Civil War and Reconstruction, formed the foundation for Dixon's fame. *The Leopard's Spots: a Romance of the White Man's Burden, 1865–1900* is a story of the trying conditions in the South immediately following the Civil War. Critics either lauded the book or violently condemned it. Foreshadowing the reception of his later novels, one writer castigated Dixon for "stirring enmity between race and race," and called the author "the high priest of lawlessness, the prophet of anarchy." The work's basic thesis is the inferiority of the Negro race and the necessity for white domination, or the permanent separation of the races. As portrayed by Dixon, the emancipated Negro was most interested in sexual union with white women.

The Leopard's Spots won immediate popularity. Sales exceeded a million copies, earned royalties amounting to several hundred thousand dollars for the author, and helped to establish Doubleday, Page as a major publisher. Also, the way was paved for the even more spectacular success of *The Clansman*. Some five thousand books and pamphlets were searched by Dixon for source material for the latter work. The actual writing and preparation of the manuscript required only thirty days. As historical background, the author recalled boyhood experiences and stories that had been told him as a youth. He could not have possessed any first-hand knowledge of the events narrated in the first section of the book, since he was less than two years old when they occurred, and he was but six when the final scene was enacted.

The Clansman is divided into four parts. For Book I, "The Assassination," the scene is laid in Washington, D.C., immediately after the war's end. In a preface directed "To the Reader," Dixon declares, "I have sought to preserve in this romance both the letter and the spirit of this remarkable period. The men who enact the drama of fierce revenge into which I have woven a double love-story are historical figures. I have merely changed their names without taking a liberty with any essential historic fact." He adds, "How the young South, led by the reincarnated souls of the clansmen of Old Scotland, went forth under this cover and against overwhelming odds, daring exile, imprisonment and a felon's death, and saved the life of a people, forms one of the most dramatic chapters in the history of the Aryan race."

At the beginning of *The Clansman*, a young Confederate soldier, Ben Cameron, is in a Washington hospital, seriously wounded, and being nursed by a Northern girl, Elsie Stoneman, the daughter of old Austin Stoneman—a thin disguise for Thaddeus Stevens, a dominant figure in Congress. Stoneman is depicted as a brilliant but diabolical man determined to gain full control of the government, a Radical Republican from Pennsylvania. His hatred for the South and the former Confederates is pathological.

The fairness of Dixon's portrait of Thaddeus Stevens, alias Stoneman, is open to serious question. Dixon makes him out to be a widower, though he was never married, to have had a son and a daughter, though he was a childless bachelor, and to have had for a mistress a vicious mulatto woman, for which there is no historical evidence. The last charge, blown up to lurid proportions by Stevens's enemies, was based on the fact that for the last twenty years of his life he had a faithful housekeeper, a colored widow named Lydia Smith, who may or may not have also been his mistress. Furthermore, justification seems lacking for representing Stevens as consistently malignant and vindictive, mercilessly revengeful. Dixon, however, never yielded an inch, replying to his critics: "I drew of old Thaddeus Stevens the first full-length portrait in history. I showed him to be what he was, the greatest and vilest man who ever trod the halls of the American Congress. I dare my critic to come out from under his cover and put his finger on a single word, line, sentence, paragraph, page, or chapter in 'The Clansman' in which I have done Thad Stevens an injustice. If he succeeds, I will give a thousand dollars to endow a chair of Greek for any negro college he may name, for I take him to be a 'missionary' to the South."[2]

Two chapters are devoted by Dixon to Stevens's mythical mistress, "the strange brown woman who held the keys of his house as the first lady of the land. . . . No more curious or sinister figure ever cast a shadow across the history of a great nation than did this mulatto woman in the most corrupt hour of American life."

The Washington chapters of *The Clansman* picture the chaotic conditions after the war and the efforts of Lincoln and other leaders to find solutions to the pressing problems. President Lincoln is treated with sympathy and understanding, as he strives to bring about reconciliation with the South and to bind up the wounds of war. His opponents are shown as bitter, malevolent, short-sighted men.

An article by Frances Oakes, "Whitman and Dixon: a Strange Case of Borrowing," reveals that Dixon drew extensively upon Walt Whitman's *Specimen Days* and other writings, frequently word for word, to describe the Washington scene during the postwar days. One of the sources for Dixon's description of the death of Lincoln in *The Clansman* is Whitman's often-delivered oration, "Death of Abraham Lincoln."[3]

Book II, "The Revolution," in *The Clansman* deals with events following Lincoln's assassination, the outburst of anger and grief in the North, the accession to the presidency of Andrew Johnson—

shown as a weak, misguided creature unable to resist the designs of diabolical men by whom he was surrounded—and the unsuccessful attempt by Stoneman and his cohorts to remove the president by impeachment. Nevertheless, Stoneman now was in full control of the Congress and "he began to plot the most cruel and awful vengeance in human history." Previously, "the giant figure in the White House [Lincoln] alone had dared to brook his anger and block the way." Henceforth, the Southern states were to be treated as conquered provinces. "The life of our party," Stoneman declaimed ,"demands that the Negro be given the ballot and made the ruler of the South. This can be done only by the extermination of its landed aristocracy, that their mothers shall not breed another race of traitors. This is not vengeance. It is justice, it is patriotism, it is the highest wisdom and humanity." The only solution for the race problem, Stoneman declared, was for the Negro to "rule the land of his bondage," to "put a ballot in the hands of every Negro, and a bayonet at the breast of every white man from the James to the Rio Grande."

Book III, "The Reign of Terror," shifts the scene to Piedmont, South Carolina, "a favorite summer resort of Charleston people before the war," bordering on the North Carolina line. It was also the home of the Camerons. Austin Stoneman, broken in health by the fierce battles in Congress, has been urged by his doctor to move to the South, and he, his son and daughter settle in Piedmont. The "double love-story" referred to by Dixon develops, with one romance between Phil Stoneman and Margaret Cameron and another between Elsie Stoneman and Ben Cameron—in both cases without the knowledge or consent of Austin Stoneman.

The Clansman treats at length of the poverty, shame, and degradation suffered by the Southerners at the hands of the Negroes and their unscrupulous Northern allies, the carpetbaggers and scalawags. Ben and Margaret's father, Dr. Cameron, appeals to Stoneman for his intervention, informing him that "The Negro is the master of our State, county, city, and town governments. Every school, college, hospital, asylum, and poorhouse is his prey. Negro insolence grows beyond endurance. Their women are taught to insult their old mistresses and mock their poverty as they pass in their old, faded dresses. Yesterday a black driver struck a white child of six with his whip, and when the mother protested, she was arrested by a Negro policeman, taken before a Negro magistrate, and fined $10 for 'insulting a freedman.'"

Dr. Cameron went on to state that the school commissioner was a Negro who could neither read nor write, the tax rate had become ruinous, and "eighty thousand armed Negro troops, answerable to no authority save the savage instincts of their officers, terrorize the State." Dixon's racial venom explodes when he has Dr. Cameron say, "For a thick-lipped, flat-nosed, spindle-shanked Negro, exuding his nauseating animal odor, to shout in derision over the hearths and homes of white men and women is an atrocity too monstrous for belief."

But Stoneman was unyielding. "Deep down in his strange soul he was drunk with the joy of a triumphant vengeance he had carried locked in the depths of his being, yet the intensity of this man's suffering for a people's cause surprised and distressed him as all individual pain hurt him."

Dixon's intense dislike of the Negro is illustrated in his description of a black trooper: "He had the short, heavy-set neck of the lower order of animals. His skin was coal black, his lips so thick they curled both ways up and down with crooked blood-marks across them. His nose was flat, and its enormous nostrils seemed in perpetual dilation. The sinister bead eyes, with brown splotches in their whites, were set wide apart and gleamed ape-like under his scant brows. His enormous cheekbones and jaws seemed to protrude beyond the ears and almost hide them." Even more rabid terms are used in characterizing Alec, one of the Negro polling officials in a Reconstruction election, whose appearance is compared to that of an "elderly monkey."

In contrast, the flower and symbol of Southern womanhood, Margaret Cameron, wins a paean of praise: "Everything about her was plain and smooth, graceful and gracious. Her face was large—the lovely oval type—and her luxuriant hair, parted in the middle, fell downward in two great waves. Tall, stately, handsome, her dark rare Southern beauty full of subtle languor and indolent grace, she was to Phil a revelation. The coarse black dress that clung closely to her figure seemed alive when she moved, vital with her beauty. The musical cadences of her voice were vibrant with feeling, sweet, tender, and homelike. And the odour of the rose she wore pinned on her breast he could swear was the perfume of her breath."

The most horrifying incident in *The Clansman* is the rape of a young white girl, Marian Lenoir, by Gus, a brutal, sensual Negro officer. Because of her shame, she and her mother commit suicide by jumping from the local lover's leap. Through a scientific miracle, doubtless unknown to the medical world, Dr. Cameron identifies the attacker by the use of a microscope, with which he sees the image of the Negro rapist imprinted upon the retina of the dead mother's eye. In the doctor's words, he saw "the bestial figure of a Negro—his huge black hand plainly defined—the upper part of the face is dim, as if obscured by a gray mist of dawn—but the massive jaws and lips are clear—merciful God!—yes!—it's Gus."

At this point the newly organized Ku Klux Klan takes charge. The coroner's jury had ruled that the mother and daughter had been killed by accidentally falling over the cliff. When Gus, who had fled to the state capital, learned of the verdict he started to return home by train. Three miles before reaching his destination, however, he is persuaded by a ruse to leave the train and is seized by members of the Klan. After a trial, during which he is hypnotized by Dr. Cameron and reenacts the crime, he is executed and his body, in full uniform, is thrown on the lawn of the black lieutenant governor's home.

The discovery of the body of the captain of the African Guards, with the letters K.K.K. written in red ink pinned to his breast, "sent a thrill of terror to the triumphant leagues. . . . For the first time since the dawn of Black Rule Negroes began to yield to white men and women the right of way on the streets." In further rapid action, the Klan forces the Negroes to surrender the thousands of arms which had been supplied to them by the state and national governments.

Stoneman's reaction was immediate. A telegram was sent to the White House and next morning President Grant issued a proclamation declaring the nine Scotch-Irish counties of South Carolina in a state of insurrection and ordered an army corps of five thousand men to report there for duty, pending the possibility of martial law and suspension of the writ of habeas corpus. The U.S. regulars, however, were soldiers from the West, who began to fraternize with the rebels. Seeing matters getting further out of hand, Stoneman shot off another telegram to the White House, following which martial law was proclaimed, the writ of habeas corpus suspended, and two companies of Negro soldiers sent in from the state capital to crush the spirit of the insurgents.

The next major crisis occurs when two Negro troopers, "fighting drunk," come into the hotel where Margaret Cameron and Phil Stoneman are having dinner. One of the Negroes begins to act in a familiar manner with Margaret. When she attempts to resist and screams, Phil rushes into the room with drawn revolver; one of the Negroes fires at him, misses, and the next moment drops dead with a bullet through his heart. Phil's father thinks that Ben Cameron committed the killing, and orders him arrested and executed. At the last moment Ben and Phil exchange places in the death cell, and old Stoneman is almost insane with grief when he hears that his own son is about to be killed. Phil is saved by the Ku Klux Klan, which takes him by force from the execution squadron.

The Clansman ends with Stoneman acknowledging his errors and expressing the deepest gratitude to the Klan for rescuing his son. A pending election is certain to be won by the Klan's forces, and Ben delivers an exultant declaration, "Civilization has been saved, and the South redeemed from shame."

Sales of The Clansman surpassed even the spectacular success of The Leopard's Spots. Before many months, more than a million copies were sold. But the novel was only the beginning. The book was to have other incarnations. The Clansman was rewritten by Dixon as a stage play, with a plot which followed substantially the original work. When the stage version went on tour, it was advertised as "The Greatest Play of the South . . . A Daring, Thrilling Romance of the Ku Klux Klan . . . A Splendid Scenic Production," etc. As the company toured the Southern states it was received by enthusiastic, sell-out audiences at every stop. Despite its phenomenal success, newspaper reviews of the play were often unfavorable. A writer for the Richmond Times-Dispatch commented that "uncontrolled desires, primal passions, race hatred and race supremacy are the warp of the Clansman."

In the North, though race riots had been predicted, The Clans-

man was performed without incident in New York. A riot stopped the Philadelphia showing, but the play was seen by capacity audiences in Brooklyn, Chicago, Washington, Baltimore, and elsewhere. For five years, two companies toured the country.

The Clansman's second reincarnation, surpassing anything which had preceded it, was as a motion-picture extravaganza, *The Birth of a Nation*, the first of the spectaculars for which Hollywood was later to become famous. To forestall expected opposition, Dixon arranged to have the film previewed by his old friend in the White House, Woodrow Wilson, who unhesitatingly paid it a high tribute. "It is like writing history with lightning," said Wilson, "and my only regret is that it is so terribly true." But powerful forces were arrayed on the other side, Oswald Garrison Villard, editor of the New York *Evening Post*, and Moorfield Storey, president of the American Bar Association, were fearful of the picture's racial theme and made strenuous efforts to ban it from public exhibition. Riots and demonstrations marked presentations in New York, Boston, Chicago, and elsewhere, but the show went on. *The Birth of a Nation* was a national sensation, millions viewed it, and Dixon became wealthy from the proceeds. There was praise among the critics for the dramatic story and the extraordinary photographic effects. Others condemned it outright. Francis Hackett, writing in the *New Republic*, for example, denounced the film because it provoked "hatred and contempt for the Negro. . . . It degrades the censors that passed it and the white race that endures it."[4]

The general spirit of *The Birth of a Nation* conforms to *The Clansman*, though there are variations in details. Thaddeus Stevens remains a diabolical figure. Shocking scenes of looting and lawlessness tell the story of Reconstruction, and a bitterly biased view of the Negro is presented. Segregation forever is a dominant theme.

Raymond A. Cook, Dixon's principal biographer, points out that the same stereotypes appear in all three of Dixon's Reconstruction novels—*The Leopard's Spots*, *The Clansman*, and *The Traitor*. According to Cook's analysis, "In each novel, the hero, in order to win his sweetheart, must overcome the objections of a stern father. Each hero is a spokesman and leader of the Ku Klux Klan. All three of the novels are laid largely in the Piedmont region of the Carolinas, and each novel focuses its attention on the inhabitants of small towns. The Northerner who sympathizes with the South is treated sympathetically, but those who champion the Negro cause are invariably treated as 'scalawags' or 'carpetbaggers.'"[5]

A perceptive insight comes from another critic, F. Garvin Davenport, Jr., who observed, "By 1900 it seemed evident to many white Americans that their Anglo-Saxon heritage of progress and a white man's democracy was in danger of being submerged by a tide of color." There were not only the blacks of the South but several million colored people who had become wards of the United States after the Spanish-American War.[6] The concept of the racial inferiority of all colored peoples everywhere, preached by Dixon, made his credo acceptable to many otherwise fair-minded Americans.

Dixon was an extraordinarily poor businessman. Through his novels and films, he became a multimillionaire, but then, through speculating on the New York Stock Exchange and a variety of unprofitable schemes, he ended up nearly penniless, forced to depend for a living in his last years on a clerkship in the United States District Court at Raleigh, North Carolina.

Antebellum South

ULRICH BONNELL PHILLIPS'S
Life and Labor in the Old South

A leading American historian, Richard Hofstadter, whose views are widely dissimilar from Phillips's, states, "No single writer has been more influential in establishing patterns of belief about the plantation system of the Old South among scholars and teachers than the late Ulrich Bonnell Phillips. His *American Negro Slavery* and *Life and Labor in the Old South* are the most widely read scholarly studies of the slave system, and have become classic sources of information and propaganda about antebellum Southern life."[1] Other critics, friendly and unfriendly, are in general agreement with Hofstadter's judgment.

Early in his career, Phillips, a native-born Georgian, expressed resentment that "the history of the United States has been written by Boston, and largely written wrong." Southern history in particular, he felt, had been misunderstood and misjudged, and there had been few, if any, Southern historians qualified to set the record straight. "A study of the conditions of the Old South from the inside," Phillips asserted, "readily shows an immense number of errors of interpretation by the old school of historians." Southern writers had been preoccupied with state and local history, pious biographies, and rambling memoirs. Another historian, Wood Gray, commented, "Most of what had been published bore the imprint of the sword and magnolia cult; the aroma of the 'lost cause' lingered in their pages."

Ulrich Phillips dedicated his career to a reexamination and reinterpretation of particular phases of Southern history, wholly objective and untainted, he hoped, by any sectional biases.

Phillips's active years were all spent in academic settings. Following his graduation from the University of Georgia and graduate study at the University of Chicago and Columbia University, he served successively on the faculties of the University of Wisconsin, Tulane University, the University of Michigan, and, until his death in 1934, Yale University. His mentors included some of the most distinguished American historians and social scientists of his time: Frederick Jackson Turner, William A. Dunning, John W. Burgess, James Harvey Robinson, Edwin R. A. Seligman, and John Bassett Moore, among others.

Spurred on by his resolve to rewrite Southern history, in order to correct the neglect and distortions of earlier writers, Phillips spent thirty-two productive years as an active scholar, during which he published an estimated forty-eight hundred printed pages, mainly relating to the Old South. Most widely known, most readable, and of chief general interest is his *Life and Labor in the Old South*. The title is a bit too comprehensive for the contents. One reviewer suggested that the work should have been called *Plantation Life and Labor in the Old South*, for that is its primary theme.

In his first chapter, "The Land of Dixie," Phillips sets the tone of his book by introducing his conception of the antebellum South and climatic influences on its development: "Let us begin by discussing the weather, for that has been the chief agency in making the South distinctive. It fostered the cultivation of the staple crops, which promoted the plantation system, which brought the importation of negroes, which not only gave rise to chattel slavery but created a lasting race problem. These led to controversy and regional rivalry for power, which produced apprehensive reactions and culminated in a stroke for independence. Thus we have the house that Jack built, otherwise known for some years as the Confederate States of America."[2]

Phillips then proceeds to analyze the South's various climatic belts, seeing in them explanations for the distinctive features of

Southern life and culture. Climate was a controlling factor in the length of growing seasons and dictated the types of crops to be planted in various regions. Hot weather is blamed for other Southern characteristics: eating habits, laziness, slow speech, easygoing ways, and the prevalence of hookworm. "The capabilities of every part of the far-flung Southern land, plains and hills, mountains and valleys," the author remarks, "had to be learned through the painful process of trial and error."

Further background for his central thesis is provided in Phillips's next four chapters, devoted to the Southern topography and soil and to summaries of the effect of environment upon the settlement of Virginia, Maryland, the Carolinas, and Georgia, and to the advance from the colonial backcountry across the mountains into the bluegrass of Kentucky and Tennessee and on into Missouri. A separate chapter, "The Old Dominion," pictures Virginia during its first two centuries as undergoing a steady process of change, with "a great increase of slave imports and a dwindling influx of servants; a multiplication of white and black through fecundity and salubrity; a shift of tobacco culture to the Piedmont, whither thousands of lowlanders migrated; a meeting and a bit of mingling with other thousands with contrasting traditions from Pennsylvania; a rise of towns at the limits of ocean shipping on the rivers; and a most remarkable growth of gentle breeding and public spirit."[3]

Maryland, North and South Carolina, and Georgia, called by Phillips "the younger colonies," were undergoing similar transformations. The nation's subsequent expansion incorporated Florida and the entire western area to Texas, the history of which Phillips skims over in rather cursory fashion to arrive at the heart of his book. His chief attention is to the development of the plantation regions, their mode of life and their problems, the handling of the great staple crops, the economic and social aspects of slavery, and studies of individual planters of Virginia, the Southeast, and the Southwest, and their overseers.

Throughout *Life and Labor*, Phillips's chief focus is on Southern agriculture and agricultural society, especially the plantations and plantation economy, the masters and the Negro slaves. Detailed consideration of the principal crops begins with a chapter on the Cotton Belt. In the late eighteenth century, the invention in

England of machines to spin and weave cotton at a rapid rate spurred an almost unlimited demand for the staple. Eli Whitney's invention of the cotton gin forged another important link in the industry, by saving a vast amount of manual labor. Cotton culture spread rapidly "from Maryland to Mississippi, from Virginia to Alabama, from Missouri to Texas," as Phillips expressed it. One result of the prodigious output was frequent price breaks, economic depressions, and bankruptcies. Phillips notes that "so great was the space, the freshness and fertility and so rapid the transit of a lusty population,"[4] that the region draining into the Gulf of Mexico surpassed the Atlantic slope in cotton production before 1830, and by 1860 was furnishing three-fourths of the whole country's output. Also, about three-fourths of all slaves employed in agriculture were working in cotton fields, along with nearly as many whites. Phillips concludes, however, that "the cotton belt differed not much from the Upper South except for its comparative immaturity and the greater proportion of Negroes in its population."[5]

Other elements in the staple economy, to which Phillips devotes a chapter, were tobacco, rice, indigo, and cane sugar. The spread of the plantation system was directly related to the nature of the crops. Sugarcane could be grown profitably only on large plantations; the sugar manufacturing process was a part of production which the small farmer could not manage. Tobacco, on the other hand, required no machine process and could not be grown profitably in large quantities, in part because of the excessive hand labor it demanded. Wheat did not have tobacco's limitations, for it required less attention than any other staple crop, and for that reason was a "poorer prospect for Southern expansion," according to Phillips, because "its work season occupied but a small part of the year" and was therefore unsuitable for year-round slave labor. Cotton "was adapted to cultivation on any scale great or small," so that "one-horse farmers and hundred-slave planters" competed on fairly even terms, acre for acre. Thus cotton, for a variety of reasons, became the most widely grown crop of all.

Transportation in the antebellum era was a major problem. Bulk shipments of cotton, tobacco, rice, and sugar were often sent considerable distances overland to reach the best markets. The highways were primitive, at times almost impassable. The early railroads, linking towns and cities, helped to alleviate the situation. Their main effect, Phillips notes, was "the broadening of the plantation area and the intensification of staple agriculture." In fact, he adds, "they brought ruin to some of the Piedmont cotton factories by putting the distant specialized mills into competition with local plants which had been meeting home needs by making diverse kinds of cloth."[6] The three principal elements in rail traffic, as seen by Phillips, were "an outward flow of the staple to markets which were mainly overseas; an inward flow of manufactured goods mainly from New York; and an inward flow of foodstuffs from the Northwest."[7]

Of major significance, too, was water transport. The rapid growth of seaports and river towns could be attributed to commerce from inland settlements. Richmond, Charleston, Savannah, Atlanta, Fayetteville, Columbia, Augusta, Macon, Columbus, Montgomery, New Orleans, and many other communities located on navigable waterways became trade centers. Slave traders and their coffles (trains of slaves fastened together) used sea lanes and riverboats extensively, as well as long overland roads and railroads.

In a chapter on slavery, "The Peculiar Institution," and in succeeding sections on the economics of slave labor and the life of the slaves, Phillips presents his views on the slavery system and traces its historical evolution. Phillips's critics have drawn ammunition from these chapters to support charges of bias and preconceived opinions. Concerning slave traders, for example, the author asserts, "The dealers were not full of the milk of human kindness or they would not have entered upon their calling. On the other hand they cannot have been fiends in human form, for such would have gone speedily bankrupt . . . sundry citizens of solid worth and esteem can be identified as regular participants."[8] Further on, Phillips equates slavery with the predicament of divorced husbands who are sent to prison for failure to pay alimony.

Historically, Phillips shows, slavery in Africa was an ancient institution, along with polygamy, human sacrifice, cannibalism, and other primitive customs. The tribes from which slaves were recruited inhabited every coast south of the Sahara and most of the interior regions, though the west coast and its hinterland were the main field of operation. Individual slaves were equally diverse in character, ranging in stature "from dwarfs well-nigh to giants, in complexion from dark brown to an almost perfect black, in facial contour from a type approaching the Caucasian to one suggesting an orang-outang."[9]

His readers are reminded by Phillips that even in America slavery had not always been confined to the South. During the eighteenth century, generally referred to as an age of enlightenment, slavery was legalized throughout the Western Hemisphere and had existed in all the Northern states from Maine to Pennsylvania. During the colonial period, Phillips observed about the New Englanders that shrewd in consequence of their poverty, self-righteous in consequence of their religion, they took their slave-trading and their slaveholding as part of their day's work and as part of God's goodness to His elect."[10] As Phillips saw it, the initial sin of the slave trade had been committed by non-Southerners.

Phillips's picture of plantation life runs the gamut from the harshly realistic to the idyllic. Its main facets, as he describes them, were these: the plantation force was a conscript army, living in barracks and on constant "fatigue," employing both men and women and militarylike in its organization; the plantation was "a homestead, isolated, permanent and peopled by a social group with a common interest in achieving and maintaining social order"; the plantation was a factory "in which robust laborers were essential to profits"; the plantation was a school, in which talented slaves were given special instruction, and many youths trained in the crafts and taught to read and write, despite laws to the contrary; the plantation was "a parish, or perhaps a chapel of ease," providing the slaves with religious teaching; the plantation was "a pageant and a variety show in alternation," with dancing, singing, baptizings, hunting, and a variety of other amusements; and the plantation was "a matrimonial bureau, something of a harem perhaps, a copious nursery, and a divorce court."[11]

The economics of slavery are dealt with by Phillips in his chapter "The Costs of Labor." He charts available statistics and reaches the conclusion that after the abolition of the foreign slave trade by Congress in 1807 the margin of profit under even the most favorable circumstances became increasingly doubtful. After the extension of the slave plantation system to new cotton lands in the lower South and Southwest, an increased demand for Negroes was faced with a limited supply, forcing prices up beyond the probable value of their services. Ownership of slaves could hardly be justified unless year-round employment could be found for them, a fact which bound the slaveholders to staple production and cutthroat competition with other producers. In Phillips's judgment, a "proclivity for buying slaves was the worst feature of the regime from an economic point of view, for it drained capital out of every developing district and froze the local assets into the one form of investment."[12]

Phillips obviously drew extensively upon Frederick Olmsted's findings reported in the latter's *The Cotton Kingdom*, though he criticized the Northern observer as prejudiced against the South. Olmsted had demonstrated that slavery was inefficient and uneconomical. Both men agreed, however, that a major reason for the continued existence of the system was Southerners' fear of racial conflict if the slaves should be freed. Olmsted took emphatic exception to the argument, used by Phillips and others, that the climate dictated the use of slaves in the South and the slave plantation was a kindly patriarchal institution. He was convinced of the presence of cruelty on the large plantations and believed that it was inherent in the institution as a whole.

On the other hand, Phillips could not fairly be accused of suppressing evidence of absconding, revolts, miscegenation, or other instances of mistreatment of blacks by whites. Concubinage, he wrote, "was flagrantly prevalent in the Creole section of Louisiana, and was at least sporadic from New England to Texas." Group rebellions cited by Phillips, however, were relatively few, a fact which led Herbert Aptheker, in his *American Negro Slave Revolts*, to assert that Phillips presented limited data in order to show that the Negro suffered from "inherited ineptitude," and was stupid, negligent, docile, inconstant, dilatory, and "by racial quality submissive." Actually, Aptheker insisted, "discontent and rebelliousness were not only extremely common, but indeed characteristic of American Negro slaves." Records of some two hundred and fifty slave revolts and conspiracies were found by Aptheker.[13]

Another historian critical of Phillips's findings is Richard Hofstadter, who maintained that "his casual treatment of the slave's

resistance to slavery and in particular of slave revolts was inadequate, and highly misleading, not merely as to the character of the
slave but also upon critical aspects of race relations." That the
slave's condition was no worse, Hofstadter believed, was due not
to "the master's benevolence but to the slave's resistance to extreme
exploitation."[14]

Nevertheless, Phillips insists that the slave was on the whole
not ill used. Generalizations, pro and con, are of doubtful validity.
Aside from the ethical and philosophical aspects of slavery, the
evidence is contradictory on how long and hard slaves were worked,
how severely they were punished, how well they were fed, housed,
and clothed, and how carefully they were attended during illness. A
noted historian, Kenneth M. Stampp, suggests, "The only gener-
alization that can be made with relative confidence is that some
masters were harsh and frugal, others were mild and generous, and
the rest ran the whole gamut in between."

The fear of Negro revolts and uprisings led to the enactment
of strict laws by Southern legislatures to make certain, as Phillips
puts it, "that the South should continue to be a white man's
country." To prevent propaganda against slavery from reaching the
blacks, they were kept incommunicado as far as possible, and
usually prevented from learning to read and write. On the other
hand, Phillips notes, "When times were quiet, as they generally
were, burdensome statutes were conveniently forgotten."[15]

Phillips's conception of the plantation system may be summarized as follows: first, the plantation itself was simply a large-scale
capitalistic agricultural unit devoted primarily to the production of
commodities for the market; second, slavery was a system of labor,
over which the employer held complete authority and responsibility; and, finally, there was the Negro slave, a savage with an alien
background. Climate and land endowed the South with exceptional resources for producing crops in great demand. Black labor
had been resorted to because of the shortage of work forces of other
races. A system of slavery was required to make Negro labor
economically effective and socially controllable.

The most frequently stated criticism of *Life and Labor in the Old
South* is that Phillips drew his materials from the records of the
largest plantations. By omitting the smaller units, he was actually

using a sample of about ten percent of all the slaves and less than one percent of all the slaveholders. For that reason, Hofstadter points out, "His picture of slavery and slaveholders in the rural South was drawn chiefly from types of plantations that were not at all representative of the common slaveholding unit."[16] The chief reason for the rather lopsided approach, as Phillips himself conceded, was that the primary sources for the larger units are much better preserved. The smaller plantations and small slaveholding farmers, who were far more typical, seldom kept diaries and formal records, and therefore they received considerably less attention from Phillips. "It is regrettable," he wrote, "that data descriptive of small plantations and farms are very scant. Such documents as exist point unmistakably to informality of control and intimacy of white and black personnel on such units." Phillips differentiates between the so-called "poor white trash" and the more respectable nonslaveholding farmers of the South. The former, the "listless, uncouth, shambling refugees from the world of competition were never enumerated, but there is cogent reason to believe that they comprised only a small portion of the nonslaveholding population."[17]

In any event, only one chapter of *Life and Labor* is devoted to the small farm and "the plain people." Yet the great majority of the white people of the South were farmers with small holdings. There were six million nonslaveholders, comprising three-fourths of the white population. Other important elements in the economic and social development of the Old South are also neglected by Phillips. There is practically nothing about such industries as mining, lumbering, milling, and manufacturing, the import-export trade, and the building of railroads. Manufacturers, ironmasters, merchants, bankers, professional men, educational leaders, and similar key figures are omitted. Phillips gave almost exclusive attention to the plantation, passing over the Southern towns and cities, except for New Orleans, which he included because it was a principal slave-trading center.

Obtaining information about the slaves and masters on the smaller holdings is difficult, but a comprehensive view of the slave system, it is generally agreed, can hardly be drawn without a study of this aspect. Historians since Phillips's time have found county records, court records, and census returns valuable for the purpose.

A further deficiency in the completeness of Phillips's account is the at least partial omission of a number of slaveholding states. The plantations with which he was concerned were in Virginia, North and South Carolina, Georgia, Alabama, Louisiana, and Mississippi. Largely excluded were Maryland, Delaware, Florida, Tennessee, Missouri, Kentucky, and Texas. Though in total these states held a large number of slaves, according to census records, major plantations were comparatively few and a majority of the slaves were owned in small lots. In any case, it is likely that Phillips never intended to write a general cultural history of the South. As an intensified study of one major phase of the Southern story, however, *Life and Labor* continues to rank as a work of outstanding significance.

Probably no other historian up to his time has made as extensive use of plantation records as Phillips. To him, they were a major source of information. He made frequent expeditions into the South in search of plantation diaries, journals, account books, correspondence, rare imprints, and family records. Phillips also made some use of farm journals, newspapers, and the accounts of travelers in the South.

Some of Phillips's principal findings have been rejected or substantially modified by later scholars. The critics are deeply skeptical of the overall impression left by his writings—that the institution of slavery was a civilizing factor, slaveholders were kindly and sympathetic masters, slaves were happy and contented laborers, and that the plantation system was an efficient method of transforming crude and inept brawn into productive enterprise—even though Phillips put forward all these concepts with qualifying limitations. A new scholarship repudiated the belief in racial inferiority and found other causes for the economic, social, and cultural backwardness of nonwhite people. Phillips was quite unable to view the institution of slavery through the eyes of the Negro, and hence never deviated from his belief in the inherent inferiority of the Negro race, nor from his understanding that the blacks were accustomed to a lower status, and thus slavery did not bear heavily upon them. The Negro's smoldering, and sometimes open, hostility to slavery appeared to be a fact of which Phillips was largely unaware.

A more friendly appraisal of Phillips's historical contributions, from a Southern viewpoint, appeared in the *Chattanooga News* at the time of his death:

The old South was far more than a place of moonlight and roses; there was more than the scent of oleander in the air. In part, it was a patriarchal society, with the courage and crudeness of the frontier. Dr. Phillips saw not one South but a dozen, and not one slavery system, but two at least, one the commercial, with its coffles, slave jails and auction blocks, and the other with patriarchal relations involving a high sense of duty from the big house to the cabin. Furthermore, he rejected the theory that the Civil War was any "irrepressible conflict," and laid the responsibility for it upon blunder and chance. Rejecting the emotional tirades of the Abolitionists, and equally discounting the sugary sentimentality and the moonlight and roses school, the Yale historian sought truth and understanding.[18]

Ulrich Phillips's influence on Southern historiography, despite differing opinions among recent critics, has been profound. His limitations are acknowledged among objective scholars, but unquestionably he improved the quality of history writing about the South and stimulated other historians, North and South, to undertake research and writing on the region.

Nostalgia for Never-Never Land

TWELVE SOUTHERNERS' *I'll Take My Stand*

Some form of agrarianism has flourished in every period of American history, and indeed in the history of every other nation, beginning with ancient Greece. From the second century B.C., for example, Cato's *On Agriculture* offers several disparaging remarks on those engaged in commerce and banking, concluding that the "good husbandman" is a far more worthy individual. "It is," he writes, "from the farming class that the bravest men and the sturdiest soldiers come, their calling is most highly respected, their livelihood is most assured and is looked on with the least hostility, and those who are engaged in that pursuit are least inclined to be disaffected."

During the colonial era, agricultural interests dominated the legislatures of the Southern states almost exclusively. A prominent Southern historian, Benjamin B. Kendrick, pointed out that "so far as the South was concerned the American Revolution itself was an agrarian movement," a protest against policies formulated in the interest of the British commercial classes.[1] Thomas Jefferson and his followers argued that agriculture is the industry basic to all others, and Jefferson built his political organization on a foundation of western-frontier farmers and a majority of the Southern planters. At the end of the Civil War, or course, the Southern planters lost everything: their government, most of their landed property, all their slave property, and their own peculiar form of agricultural organization.

It was against this background that in 1930 a group of Southern writers, centered in Nashville, Tennessee, at Vanderbilt University, produced *I'll Take My Stand: the South and the Agrarian Tradition*, a work which has since had considerable influence on other writers and thinkers about the South and its problems. The general purpose of the book was to promote the concept of an agricultural economy and a regional culture modeled on that of the South before the Civil War. One of the foremost Southern literary critics, Louis D. Rubin, Jr., in an introduction to a new edition of *I'll Take My Stand*, summed up the book's reception and present status: "Not a single writer about the modern South has failed to mention and discuss it. From the very beginning it has been singled out for praise or blame. Some critics have termed it reactionary, even semi-fascistic. Others have considered it a misguided, romantic attempt to re-create an idyllic utopia that never really existed. Still others have seen it as a voice crying in the wilderness. Ridiculed, condemned, championed, it has been everything except ignored, for that it cannot be by anyone who wants to understand a complex American region."[2]

The dozen contributors do not speak with a single voice, and no attempt was made to persuade them to do so. In fact, there is considerable diversity of views. The authors are consistent, however, in their desire to maintain the Southern heritage of "decent formality and tolerant social balance," of quiet, rural, tradition-ordered, individualistic decorum, "not because they belong to the South, but because the South belongs to them." The enemies are identified as the promoters of industrialism, progressism, dollar mania, strenuousness, and curt, brisk, and blatant Americanism. To these Southern agrarians, the United States seemed entirely too devoted to material things, to a get-rich-quick, boom-or-bust economy. Mass culture at the lowest level was debasing artistic taste, they declared, and the concentration on industrial development was causing the fine arts to be relegated to a peripheral, nonessential, merely diversionary role. An evocation of certain traditions of the Old South could perhaps provide the region and the nation with proper perspective and a better-balanced culture. Among the skeptics was a *New York Times* editor, who described the essayists as "twelve Canutes without any Saxon conquests to their credit, bidding the waves of the industrial North Sea to fall back."[3]

John Crowe Ransom introduces *I'll Take My Stand* with "A Statement of Principles." Though the twelve articles are not intended to be presented as an integrated whole, they all tend, in Ransom's words, "to support a Southern way of life against what may be called the American or prevailing way; and all much as agree that the best terms in which to represent the distinction are contained in the phrase, Agrarian *versus* Industrial."[4] There is no thought of making the South an independent political entity—an idea vanquished by the Civil War. But, Ransom insists, the South need not surrender its moral, social, and economic autonomy. Especially it should reject being seduced by the industrial gospel and succumbing to the blight of industrialism.

In the lead essay, "Reconstructed but Unregenerate," also by Ransom, the claim is made that Southern culture was built upon "European principles," the chief features of which are to encourage the right relations with nature and one's fellow men, to respect leisure, and to devote energy to "the free life of the mind." Following the European example, the Old South had enjoyed "the social arts of dress, conversation, manners, the table, the hunt, politics, oratory, and the pulpit."[5] Ransom acknowledged that a certain amount of industrialism was inevitable, for the sake of the region's prosperity, but that it should be kept within strict bounds. The South should reject blatant materialism, noisy salesmanship, and dollar-chasing. Instead, it should unite with Western agrarians to work for the preservation of rural life in America.

John L. Stewart, in his work *The Burden of Time*, raises serious doubts about the validity of Ransom's views. He notes that the old planter aristocrats were a highly acquisitive breed and that the leisure so extravagantly praised "was simply vacant idleness made possible for the upper classes by slavery and later by a labor surplus and forced upon the lower classes by poverty, malnutrition, and the growth cycles of staple crops."[6] Equally despicable in Stewart's judgment were the intolerance of the Ku Klux Klan and the fundamentalist sects and the harsh censorship of dissenting social criticism in the antebellum period. Ransom and other agrarians were also inclined to ignore the eroded farmlands and destroyed forests characteristic of the old plantation system. Ransom offers a semi-apology for the institution of slavery. "Slavery was a feature monstrous enough in theory," he concedes, "but, more often than not, humane in practice; and it is impossible to believe that its abolition alone could have effected any great revolution in society."[7]

Donald Davidson's "A Mirror for Artists," the second essay, deplores the "feverish and energetic" pace of life in an industrial society, a consequence of which is that the arts become regarded as mere entertainment, or are "pursued as a kind of fashionable enterprise," not because of any genuine interest but out of a feeling of obligation to culture. Mass methods of reproduction and distribution have, in Davidson's opinion, served to spread bad art. The industrialists in art make their appeal to the lowest common denominator, and turn to mass production for maximum profits. In short, Davidson does not believe that the arts are cherished in an industrial civilization. Such vitality as they show, he suggests, "is probably not a mark of abundant health, but of a lingering and lusty capacity to survive every disaster and disease short of complete extinction."[8]

The solution for the South proposed by Davidson is for the artist to derive his inspiration and strength from the region. For the South specifically, this would mean drawing upon distinctly Southern architecture, the folk arts—ballads, country songs and dances, hymns and spirituals, folktales, and such folk crafts as weaving, quilting, and furniture making—and encouragement for the more sophisticated arts, such as Southern contributions to literature. Davidson's claim that art flourishes best in an agrarian society is at least questionable, and he admits by implication that the actual performance of Southern art had not been impressive—a fact that he is inclined to blame on the interruption of the Civil War.

Historian Frank Lawrence Owsley revives and reviews the old

controversies on the causes of the Civil War in his essay, "The Irrepressible Conflict." Owsley seeks to demonstrate that the popular belief the Civil War was fought over slavery was a gross oversimplification. On the contrary, he argues, the factors which finally caused the war grew out of two fundamental differences existing between the two sections: the North was commercial and industrial, the South was agrarian. Owsley thought that the Southern championship of states' rights, Northern demands for high tariffs, and the steady attrition of Southern political power by the constant admission of new states were also significant issues, but "the fundamental and passionate ideal for which the South stood and fell was the ideal of an agrarian society."[9]

Even more nostalgic for the good life of an old-fashioned Southern farm was Andrew Nelson Lytle in his essay, "The Hind Tit." Lytle had an intense dislike of Northern cities and a deep love of the Southern region and its folkways. He insisted that the farmer's charms, signs, and omens "are just as useful and necessary to an agrarian economy as the same attempts which come from the chemist's laboratory in an industrial society, and far wiser, because they understand their inadequacy, while the hypotheses of science do not."[10] Lytle gave stern warning against the evils of an industrial society: "The agrarian South, whose culture was impoverished but not destroyed by the war and its aftermath, should dread industrialism like a pizen snake."[11] In effect, a boycott of the products of a money system is urged by Lytle, who would have the farmer grow his own food, kill his own meat, make his wool and cotton into clothes, grow corn and hay for his stock, draw milk and butter from his cows, eggs from his hens, water from the ground, and fuel from the woodlot. Native handicrafts should be revived; for recreation the old fiddle would replace the radio, and play parties and square dances substitute for the movies. John L. Stewart believed that Lytle caused the agrarian cause "incalculable harm" by overstating his case, revealing "the insufferable limitations it seemed to put upon the human spirit."[12]

A more down-to-earth, realistic viewpoint is presented by Herman Clarence Nixon in a solid piece entitled "Whither Southern Economy?" Nixon recognizes the fact of rapidly increasing industrialization of the Southern region, though he expresses unhappiness at some of its manifestations. The South was worshipping industrial gods, he feared, "at a time when dollar-chasing industrialism is being weighed in the balance and found wanting in America and Europe."[13] The Old South was working toward a balanced industry and a reformed agriculture, according to Nixon, when the Civil War upset the evolutionary process. As he saw it, "In disrupting and disorganizing the economic life of the South, the Civil War jolted from power and status the most articulate agrarian group known to American history, leaving no effective check to an industrial dominance in national public policy, particularly in tariff matters."[14] Nixon pleads for the development of Southern agriculture and industry, side by side and properly balanced, with neither subordinate to the other. "From a dull industrialization," he concludes, "Southern civilization should be preserved with its supporting agrarian economy."[15]

Robert Penn Warren's "The Briar Patch" is concerned with sensitive issues of race relations and the future of the black race in the South. A brief historical survey sketches the role of the Negro in America from 1619, when the first slaves were landed at Jamestown. The sometimes disastrous effects of the Reconstruction era on the freed slaves, the problems of Negro education following the Civil War, discriminatory practices in nearly all aspects of life, and the Negro's economic difficulties down to the present are among Warren's themes. Of particular concern to him is conflict between white and black labor. Like Frederick Douglass more than a century earlier, he observed that the poor white was as much the victim of the slave system as the Negro, and their fates are linked together: "The well-being and adjustment of one depends on that of the other." Any plan for maintaining a high level of agrarian culture, Warren holds, has to make a place for the Negro.

Lyle H. Lanier offers "A Critique of the Philosophy of Progress," from the point of view of the trained social scientist. The historical roots of the concept of progress are traced, after which the author notes the manner in which the doctrine has become perverted and twisted to mean an accelerated consumption of new products, and a carefully nurtured idea that the self-interest and welfare of the individual are identical with those of large corporations, or "what's good for General Motors is good for the country."

This questionable tenet is used by the corporations to resist public regulation, as a license to expand without limit and to overproduce, bringing on depressions. Lanier argues for restoration of agriculture to a position of respect and power, in the belief that the yeoman farmer would have a moderating and balancing influence on the national economy and culture.

The remaining essays include John Gould Fletcher's "Education, Past and Present," with "a brief glance at Southern educational history," and generally deploring the low quality of modern schools at all levels; Allen Tate's "Remarks on the Southern Religion"; John Donald Wade's "The Life and Death of Cousin Lucius," characterized by Stewart as "a maudlin and snobbish portrait of a Georgian Colonel Carter"; and Henry Blue Kline's "William Remington: A Study in Individualism," which Stewart calls "an even more sentimental defense of a feeble dilettante ill at ease in a world of businessmen, engineers, and moviegoers."[16]

The concluding chapter, "Not in Memoriam, But in Defense," is Stark Young's contribution. Young provides some needed perspective by stating, "If anything is clear, it is that we can never go back, and neither this essay nor any intelligent person that I know in the South desires a literal restoration of the old Southern life, even if that were possible; dead days are gone, and if by some chance they should return, we should find them intolerable."[17] Further and probably accelerated industrialization of the South was regarded as inescapable by Young. The basic question was how to adjust to it while preserving the most precious values of the traditional Southern culture. "It all comes down to the most practical of all points," Young declares. "What is the end of living? What is the end of living that, regardless of all the progress, optimism, and noise, must be the answer to the civilization in the South?"[18]

A similar view was expressed by Louis Rubin some thirty years after *I'll Take My Stand* first made its appearance. Rubin notes that the book was written by men of letters, chiefly poets, who were concerned with more than the economic and social well-being of any one region. The South and the nation had become too obsessed with material possessions. So-called "progress" or "industrialism" as seen by the agrarians "stifled the aesthetic impulse, rendered impotent the religious impulse, and converted man's days into a frantic and frenzied drive for the often tawdry conveniences of modernism."[19] It was the sacrifice of humanistic values the authors of *I'll Take My Stand* were protesting. What matters to them, Rubin writes, "is the vision of a more harmonious, esthetically and spiritually rewarding kind of human existence that the book holds up."[20]

One reviewer, Henry Hazlitt, judged the book more harshly, seeing in it "the rationalization of a nostalgia for ancestral ways rather than a rational approach to real problems."[21] The Old South, farming and farm labor are seen through a sentimental haze, according to Hazlitt, and he held there had in fact been no flowering of art, music, and literature. Such culture as the South possessed, he believed, rested on slavery and was confined to a small privileged upper class. Hazlitt objects, too, to the central thesis of *I'll Take My Stand*, that industrialism and agrarianism are essentially antagonistic, while actually they are, and should be, complementary.

How homogeneous was the Old South? Is it safe to generalize? Certainly the region and its people were molded by certain common forces: the climate, an economy based on staple crops, and a large slave population. The people were unified, too, by Northern attacks on slavery, the plantation system, and Southern beliefs. On the other hand, the population was, for the most part, lower- and middle-class, of humble origins. Any large group of gentry, with a background of elegance and privilege, was largely, though not entirely, a myth, as W. J. Cash makes clear. There was, however, a long tradition of chivalry, partly inspired no doubt by a reading of Sir Walter Scott's novels, emphasizing courtesy, decorum, hospitality, and a certain indifference to money and the pursuit of money. To this extent, at least, the validity of the view of the authors of *I'll Take My Stand* is established.

In his essay on education, John Gould Fletcher offers a quotation from Confucius which seems to sum up perfectly the book's aim: "When balance and harmony are carried to the point of perfection, heaven and earth are in a state of perfect tranquillity, and all beings receive their perfect development."[22]

23.

Regional Inventory

HOWARD W. ODUM'S *Southern Regions*
of the United States

An editorial in the *Washington Post* commented, "Howard W. Odum
was the Eli Whitney of the Modern South. He inspired a revolution.
Certainly there was no one—unless it was Franklin Roosevelt—
whose influence was greater than Odum's on the development of
the region below the Potomac."[1] Thus is summed up the career
of one of the most remarkable and versatile figures to emerge in
the South in the twentieth century—teacher, sociologist, folklorist,
prose poet, administrator, promoter, and master breeder of pedi-
greed Jersey cattle.

Born in 1884, Odum grew up as a farm boy in post-Reconstruction Georgia, and graduated from Emory College and the
University of Mississippi (majoring in Greek, Latin, and English).
He proceeded subsequently to Clark University for a Ph.D. in
psychology with G. Stanley Hall, and to Columbia University for a
second Ph.D. in sociology, with Franklin H. Giddings. After brief
stays on the faculties of the University of Georgia and Emory
University, he transferred to the University of North Carolina,
where for the next thirty-four years he was a human dynamo in the
promotion and organization of scholarly research and teaching in
the social sciences.

Odum's influence through his writings was great. He was the

author of some twenty-two books and two hundred articles and brochures. Early works included *Social and Mental Traits of the Negro* and a trilogy based on Negro folk culture: *Rainbow Round My Shoulder, Wings on My Feet,* and *Cold Blue Moon.* His profound concern with interracial relations and the plight of the Southern blacks was lifelong.

Of Odum's numerous contributions to sociological literature his researches in regionalism, and especially his work *Southern Regions of the United States,* are best known and have had the greatest impact. His aim was to account for regional divergences in the nation. In what ways was the South different from other major regions of the United States, and how had these variations affected its development?

Southern Regions and a complementary work, *American Regionalism,* issued two years later, state Odum's conclusion that the whole country is divided into six principal regions: "The Middle States and Their 'Middle West', the Northeast and Its New England, the Southeast and Its 'Old South', the Far West and Its California, the Northwest and Its Great Plains, the Southwest and Its Texas." Odum begins by showing that the South, for purposes of social study and planning for future development, must be divided into two regions: the Southeast and the Southwest. The former embraces Virginia, the Carolinas, Georgia, Florida, Kentucky, Tennessee, Alabama, Mississippi, Louisiana, and Arkansas. The Southwest is made up of Oklahoma, Texas, New Mexico, and Arizona. *Southern Regions* deals in the main with the Southeast.

The definition of a region is arrived at by Odum through the application of about seven hundred indices—economic, geographical, and cultural. He emphasizes the point that no adequate understanding of the South, or of any other region, can be gained except by comparisons with other regions. Out of the seven hundred characteristics examined, each Southeastern state was found to be like the others in more than three hundred and fifty ways, and separate and distinct from the others in a minority of these characteristics. Similar criteria define the other five regions of the nation. Each region, Odum states, "is an empire of territory and wealth in itself. Each is greater and more self-sufficing than many nations of the world. Each is incurably sentimental and patriotic about its own virtues and assets."

The importance of the regional approach is stressed through-out Odum's writings. Only in this way, he was convinced, would it be possible "to build permanent foundations for national unity, to attain social and mental freedom, to develop creative research and discovery, or to achieve economic rehabilitation, sound legislation aptly adopted, and strong autonomous movements well integrated with the new public administration."

Regionalism, according to Odum, is a vastly different concept from sectionalism. In the 1890s, Frederick Jackson Turner had revolutionized the teaching of American history by showing the significance of the frontier. With the frontier gone as an active force, Turner believed that the development of sections would be the future national trend and a permanent feature of the American scene. By the beginning of the twentieth century the United States, in effect, had become a congeries of sections, with diverse and often conflicting interests.

Sectionalism was seen by Odum as an evil force, bringing division and conflict, and therefore he felt it should be rejected. Thus his approach is consistently from the regional-national in-stead of the local-sectional point of view. The regional concept would enable the South to make its unique contribution to the national whole. The older sectionalism, more prevalent in the South than in any other area of the country, was viewed by Odum as narrow and constricting. The regional idea, on the other hand, would avoid "any hypotheses of a self-contained or self-sufficing South, and would stimulate a greater degree of Federal interest and participation on the part of the South." The goal should be the integration of each region into the nation, recognizing differences and encouraging diversity, but making the general national welfare paramount. Odum's indictment of sectionalism in its Southern manifestations is strongly expressed; it had conditioned the region, he says, "to isolation, individualism, ingrowing patriotism, cultural inbreeding, civic immaturity and social inadequacy."

Regionalism as defined by Odum is far more, however, than a rejection of sectionalism. It has important implications for litera-ture, geography, history, ecology, anthropology, psychology, eco-nomics, political science, and sociology. These multiple facets are examined in detail in *Southern Regions*, supported by an enormous body of maps, charts, and other statistical data. In essence, the work is a description and appraisal of the South as Odum found it in the mid-1930s. Within this framework are analyzed natural resources, agriculture, industries, transportation, population, education, politics, religion, and general culture.

Five major types of resources are appraised in *Southern Regions*. Of these, Odum states, "the conclusion seems justified that the Southeast excels in the two primary resources; namely natural wealth and human wealth, while it lags in the secondary resources of technology, artificial wealth, and institutional services." An appalling picture is painted in *Southern Regions* of the waste of the land. The value of the two greatest geographic assets, soil and rainfall, had been steadily depleted for generations by uncounted millions of acres of eroded land. This neglect, Odum noted, was "threatening to make the region impotent for a rich agrarian culture and incapable of supporting industrial and commercial activities." Statistically, 97,000,000 acres, or 61 percent, of the nation's 150,000,000 acres of eroded land were in the South. Another 5,000,000 acres of bottomland had been affected by the filling of stream beds and overflow, while thousands of acres of arable land had been ruined or damaged by sand and gravel from the hillsides. The fertility of the soil had been destroyed in broad areas by over-cropping. The one-crop economy—cotton or tobacco—was the chief culprit.

None of these facts was exactly a new discovery. The evils of the one-crop system in the South had been recognized and condemned by writers on agriculture since the time of Thomas Jefferson, or earlier. As far back as the Jamestown colony in the seventeenth century, there were laws against planting too much tobacco. Later observers who perceived the disastrous results of the land wastage included Fanny Kemble, Frederick Olmsted, Hinton Helper, and Ulrich Phillips, but their voices were largely unheard or unheeded, because the entire economic structure was built upon the single crop, mainly cotton, and, short of a revolution, the system was unchangeable.

The waste of natural resources in the South was equally ruinous in the destruction of forests. In the beginning there were in the Southeast 125,000,000 acres of longleaf pine, an exceptionally valuable wood. At Odum's writing, about four-fifths of the total was gone. Immense quantities were simply piled in heaps and burned, to clear the land, and not used for lumber at all. The hardwoods of the uplands fared little better; hillsides more suitable for pasturage or forests were plowed up for agriculture, swiftly eroded, and left essentially ruined.

On the basis of his numerous indices, Odum reaches the judgment that the Southeast, in comparison with other regions, lags in every item of a twelve-point scale in its farm economy: farm ownership, balanced animal and plant production, balanced plant crops, enrichment of land and increasing of values, adequate home-grown feeds, efficient cultivation, adequate fencing, well-planned fields and forest areas, adequate housing for animals and tools, farm management and accounting, care in preparation of commodities for market, and motivation for the enrichment of farm life, mea-sured by the type of housing, household equipment, and cooperative arrangements.

When Odum was writing, in the 1930s, the South was still predominantly rural, but the urban population was steadily increas-ing and industries were growing up in the midst of the agrarian setting, chiefly for textiles, tobacco, and furniture manufacturing. Nevertheless, if tested by employment of labor in manufacturing industries, the Southeast was not a leader in any of the nation's ten major industries: cotton goods, foundry and machine shops, steam-railroad repair shops, steel works, and rolling mills, lumber and lumber products, boots and shoes, bread and bakery products, electrical machinery, knit goods, and women's clothing. In per capita wealth and on the basis of other indices of income and wealth, the South ranked low among the nation's six regions.

The special characteristics of the South's population are ana-lyzed by Odum. Of a total population of 25,000,000, when *Southern Regions* was published, nearly 8,000,000 were Negroes, twice as many as in all the rest of the country combined—a distribution which has changed drastically, of course, in the intervening years. The South was the most thoroughly American region in the sense that a great majority of its people were native born and its white race was of British descent, except for limited German, French, and Spanish infiltrations. The typical Southerner's culture was also British from the point of view of religion, politics, economic ideas, and social and legal codes. Another significant fact revealed by Odum's studies was that the people of the South were markedly younger than those of any other section, and the region's birthrate was the highest of any in the nation.

The human resources lost through emigration from the South was a matter of serious concern to Odum. During the first thirty years of the twentieth century, more than 3,500,000 of those born in the Southeast had moved to other regions; the loss was not compensated for by in-migration. The money value of this human wealth was estimated by Odum as the equivalent of the existing national debt. The loss, representing some of the best and the brightest individuals, especially among the young, was explicable by the lack of opportunities in the South.

Another explanation was the quality of Southern education. Odum stresses that despite the fact the region "has made great strides in its educational endeavors, increasing its quantitative achievement a hundredfold, straining its financial capacities to the limit, and making contributions in creative effort," it still "ranks lowest of all the regions in most aspects of its educational equipment and work." Among the reasons were the extraordinarily large proportion of school-age children in the population, the burden of supporting a dual system of education for the whites and the Negroes, and in higher education maintaining a tripartite system of colleges for white men, white women, and for blacks. Handicaps in Odum's view too were the multiplicity of institutions representing religious denominations and their opposition to public higher education, and the lack, at that time, of even one first-class university in the entire region. Nevertheless, the Southeast was appropriating a greater percentage of its total income for higher education than the rest of the nation. Important deficiencies in the existing system, Odum felt, were that the South had no college of agriculture or engineering of first rank and offered no advanced instruction in such fields as politics, business, industry, and land utilization.

Another critical gap in the region's resources was deplored by Odum: "Perhaps no deficiency in the Southeast is more marked than its lack of books and libraries and the consequent absence of reading habits. What lack of many techniques on farm and in factory is to the development of wealth, the lack of reading may very well be to the development of the youth of the land." The situation is documented by Odum with comparative figures on per capita expenditures for libraries, registered library users, circulation of books per capita, and the number of urban and rural people with and without public library service.

Politics and politicians have played a dominant role in its affairs throughout the South's history. Odum divides the historical background into two periods: pre-1860 and post–Civil War. There is a remarkable contrast between the two eras, the first marked by statesmanship in high places (fourteen of the seventeen presidents up to 1850 were native or resident Southerners), the second by what Odum describes as a record of "demagoguery in low places." Symbols of the period after 1870, and illustrative of the South's political dilemma, were such rabble-rousing characters as Jeff Davis of Arkansas, Huey Long of Louisiana, Vardeman and Bilbo of Mississippi, Heflin of Alabama, Tom Watson and Gene Talmadge of Georgia, and Cole Blease of South Carolina. Largely unqualified by education and training to deal with economic and social issues were most of the governors and legislators of the Southern states. A highly complicating factor in the situation was the disfranchisement, in practice, of one-third of the population, the black race.

Charles Puckett, in reviewing *Southern Regions* for the *New York Times*, questions whether Odum is quite fair to Southern politicians, particularly to the Southern representation in Congress after Woodrow Wilson became president. "Granted," writes Puckett, "that the South has been afflicted with a considerable (perhaps an excess) share of hill-billy rabble raisers, it is nevertheless the case that it has had in the Senate and House many men of substantial character and ability."[2]

Odum brings his analytical methods to bear also on the South's public and private social services. Here again all the statistical evidence points toward low per capita contributions for religious and social services, bad penal practices, niggardly expenditures for public welfare and old-age pensions, inadequate support for hospitals—general institutions, as well as those for the insane and feeble-minded—low expenditures for the prevention and treatment of communicable diseases, and a bottom rank for per capita expenditures for industrial welfare. Odum notes, however, that "there have been many examples of distinctive contributions and pioneering efforts, such as those in public welfare administration, social service conferences, and community organization and citizens' committees."

Religion, like politics, Odum observes, is closely interwoven in the fabric of Southern culture. The Southeast outranks the other regions of the country, he finds, "in its church membership, in its Protestant representation, in its church colleges, in the position which the church holds in the community, and in its general influence upon social policy." Some critics have suggested that the obvious deficiencies of the South can be attributed to the markedly religious character of the population. Odum's analysis, however, supports a comment by Gerald W. Johnson: "The truth seems to be rather that the characteristic religion of the region is more affected by its general culture than the general culture is affected by the religion. . . . The attitude of the churches on social questions is determined by the general culture of the region, not the attitude of the people by that of the churches."[3]

Contradicting H. L. Mencken's description of the South as "the Sahara of the Bozart," Odum reports that in the field of literature and drama the Southeast had achieved an increasingly merited distinction. "Of more than 1,000 volumes of fiction in the decade from 1920 to 1930 featuring regional Americana," he notes, "the Southeast predominated in titles largely by Southern authors in which the folk-regional character of the Negro, the poorer whites, the old South, the conflict between the old and the new South, and between the Negro and the whites was depicted variously." During that period there were a dozen Pulitzer prizes awarded to Southerners for fiction, drama, and editorials, and numerous adoptions and awards were made by book clubs and others. Unfortunately, more than ninety percent of the awards for distinction came after the authors had left the region.

When *Southern Regions* was published, in 1936, the Tennessee Valley Authority had been in existence only three years. The TVA was established by the Roosevelt administration for the purpose of promoting the unified development of the resources of the Tennessee River basin, an area that includes parts of Tennessee, Kentucky, Mississippi, Alabama, Georgia, North Carolina, and Virginia. The chief concerns were water control to prevent floods and improve navigation, production and transmission of electric power, fertilizer research, and conservation and recreation programs. Obviously deeply intrigued by the experiment and its potential for improvement in many problem areas of the South, Odum deals in detail with the significance of the TVA and its future prospects.

In a recapitulation of the Southern situation as revealed in researches for *Southern Regions*, Odum reports: "As to resources— superabundance; as to science, skills, technology, organization— deficiency; as to general economy—waste; as to culture—richness, with immaturity and multiple handicaps; as to trends—hesitancy and relative retrogression in many aspects of culture."

Having presented the facts about the Southeastern and Southwestern regions and their relation to the nation, Odum proceeds to a discussion of what should be done. A basic consideration, he concludes, is that "unless there is a definite change in regional economy there will be retrogression in agriculture, in industry, and in general culture and institutions." Further, "regional reconstruction can be successfully achieved only in relation to national integration and interregional adjustments." Gradual progress would be made, Odum believed, through state planning boards, through assistance from national and regional planning boards, and by way of general promotion and educational work. He was convinced that a first essential was for the South to face facts realistically and become fully aware of the critical nature of its dilemmas. A second step would be to avoid internal jealousies and rivalries among states and institutions, and, finally, there should be a willingness to pay the price of progress.

In Odum's opinion, the problems facing the Southeast fell into four groups, each with its own predicaments: agriculture, industry, politics and government, and institutions of learning, the last including the whole field of higher education and of research. Though no definite priorities are proposed for the solution of problems relevant to each area, on the basis of Odum's own emphases, it would appear that agrarian reform and policies should receive first attention, followed by the fourth: a strong educational system. The second and third were dependent on solutions developed for these other two areas.

A time schedule of twelve years is drawn up by Odum as a minimum period for a program of regional development in relation to the national culture and to meet the special objectives set for the Southeast. During the first six years attention would be concentrated on agriculture, land utilization, and forestry, specifically on crop rotation, soil erosion, rural rehabilitation, changes from tenant farming to land ownership, and experiments in livestock breeding and seed production. In the field of industry, there would be experimentation in part-time industry and farming, in small industries, and the training and apprenticing of workers for various skills. New programs for high schools and junior colleges, in upper and lower college curricula, and in research would enable educational institutions to make significant contributions on a more advanced level of activities in the same fields, profiting by previous developments and experience.

In an eloquent summing-up, Odum states:

The South, now facing its own peculiar crises in the midst of and in relation to national recovery, appears almost equally capable of making the best or the worst of all possible contributions to the general culture of the next generation. That is, its contributions might be of the lowest as well as of the highest order; might add to the nation's burden as well as enhance its riches; might contribute to national conflict as well as national unity; might afford the shortest road to revolution or the quickest steps to fascism, as well as a logical part of an orderly planned reconstruction economy.

A biographical sketch of Odum by two of his colleagues, Rupert B. Vance and Katharine Jocker, for *Social Forces*, the journal founded by Odum in 1922, notes: "For a work of such size and complexity [*Southern Regions of the United States*] the public's reception was little short of amazing. It became a basic book in courses and seminars, had an important impact on policy and thought, went through four printings and had books, commentaries, and pamphlets written about it. . . . In retrospect regionalism represents the high point of Odum's achievement and influence."[4]

Another writer, George B. Tindall, in his piece "The Significance of Howard W. Odum to Southern History," offers a similar view: "The influence of Odum's regionalism in Southern thought would be difficult to trace. Suffice it to say here that at least thousands, possibly millions, of Southerners were exposed to it either directly or through pamphlets, monographs, or teachers having their origin in that school of thought. His magnum opus, *Southern Regions*, went through four printings and enjoyed such wide popularity as a textbook that a large portion of a generation of college students became familiar with the general outlines of the idea."[5] Tindall observes that the concept has had a considerable impact on the social sciences in general, attested to by the monumental bibliography of regionalism.

A pertinent question to ask is to what extent the mass of factual data compiled by Odum for *Southern Regions* has become outdated. In the past forty years, since publication of the book, vast changes have occurred in virtually every phase of Southern life and culture, in agriculture, industry, education, per capita wealth, social services, government finance, and numerous other aspects. An exodus of blacks from the South to other regions has made the Negro a national and not a largely regional concern. A need for updating his findings was recognized by Odum himself. Left unfinished at his death in 1954 was a major work, *Mid-Century South: New Southern Regions in the United States*. As offering a method of analysis of a region's resources and problems, the original work remains of first importance, and it provides valuable historical perspective for future sociologists, economists, political scientists, and other scholars and students.

Tindall comments that in Howard Odum "the folk heritage of the New South coalesced with intellectual insights into new concepts of universal import. He was a rare academic specimen whose scholarship had practical implications which he himself sought to apply in social action."[6] A noted sociologist, William F. Ogburn, adds: "Notable among Odum's personal traits were boldness, initiative, leadership, kindness and loyalty."[7] Odum's keen, analytical mind made him the most perceptive observer of the Southern scene as a whole during the first half of the present century.

Nation within a Nation

W. J. CASH'S *The Mind of the South*

Over the years the South as a region has been analyzed, examined, dissected, and surveyed more thoroughly than any other section of the United States. Noteworthy examples are Odum's *Southern Regions of the United States*, Vance's *Human Geography of the South*, Daniels's *A Southerner Discovers the South*, and Mims's *The Advancing South*. W. J. Cash's *The Mind of the South* takes a different approach from previous studies; it is an attempt to penetrate the mentality of the South, to explain the psychological factors that have shaped the thinking of Southerners since the American Revolution.

Cash returns a positive answer to the question of whether the South is fundamentally different from other regions of the United States. While conceding that there are enormous physical and social differences among the former Confederate states, he insists that "the South is another land, sharply differentiated from the rest of the American nation, and exhibiting within itself a remarkable homogeneity." Common to an overwhelming majority of Southern white people, according to Cash, is "a complex of established relationships and habits of thought, sentiments, prejudices, standards and values, and association of ideas."

Carl Carmer, a Southerner by adoption, once made the remark that "the Congo is not more different from Massachusetts or Kansas or California than Alabama." Carmer could as logically have pointed out the divergences between Mississippi and North Carolina. "Nevertheless," asserts Cash, "if it can be said that there are many Souths, the fact remains that there is also one South," formed by the peculiar history of the region. To validate and to illuminate his basic premise, Cash presents a fascinating ideological and social history of the South from colonial times until the beginning of World War II. The emphasis, contrary to the book's title, is sociological, rather than psychological or intellectual.

Cash begins by rejecting two commonly accepted legends—the Old South and the New South. The Old South, he finds is "a sort of stage piece out of the eighteenth century" picturing a culture of elegant gentlemen and lovely ladies moving "against a background of rose gardens and dueling grounds," dwelling "in large and stately mansions, preferably white and with columns and Grecian entablature." This ruling class of cavaliers possessed vast estates and innumerable slaves, and was constantly engaged in brilliant social activities.

Beneath the elite class, the myth goes, were the poor whites, sometimes referred to as "white trash," physically inferior and descended from convict servants, redemptioners, and debtors, with a sprinkling of European peasants and farm laborers and immigrants from European slums.

The legend of the Old South is dismissed by Cash, in large part, though he does not find it to be unadulterated moonshine. There were enough genuine aristocrats to provide a basis for the legend, but the colonial gentry were a much more homespun lot than one would gather from a visit to the Williamsburg restoration or from listening to members of the Colonial Dames. The frontier tradition remained strong and there was no great gap between the owners of large plantations and the common whites. In fact, the two were frequently blood relations. By accident, fate, and the process of natural selection, the nonplantation, nonslaveholding whites were "the less industrious and thrifty, the less ambitious and pushing, the less cunning and lucky."

The number of great plantation owners as of 1860 was estimated by W. E. Dodd, American historian, at no more than four or five thousand throughout the South.[1] Cash guesses that "the total number of families in Virginia, South Carolina, Louisiana—in all the regions of the little aristocracies—who were rationally to be reckoned as proper aristocrats came to less than five hundred—and maybe not more than half that number."

A common bond held the aristocrats and the poor whites together; they both belonged to the master race and shared the "vastly ego-warming and ego-expanding distinction between the white man and the black." No matter what his station in life, the white man would always be a member of the dominant race. "And before that vast and capacious distinction," Cash points out, "all others were foreshortened, dwarfed, and all but obliterated." Thus was democracy preserved, insofar as the white man was concerned.

Prevailing notions about the New South are as full of errors as are those about the Old. Cash maintains that a legend has arisen based on the mistaken view that the Civil War simply obliterated the civilization and culture of the antebellum era and established a new order dominated by industrialism. As seen by Cash, the distinction between the Old and the New South is largely imaginary. The South is substantially what it always was, if allowance is made for modifications in its environment brought about by industrialization and commercialization. His view was that the mind of the South survived virtually unchanged into recent times in its attitude toward race and politics, its intolerance toward "wrong thinking," its religious conservatism. A striking instance is the cotton-mill village, found by Cash to be organized along lines quite similar to the plantation; furthermore, the owners' views of their workers closely paralleled those of the great plantation proprietors. From this conclusion stems Cash's argument that industrialism did not lead to a revolution in the South's ingrained ideology, but placed more power in the hands of "the hard, pushing, horse-trading type of man" and confirmed the exaggerated individualism of the Old South.

Excessive individualism as a factor in the development of the Southern mind is constantly stressed by Cash. The impact of the frontier may be clearly discerned here, a rough-and-ready setting in which every man was forced to stand on his own feet in order to survive. Independence and self-sufficiency worked against the development of law and order. As Cash notes, the Southerner has "an intense distrust of, and indeed, downright aversion to, any actual exercise of authority beyond the barest minimum essential to the existence of the social organism." As a natural corollary, the Southerner is quick to resent any encroachment on his freedom of action and to boast "that he would knock hell out of whoever dared to cross him." Hence we see "the perpetuation and acceleration of the tendency to violence which had grown up in the Southern backwoods as it naturally grows up on all frontiers." Also traceable to the frontier mentality is the tradition of vigilantism, represented in the South by multiple lynchings in the nineteenth and early twentieth centuries.

Cash's belief in the impact of the frontier on Southern history is as confirmed as Frederick Jackson Turner's on American history as a whole. The plantation system did not become fully established until about 1820, and forty years later the Civil War erupted. "It is impossible to conceive the great South as being, on the whole," Cash writes, "more than a few steps removed from the frontier stage at the beginning of the Civil War . . . the mere physical process of subduing the vast territory which was involved, the essential frontier process of wresting a stable foothold from a hostile environment, must have consumed most of the years down to 1840."

Beyond extreme individualism, a second characteristic of the Southerner dealt with at length by Cash is the strong tendency toward romanticism and hedonism, that is, the credo that pleasure is the chief good in life. The Southerner spurns realism, lives much in a self-created world of imagination and fantasy, and "he likes naively to play, to expand his ego, his senses, his emotions . . . he will accept what pleases him and reject what does not . . . and in general he will prefer the extravagant, the flashing, and the brightly colored." Aspects of this attitude are contempt for certain types of hard labor, referred to as "nigger work"; devotion to horse racing, listening to brass bands, making love, dancing, and extravagant play; and a fondness for rhetoric, especially the high-flown oratory of demagogic politicians.

Cash credits association with the Negro as having influenced and strengthened the Southern white man's pleasure-loving instincts. "The Negro is notoriously one of the world's greatest romantics and one of the world's greatest hedonists," Cash comments; "he is sometimes capable of a remarkable realism. But in the main he is a creature of grandiloquent imagination, of facile emotion, and, above everything else under heaven, of enjoyment."

Romanticism and escapism also account for the South's religious pattern, as described by Cash. The Southerner's "chief blood-strain was likely to be the Celtic—of all Western strains the most susceptible to suggestions of the supernatural." Consequently, "what our Southerner required was a faith as simple and emotional as himself. A faith to draw men together in hordes, to terrify them with Apocalyptic rhetoric, to cast them into the pit, rescue them, and at last bring them shouting into the fold of Grace." For these reasons, the appeal of the revivalistic sects—the Methodists, the Baptists, and the Presbyterian—to the Southern mind is obvious, according to Cash.

The Anglican tradition of religious tolerance held little appeal for the "fierce Celt-blooded primitive." By Andrew Jackson's time, the power of the evangelists over the whole Southern mind was so great that "skepticism of any sort in religion was anathema, and lack of frenetic zeal was being set down for heresy." The end result was "adherence to a code that was increasingly Mosaic in its sternness." Without being a hypocrite, however, the Southerner continued to practice his hedonistic philosophy, successfully "uniting the two incompatible tendencies in his single person."

Toward the institution of slavery, the churches displayed a curious ambivalence. The evangelical religious sects had all begun by denouncing it. Before 1830, a majority of the abolition societies were in the South. But when the South was placed on the defensive by bitter attacks from the North, viewpoints began to change, and justifications for slavery, characteristically moralistic and romantic in nature, began to emerge. To palliate what Cash calls "that eternal uneasiness of the South's conscience over slavery," churchmen began referring to it as a "providential trust" and "God's plan for instructing the black man in the Gospel and securing him entry into eternal bliss." A taboo on criticism of slavery inevitably followed.

In a later era, Calvinistic religion in the South, a kind of Southern version of Puritanism, became Fundamentalism and led to such phenomena as the Dayton "monkey trial," and further impediments to intellectual progress.

The suppression of dissident thought in the South, called "the savage ideal" by Cash, was originally directed toward stifling any critical discussion of the slave system, but in time an exacerbated sense of honor was turned in fury against all forms of criticism. The "ideal" was attained when "men became in all their attitudes, professions, and actions, virtual replicas of one another." One manifestation was the hazardous lives led by newspaper editors. "For, from John Hampden Pleasants of the Richmond *Whig* down," Cash writes, "the record is rich in entries of 'fatally wounded in a duel,' or 'shot dead in the streets.' On the *Vicksburg Journal*, indeed, the mortality by violence actually reached the total of five editors in thirteen years!"

Southern legislators and fundamentalists preachers have never experienced any difficulty, according to Cash, in justifying and rationalizing their campaigns to curtail freedom of speech, freedom of the press or of teaching, and liberal movements. When threatening scientific or social ideas are put down, excuses have varied from the fear of slave revolts, in the antebellum period, to the protection of school children against dangerous thoughts, in recent times.

From colonial days forward, miscegenation was a striking feature of the slave system, beginning with the Portuguese, Spanish, and Yankee slave traders, and continuing with the Southern planters. A well-known American anthropologist, Melville Herskovits, is quoted by Cash as stating that "instead of 80 or 85% of the American Negroes being wholly of African descent, only a little over 20% are unmixed, while almost 80% show mixture with white or American Indian." The Southerners' reaction to this reality in antebellum days, Cash finds, was typically romantic; first they invented the fiction that miscegenation did not exist, and then they placed the white woman on a pedestal to compensate her for so cruelly wounding the sentiments she held most sacred. The fact of miscegenation and the Southern white man's feelings of guilt "served to intensify the old interest in gyneolatry, and to produce yet more florid notions about Southern Womanhood and Southern Virtue," Cash comments, "and so to foster yet more precious notions of modesty and decorous behavior for the Southern female to live by."

Having subjected the characteristics of the region to a rigorous analysis, Cash turns to a critical examination of the South's claim to a superior culture. By and large, the claim is disallowed. Prior to the Civil War's outbreak, the South's colleges "were no more than academies"; illiteracy was far above the American average; the only novelist of distinction, William Gilmore Simms, was snubbed; the only noteworthy painter, Washington Allston, achieved his first recognition abroad; the only poet deserving the name, Edgar Allan Poe, was left to starve; and any books except the Bible were rare, even in the homes of wealthy planters.

And so Cash arrives at a harsh judgment: "In general, the intellectual and aesthetic culture of the Old South was a superficial and jejune thing, borrowed from without and worn as a political armor and a badge of rank; and hence . . . not a true culture at all." Cash considers the situation the more amazing because the South "had enjoyed riches, rank, and a leisure perhaps unmatched elsewhere in the world, for more than a hundred years at least," and ought to have progressed to a complex and important intellectual culture. In seeking an explanation, Cash believes that conflict with the Yankees was a primary factor. The taboo on criticism of slavery, as noted, led to a ban on all analysis and inquiry, and an opposition to new ideas and to every innovation. Given his environment, the Southerner "developed no need or desire for intellectual culture in its own right—none, at least, powerful enough to drive him past his taboos on its actual achievement."

The Civil War and Reconstruction are seen by Cash as an attempt by the Yankee to achieve by force what he had failed to accomplish by political means, namely to give the "tariff gang" a free hand and to force the South into the prevailing American mold. At Appomattox the Southern world seemed to have been destroyed, but the victory was an illusion. The war "left the essential Southern mind and will . . . entirely unshaken." Reconstruction made the region more self-conscious, more united than ever, its citizens filled with fear, rage, indignation, and resentment, and patriotic passion, determined to reassert white superiority and to resume mastery of the Negro.

Out of Reconstruction and the decade or so of Negro-carpetbagger dominance developed two complexes in the Southern mind. The first was the fear of Negro rape of white women, the other fear of control of government in the South by the Yankee, operating through the Negro. Only by resorting to naked force, the white Southerners felt, could they again become the ruling class. Hence the coming of the Ku Klux Klan and the revival of a tradition of violence which has marked Southern culture virtually throughout its history. The Negro, caught in the middle, became the scapegoat. No matter how damnable the means, they were justified and even glorified if the end to be attained was good.

Paradoxically, despite widespread repression of liberal ideas and free speech, the South began, after Reconstruction, to develop a distinctive literature, as an increasing number of authors devoted themselves to the writing and publishing of novels, stories, essays, and poetry, beginning with Sidney Lanier, Joel Chandler Harris, George W. Cable, Thomas Nelson Page, and Ellen Glasgow. Later a powerful new school of writers was making itself heard at home and abroad, notably James Branch Cabell, Elizabeth Madox Roberts, Julia Peterkin, DuBose Heyward, Conrad Aiken, Roark Bradford, Thomas Wolfe, Erskine Caldwell, and William Faulkner. In the 1920s the Southern agrarians appeared, led by John Crowe Ransom, Allen Tate, and Donald Davidson, moving, as Cash notes, "toward a more clear-eyed view of the Southern world."

Then came Progress. To meet the Yankee on his own ground, and perhaps even to excel him, Southern leaders decided late in the nineteenth century that the region must industrialize. With the factory—chiefly the cotton mill—rose the myth that the South had "suffered a change of heart," had acquired "a completely new viewpoint," and henceforth would be just like Yankeedom. In fact, Cash maintains, with much supporting evidence, "there was no revolution in basic ideology and no intention of relinquishing the central Southern positions and surrendering bodily to Yankee civilization. By the beginning of the new century, for example, the South had effectively nullified the Fourteenth Amendment and formally disfranchised the Negro."

As they viewed their own actions, the cotton-mill owners and founders, mainly the old "Confederate captains," built the factories for humanitarian reasons, to salvage the sinking tenant farmer from economic ruin. In practical operation, Cash iterates again and again, "the economic benefits of the new industrialism were far from distributing themselves equitably down the social scale. Whatever the intent of the original founders of Progress, the plain truth is that everything here rested finally upon one fact alone: cheap labor."

In Cash's view the mind of the South is much obsessed with cotton. Cash was born and spent his boyhood in a South Carolina cotton-mill town, where his father operated a company store. The cotton mill's whistle calling the "lintheads" to the spindles was Cash's association with cotton—not wide fields covered with white blossoms. When he thought of cotton, Cash visualized company housing, clouds of lint, and lung diseases, and a general physical deterioration of the workers.

By the 1920s King Cotton was ill, both in the factory and on the farm, as a result of European and Japanese competition, overproduction, economic depression, loss of foreign markets, and poor management. For these conditions, the worker paid the main part of the price.

Nevertheless, Southern industry continued to expand. New England mills were lured southward by the promise of cheap, contented labor, free factory buildings and sites, and the waiving of taxes. The consequence, Cash was convinced, was that "Dixie was now being worse exploited than ever the tariff gang had dreamed of." There was increased employment, but it was "a boon purchased at the appalling price of virtually giving away the inherent resources of the section, physical and human."

Meantime, the small farmers, the tenants, and the sharecroppers—the dwellers on the land who outnumbered the industrial workers by more than two to one in 1930—were having more than their share of trouble. The depredations of the boll weevil, starting in the early 1920s, price slumps, and increasing foreign production and competition were crowding the Southern farmer to the wall. Thousands of landowners in the Deep South were reduced to bankruptcy and many more thousands of tenants and sharecroppers were driven to emigrate.

The rise and fall of labor unions in the South is traced in graphic detail by Cash. Unionism from the beginning was equated with Communism by the Southern industrialists, and even among the workers themselves there was long a curious, widespread, and active antagonism to unionization, explained in part by their old intense individualism. Faced with exploitation by Yankee manufacturers, wage cuts, and work speedups in the late 1920s and the 1930s, however, the workers reacted with strikes and attempts to form unions. The movement had too many forces arrayed against it to hope for success, including economic depression, a surplus of labor willing to serve as strikebreakers, the whole business community, the evangelical clergy, the police and other government agencies, the press with few exceptions, and the farmers. And so the strikes failed and the unions collapsed.

Cash's comments on Southern politicians are scathing. He saw demagogues of the right and left proliferating—Cotton Ed Smith of South Carolina, whipping up hatred of the Negro and preaching states' rights; Huey Long of Louisiana, declaiming "every man a king"; Bilbo of Mississippi, promoting a movement to deport all Negroes to Africa; Robert Rice Reynolds of North Carolina, leading a crusade of hatred against aliens, of which his state had the smallest proportion in the nation; "Red Gallus" Gene Talmadge, rabble-rousing hero of the crackers. More decent individuals, such as Carter Glass and Harry Byrd of Virginia and Josiah William Bailey of North Carolina, were ultraconservatives, but a few social-minded individuals were beginning to emerge, notably the Bankheads and Lister Hill of Alabama.

Cash's concluding "basic picture of the South" has been often quoted:

Proud, brave, honorable by its lights, courteous, personally generous, loyal, swift to act, often too swift, but signally effective, sometimes terrible, in its action—such was the South at its best. And such at its best it remains today, despite the great falling away in some of its virtues. Violence, intolerance, aversion and suspicion toward new ideas, an incapacity for analysis, an inclination to act from feeling rather than from thought, an exaggerated individualism and a too narrow concept of social responsibility, attachment to fictitious and false values, above all too great attachment to racial values and a tendency to justify cruelty and injustice in the name of those values, sentimentality and a lack of realism—these have been its characteristic vices in the past. And, despite changes for the better, they remain its characteristic vices today.

In a chapter of Willie Morris's *The South Today, 100 Years after Appomattox* (1965), Edwin M. Yoder, Jr., reexamines Cash's work in "W. J. Cash After a Quarter Century."[2] Yoder notes that, after twenty-five years, historians differ with Cash on several points.

Some hold that there was more to the Reconstruction period than Yankee piracy and brutal economic imperialism, and others consider Cash's bitter treatment of Southern religion as superficial and biased. Nonetheless, Yoder believes that the essential character of the South did not change radically in the quarter century after Cash described it, despite economic and social modifications, the spread of television, and jet air travel. Race remained as much a Southern preoccupation as it was before World War II, and fundamental changes in racial attitudes and practices were exceedingly slow in coming, regardless of federal legislation.

Cash believed that unionization of mill workers would herald a new day for the South, a belief that Yoder considers naive, given the fierce individualism and aversion to regimentation characteristic of the Southern poor white. In any event, the wholesale unionization predicted by Cash never came, beaten back by right-to-work laws, a mass of cheap labor out of the hills, and high-priced lawyers hired by the corporations.

Another explanation of the Southern mind, differing somewhat from Cash's analysis, is offered by C. Vann Woodward in *The Burden of Southern History*. Unlike the rest of the nation, which has been historically conditioned to victory, plenty, and optimism about the possibility of solving human problems, Woodward argues, the South has experienced defeat, poverty, and tragedy on a large scale.[3] An atmosphere of abiding tragedy permeates Southern fiction, always with a background of inability to resolve the great social dilemma of race relations.

In his biography, *W. J. Cash: Southern Prophet*, Joseph L. Morrison concludes that "during this second half of the twentieth century, it has been accepted by virtually everyone that studies of the South—and, by extension, of the Negro revolution—must begin where Cash left off."[4] Cash's work contributed to an important degree to regional self-consciousness. The pattern he designed has since influenced a multitude of investigators of regional problems, in the South and elsewhere.

25.

Reconstruction to the New Freedom

C. VANN WOODWARD'S *Origins of the New South, 1877–1913*

C. Vann Woodward, one of America's most distinguished historians, a Southerner by birth and training, has been a key figure in a thoroughgoing reinterpretation and revision of Southern history for the post–Civil War era. In scope and authority, his *Origins of the New South* supersedes all previous accounts of the region, and there is wide agreement that the general history of the United States for the period between Reconstruction and Woodrow Wilson's first term will need to be rewritten in the light of Woodward's extensive research.

At the outset, Woodward makes it clear that he dislikes the phrase "New South." It has, he writes, "the color of a slogan, a rallying cry" for those who profess to have faith in the future, marked by a kind of blind optimism, rather than concern for the past. The author defines the South to include the eleven former Confederate states plus Kentucky and, after it became a state, Oklahoma. "In some ways," he finds, "it was more distinctive as a region than it had been earlier. Politically the South achieved, on the surface at least, a unity that it had never possessed in ante-bellum times. Economically it was set apart from the rest of the nation by differentials in per capita wealth, income, and living standards that made it unique among the regions. War and Reconstruction, while removing some of the South's peculiarities, merely aggravated others and gave rise to new ones."[1]

With an infinity of detail, testimony to a vast amount of investigation, Woodward deals with the process by which the Southern states, after four desperate years of Civil War and a decade of Reconstruction turbulence, reentered the mainstream of the nation's economy and politics. The story is almost unrelievedly sordid, but, as Dumas Malone commented, "devastatingly honest and highly illuminating."[2]

The connivance of Southern politicians in the deal which put Rutherford B. Hayes in the White House and stole the election from Samuel J. Tilden, recipient of a majority of the popular votes, is fully analyzed by Woodward. The Southern congressmen who agreed not to obstruct the counting of the electoral vote in favor of Hayes explained to their constituents that they were making the sacrifice on the strength of Hayes's promise to withdraw federal troops from the South, thus insuring the overthrow of carpetbag governments in South Carolina, Louisiana, and Florida. In reality, however, many congressmen from the South were influenced by economic factors, anticipating, for example, that Hayes would be more flexible in approving certain railroad legislation.

Following the end of Reconstruction, the so-called Redeemers, heirs to the Whigs, took over. These ex-Confederate heroes promptly proceeded to turn the South over to the Northern bankers, land speculators, and industrialists. Another well-known historian, David Donald, offers a devastating appraisal: "They might talk with drawls or dress like Confederate colonels, but these captains of industry were as hard and unscrupulous as they were successful. Lending money to farmers at interest rates of 43 percent or more, exploiting mill labor at an hourly wage of not quite 3 cents in 1890, extracting favors from purchasable legislatures, these champions of the New South liked to fancy themselves as the successors of the ante-bellum gentry."[3]

The consequences of control by the robber barons was the triumph of the Northern economic system, condemning the South to a colonial economic status, to continued extreme poverty, to the substitution for slavery of a caste system, in some aspects as evil as slavery in terms of human relations, and to the inauguration of a philosophy of unbridled laissez-faire.

Fair warning had been given the Southerners in a piece from Lowell, Massachusetts, printed in 1895 by the *Manufacturers' Record*: "Our capitalists are going into your country because they see a chance to make money there, but you must not think that they will give your people the benefit of the money they make. They will come north and enrich their heirs, or set up public libraries in our country towns. . . . Your people should not be dazzled by the glamour nor caught with the jingle of northern gold, but they should exact terms from these men that will be of benefit to the communities in which they may select to establish themselves."[4] The advice came too late, even if the Southerners had listened and been inclined to heed it; by then, the post-Reconstruction leaders had already sold the South to the "low-wage, low-value-creating industries," for which, Woodward stated, "the South seems to have had a fatal attraction."

The partners for the Eastern alliance in the South were Democrats of a most conservative stripe. During the 1880s, the Southern states became, according to the *Industrial South*, a Richmond journal, a "breakwater for all fanaticism. They are the bulwark against all the storms of political passion. They send forth conservative influences."[5] As Woodward rather picturesquely phrased the situation: "It took a lot of hallooing and heading off by the conservative leaders to keep the mass of Southerners herded up the right fork. Agrarian mavericks were eternally taking off up the left fork followed by great droves that they had stampeded. With the aid of the New-South propagandists, however, and by frequent resort to repressive or demagogic devices, the right-forkers contrived to keep the South fairly faithful to the Eastern alignment—until the advent of the Populists."[6]

Whenever the entrenched conservatives were criticized for "redeeming" their states by bringing in Northern capital, an appeal to the sacred memories of the Lost Cause was generally sufficient to quiet the dissenters. A South Carolina senator, whose campaign was going badly in 1894, was advised that a winning formula was "to get General Gordon to deliver his lecture on 'the last days of the Confederacy' in visiting the country people, and get him to make an allusion to you."

Two primary goals were achieved by the whites in the South with the end of Reconstruction: the crushing of Negro power and the termination of outside political control. The memory of these achievements, Woodward points out, remained the main unifying factor. The politics of the Redeemers, he concludes, "belonged therefore to the romantic school, emphasizing race and tradition and deprecating issues of economics and self-interest."[7] Woodward adds that "it was not the Radicals nor the Confederates but the Redeemers who laid the lasting foundations in matters of race, politics, economics, and law for the modern South."[8]

Low salaries for state officials invited corruption. The extravagance of carpetbag legislatures was replaced by niggardly appropriations as the criterion of good government. Salaries were cut as much as fifty percent, many offices were abolished, and the staffs of other departments cut drastically. In the 1880s Woodward reports, only two Southern states paid their governors as much as $5,000 and four paid only $3,000. At the same time, taxation systems placed grossly inequitable burdens on the people. The poll tax was regressive, property taxes forced owners of realty to pay a disproportionate share, and assessments favored railroads, utilities, and insurance companies.

Of all agencies of government, Woodward shows that public education was hit hardest by the retrenchment policy. Some officials insisted that obligations to bondholders came ahead of funds for public schools, that taxation to support education was socialistic, and that schools should be provided for pauper children only. By 1890 the per capita expenditure for schools in the South was well under half the national average, and the average length of school terms showed a proportionate decline.

Woodward regarded the expression "Solid South" as of doubtful validity for the period covered by his history. A variety of cleavages existed: "Black-Belt gentry and hillbilly commoners," the lower South against the Appalachian region, Jacksonians against Whigs, use of intimidated Negro voters by the Redeemers in the Black Belt to maintain political dominance over white counties.

Corruption of the ballot box and outright stealing of elections were common grievances.

The most effective protest against the excesses of the new industrial overlords was made by the Populists, who championed various constructive reforms, but the gains of the Farmers' Alliance and the Populist movements were bartered away in the shabby political maneuvers of their leaders. The end result is summed up by Woodward: "With the party of white supremacy in alliance with the Negro against lower-class white men; with the Republican party of hard money and Negro rights in alliance with the Green-backers and repudiationists against the Negro and debt payers; and with agrarian anti-monopolists in alliance with the party of big business, what wonder is it that the average Southerner retreated into some form of political nihilism?"[9] For a period of years after the collapse of the Populist movements of the early 1880s, the South lapsed into what Woodward describes as "a period of po-litical torpor."

But Southern industrialization was speeding up. A great de-pression ended in 1879 and Northern and English capital began to move South. The striking contrast between the peaceful Southern workers and "the convulsed and panic-stricken, mob-ridden States of the North" was emphasized. Irresistible pressures built up for throwing open to unrestricted speculation rich Southern resources of timber, coal, and iron. Corruption in the disposal of public lands was rampant. Texas, for example, granted to twelve railroad com-panies a total of 32,400,000 acres, an area larger than the state of Indiana. Northern and foreign capital was attracted by Southern railroad development to an even greater degree than to its lands. A railroad construction boom of unprecedented proportions got under way about 1880. By 1890, more than half the railroad mileage in the South was owned by a dozen large companies, mainly directed from New York. One victim of the railroad expansion was the region's steamboats, which in previous years had carried on heavy traffic along the rivers and inland waterways.

The business revival of 1879 opened the way for the Southern iron industry. From the beginning, Northern capital was a key factor in Southern mineral development. Manufacturing of tobacco, the South's oldest staple crop, was revolutionized by mechanization in the making of cigarette, smoking, and chewing tobacco. The Duke tobacco fortune had its origin at this point. Cotton mills began to move south from New England, following the popular slogan, "Bring the factories to the field," motivated in fact largely by the availability of low-paid, docile labor. Woodward describes the drive for more cotton mills in the South as a civic crusade inspired with a vision of social salvation, the promoters piously concerned with giving "employment to the necessitous masses of poor whites." Their philanthropy paid off in enormous profits. Nevertheless, despite the rapid rise of Southern industrialization, Woodward concludes that the South as a whole did not advance in manufacturing faster than the nation as a whole.

Oblivious to the inroads of Northern capital and industry and the widespread emulation of all things Yankee, there remained a spirit of romanticism in the South, characterized by Woodward as "a cult of archaism, a nostalgic vision of the past." The United Confederate Veterans was organized in 1889 and the United Daughters of the Confederacy in 1895. Woodward doubted that any lost cause in modern history "has received the devotion lavished upon the Stars and Bars." Genealogy became an avocation for thousands. Southern achievements in the arts and sciences, however, remained at a low level. Authors of distinction, such as Sidney Lanier, Paul Hamilton Hayne, and George W. Cable, lived in dire poverty or emigrated north. Local-color themes predominated in literature, reviving plantation legends, Negro dialect folktales, and moonlight-and-magnolia stories, exemplified by Thomas Nelson Page's *In Ole Virginia*.

Following the Civil War a religious revival swept the South in the form of evangelical crusades, revivalism, camp meetings, and mass conversions. This religious ferment was found by Woodward to be the work of only two Protestant sects, the Methodists and the Baptists. The two denominations had about twice the relative strength in the South that they had in the whole country. The rupture between the great Protestant sects, North and South, remained.

Emancipation of the slaves, according to Woodward, accomplished little or nothing toward improving the lot of the Southern small farmer and poor whites. The great mass of the population, the farmers, remained in a state of wretched poverty years after the close of the war. Among the causes for this situation were the persistence of sharecropping and the lien system. Under the latter scheme the farmer had to pledge his crops to merchants for future supplies; there was no other means of getting credit. Interest rates ran from thirty to seventy percent. When the farmer signed such a mortgage, one commentator wrote, "he has usually passed into a state of helpless peonage." These conditions gave rise to the Southern Farmers Alliance, which attained considerable political success, at least temporarily.

Southern factory workers were in as sad a state as the farmers. The company store replaced the country supply store, with the result that mill workers often found that their wages had been spent or overspent when payday arrived. A system of paternalism established a great degree of dependency on the part of the workers. Wages were miserably low. Adult male workers in North Carolina were paid forty to fifty cents a day, and child labor as low as ten or twelve cents a day. The work week averaged seventy hours, without regard to age or sex. The expanding industrialization of the New South, Woodward notes, was based to a large extent upon the labor of women and children. The Negro was eliminated as a competitor by banning him from the skilled trades. Embryo labor unions, led by the Knights of Labor, were organized to improve wages and working conditions, with very limited success. Strikes were ruthlessly suppressed, but occasional concessions were wrung from the corporations.

In his discussion of the "colonial economy," Woodward writes, "The vision that inspired the Southern businessman was that of a South modeled upon the industrial Northeast." The chief aim therefore was to attract the attention and the investments of Northeastern capitalists southward. Down through the first decade of the twentieth century, Northern capital penetrated the South at an accelerated rate. The Morgans, Mellons, and Rockefellers took charge of the region's railroads, mines, furnaces, and financial institutions. Smaller railroads "were raided, bankrupted, driven to the wall, or suffered to survive, at the pleasure of the giant systems." Early in the century, Standard Oil established a monopoly over Southwestern oil, the Union Sulpher Company had complete mastery of sulphur deposits in Louisiana and Texas, the Aluminum Company of America had bought up practically all bauxite deposits in Arkansas, Georgia, Alabama, and Tennessee, and "Buck" Duke's tobacco monopoly was headquartered in New York.

Northern capital for manufactures in the South was drawn by cheap money, cheap taxation, cheap labor, cheap coal, and cheap power. Among the attractions, too, Woodward points out, were tax exemptions, municipal subsidies, freedom from wage-and-hour laws, and a promise to avoid labor troubles. The consequences of the South's economic policies were lamentable: "Cut off from the better-paying jobs and the higher opportunities, the great majority of Southerners were confined to the worn grooves of a tributary economy. Some emigrated to other sections, but the mass of them stuck to farming, mining, forestry, or some low-wage industry, whether they liked it or not. The inevitable result was further intensification of the old problems of worn-out soil, cut-over timber lands, and worked-out mines."[10]

From the end of Reconstruction onward, strong political pressures developed for the disfranchisement of Negroes and poor whites. Objections to corrupt elections were offered as justification for taking voting rights away from these elements in the population. The Negroes were to be disfranchised, it was claimed, to eliminate corruption in political life and to save the expense of purchasing black votes.

Taking the ballot away from poor whites was also a goal of powerful political forces in a number of Southern states. "The intelligence and wealth of the South" would then be in the driver's seat, to "govern in the interest of all classes." "Every unworthy white man," as well as "every unworthy negro," was to be removed from the list of registered voters. Various devices were dreamed up by compliant legislatures and constitutional conventions to accomplish the dual purpose. The two most common barriers were literacy tests and property qualifications. Another was the "grandfather clause" to create a hereditary class of voters. Most effective, probably, was the poll tax, which caused thousands to lose their suffrage. Following enactment of the new regulations, Southern voters qualified to register showed a precipitate decline, and the Negro voter was virtually eliminated. In Woodward's judgment, "White supremacy enjoyed a success second only to that of the silver panacea as a discourager of political independence and a uniter of the Solid South."[11]

Meanwhile, the walls of segregation and caste were raised higher and higher by Southern law and custom, including laws requiring separation of races in transportation facilities, ordinances segregating residential areas, and of course separate schools. Booker T. Washington helped to cool the issues with his "Atlanta Compromise," pleading for industrial education and economic opportunity for the Negro, while expressing willingness to forego, at least for a time, political rights and privileges. Despite the handicaps to which they were subjected, the blacks managed to make slow progress in various areas, but in 1913 when the Negroes celebrated a "Year of Jubilee," the fiftieth anniversary of emancipation, Woodward judged that the material progress of which they boasted "represented the rise of a colored middle class of businessmen, farmers, and professional people—the accumulations of a 'brown middle class' that had arisen out of a 'black proletariat.'"[12]

Woodward pays his respects in no uncertain terms to the rabble-rousing politicians who have long been the curse of the South—Tom Watson, Hoke Smith, James K. Vardaman, Jeff Davis of Arkansas, Benjamin Tillman, Cole Blease, Tom Heflin, and Theodore G. Bilbo—none of whom "ever rose above the level of an obscene clown," according to their enemies.

Crusaders for public education had succeeded in making some gains by the start of the new century, in part due to Northern philanthropy. Less than half of the children of school age attended regularly, because of the absence of compulsory school-attendance laws in all Southern states except Kentucky. Illiteracy among native whites was high and far higher among the colored race. Taking the lead in the educational awakening after 1900 was North Carolina, the home of such active proponents of education as Page, Alderman, McIver, and Aycock. But for all its improvements, the public education system of the South still remained far below the national average during this period. The reasons, as summed up by Woodward, were that "the peculiar Southern combination of poverty, excessive numbers of children over adults, and duplication for two races proved in the end more of a problem than Southern resources, philanthropy, and good intentions could solve."[13]

The handicaps confronting higher education were as formidable as those facing the lower schools. As described by Woodward, "a multitude of superfluous institutions hung on in a dying condition." Miserably equipped colleges competed among themselves and with high schools for students, for tuition fees, practically their only revenue. The average professor's salary in forty-four of the better white colleges in ten Southern states was estimated in 1901 to be about $840. As late as 1913, the bachelor's degrees of thirty-eight Southern women's colleges were judged equivalent to one year of college work. One Southern college president reported in 1911 that the South had "no university well enough equipped to do genuine research work, and twice as many professional and polytechnic schools as are needed, and none of them able to give our people the advantages that northern and western institutions offer."[14]

Church sects dominated numerous colleges in the South. During the first decade of the century, the Baptists controlled forty colleges, the Methodist Episcopal Church South twenty, and the largest Presbyterian sect eighteen. "Denominational war against state institutions," Woodward writes, "was waged sporadically in several states," illustrated by North Carolina in the 1890s, when the Baptist, Methodist, and Presbyterian colleges attacked the state university at Chapel Hill as a seat of godlessness and an unfair competitor of church schools. They demanded that state institutions be forced to depend on voluntary support and that all taxes for education go to the public schools. Rigid controls over the expressed views of college faculty members were exercised by church groups and academic freedom was a victim in a number of universities and colleges.

The power and influence of religion over the minds and spirit of the South were evidenced by the rapid increase in church membership, which grew from six million in 1890 to more than nine million sixteen years later. Because of low incomes, however, about half the ministers had to supplement their pay with other occupations, especially in small communities and rural areas.

Woodward concludes his wide-ranging chronicle with a chapter called "The Return of the South." He observes that at the end of the first decade of the twentieth century the South had been wandering for fifty years in a political wilderness, isolated and impotent in national politics. Agricultural, commercial, and industrial power had been recovered, but not political power and prestige. The South's solidarity, affiliated with a consistently losing party, was a chief source of weakness. The election of Woodrow Wilson, with strong Southern support, saw the beginning of a change. Four of Wilson's cabinet and many lesser officials were Southern born. Two Virginians, Walter Hines Page and Thomas Nelson Page, became ambassadors, to Britain and Italy, respectively, Chief Justice White of Louisiana presided over the Supreme Court, and Colonel House of Texas became the President's principal adviser. Nearly all the important Senate and House committees had Southern chairmen. As Woodward remarked, "The change in the atmosphere at Washington represented a revolution in the geographical distribution of power," comparable to "the resurgence of the South upon the inauguration of Jefferson and of Jackson."[15]

Notes

Introduction

    1. C. Vann Woodward, *Origins of the New South* (Baton Rouge, La., 1951), p. 22.
    2. Norman Graebner, *A History of the American People* (New York, 1970), p. 612.
    3. Ibid., p. 636.

Chapter 1

    1. Arthur D. Innes, *Leading Figures in English History* (London, 1931), p. 200.
    2. John Smith, *The Generall Historie* (London, 1624), p. 49.
    3. John Gould Fletcher, *John Smith—Also Pocahontas* (New York, 1928), pp. 126–27.
    4. Innes, *Leading Figures*, p. 204.
    5. Smith, *Generall Historie*, pp. 105–6.
    6. Ibid., p. 126.
    7. W. O. Blake, *The History of Slavery and the Slave Trade* (Columbus, Ohio, 1860), p. 98.
    8. Smith, *Generall Historie*, p. 168.
    9. Bradford Smith, *Captain John Smith: His Life and Legend* (Philadelphia, 1953), p. 263.
    10. Alexis de Tocqueville, *Democracy in America* (New York, 1946), 2:343.
    11. John Lankford, *Captain John Smith's America* (New York, 1967), p. viii.

Chapter 2

    1. Jay B. Hubbell, *The South in American Literature* (Durham, N.C., 1954), p. 45.
    2. William Byrd, *William Byrd's Histories of the Dividing Line Betwixt Virginia and North Carolina* (New York, 1967), pp. 90, 92.
    3. Ibid., p. 72.
    4. Ibid., p. 21.
    5. Ibid., p. 25.
    6. Ibid., p. 27.
    7. Ibid., p. 70.
    8. Ibid., p. 46.
    9. Pierre Marambaud, *William Byrd of Westover* (Charlottesville, Va., 1971), p. 113.
    10. Byrd, *Histories of the Dividing Line*, p. xxxix.

Chapter 3

    1. *American Literature*, 46 (January 1975):580.
    2. Thomas Jefferson, *Notes on the State of Virginia*, ed. William Peden (Chapel Hill, N.C., 1955), p. 19.

3. Gilbert Chinard, *Thomas Jefferson* (Boston, 1929), p. 121.
4. Jefferson, *Notes on Virginia*, p. 25.
5. Ibid., p. 47.
6. Ibid., p. 55.
7. Ibid., p. 58.
8. Ibid., p. 59.
9. Ibid., p. 62.
10. Ibid., p. 64.
11. Ibid., p. 64.
12. Paul Leicester Ford, *The Writings of Thomas Jefferson* (New York, 1895) 5:159.
13. Jefferson, *Notes on Virginia*, p. 83.
14. Ibid., p. 84.
15. Ibid., p. 85.
16. Ibid., p. 87.
17. Ibid., p. 87.
18. Ibid., p. 138.
19. Ibid., p. 143.
20. Ibid., p. 162.
21. Ibid., pp. 162–63.
22. Dumas Malone, *Jefferson the Virginian* (Boston, 1948), p. 383.
23. Jefferson, *Notes on Virginia*, p. 164.
24. Ibid., pp. 164–65.
25. Ibid., p. 157.
26. Ibid., p. 159.
27. Ibid., pp. 146–47.
28. Ibid., p. 174.
29. Ibid., pp. 174–75.
30. Ibid., p. 175.
31. Ibid., p. xxiii.
32. Ibid., pp. xxiv-xxv.
33. Chinard, *Thomas Jefferson*, p. 118.

Chapter 4

1. William Bartram, *Travels* (Philadelphia, 1791), p. 137.
2. Ibid., pp. 141–42.
3. Ibid., p. 142.
4. Ibid., p. 118.
5. Ibid., p. 119.
6. Ibid., p. 128.
7. Ibid., pp. 269–70.
8. Ibid., pp. 81–82.
9. Ibid., p. 123.
10. Ibid., p. 123.
11. Ibid., pp. 289–96.
12. N. B. Fagin, *William Bartram* (Baltimore, 1933), p. 81.
13. Bartram, *Travels*, p. 185.
14. Ibid., p. 213.
15. Ibid., p. 483.
16. Ibid., p. 484.
17. Ibid., p. 484.
18. Ibid., pp. 99–100.
19. Ibid., pp. 253–54.

20. J. M. Edelstein, "America's First Native Botanists," *Library of Congress Quarterly Journal of Acquisitions*, 15 (February 1958):57.

Chapter 5

1. Emily Ellsworth Ford Skeel, *Mason Locke Weems* (New York, 1929), 2:xvi.
2. Jay B. Hubbell, *The South in American Literature* (Durham, N.C., 1954), p. 231.
3. Skeel, *Weems*, 2:xiii.
4. Ibid., 2:410
5. Lawrence C. Wroth, *Parson Weems* (Baltimore, 1911), p. 7.
6. Skeel, *Weems*, 2:72.
7. Ibid., 2:120.
8. Ibid., 2:126.
9. Hubbell, *South in American Literature*, p. 233.
10. David D. Van Tassel, *Recording America's Past* (Chicago, 1960), p. 70.
11. Robert W. McLaughlin, *Fishing for Fish Not in the Pond* (Brooklyn, N.Y., 1930), pp. 35–36.
12. For full descriptions see Randolph G. Adams's "The Historical Illustrations in Weems's Washington," *Colophon*, part 8 (New York, 1931).
13. William Gilmore Simms, *Views and Reviews* (New York, 1845), 2d series, p. 125.
14. *North Carolina Historical Review*, 29(January 1952):23.
15. *John Rylands Library Bulletin*, 45(September 1962):88.
16. Michael Kraus, *A History of American History* (New York, 1937), p. 162.
17. John K. Bettersworth, "The Folk Imperative," *Phi Kappa Phi Journal*, 52 (Spring 1972):28–35.

Chapter 6

1. Walter Blair, "Six Davy Crocketts," in Leonard F. Dean, ed., *Perspectives* (New York, 1954), pp. 233–45.
2. Charles A. Beard and Mary R. Beard, *The Rise of American Civilization* (New York, 1930), p. 540.
3. James A. Shackford, Introduction, in *A Narrative of the Life of David Crockett* (Knoxville, Tenn., 1973), p. ix.
4. Vernon L. Parrington, *Main Currents in American Thought* (New York, 1927), 2:172–73.
5. Ibid., 3:391.
6. David Crockett, *A Narrative of the Life of David Crockett* (Philadelphia, 1834), p. 43.
7. Ibid., p. 49.
8. Ibid., p. 135.
9. Ibid., p. 144.
10. Ibid., p. 147.
11. Constance Rourke, *Davy Crockett* (New York, 1934), p. 128.
12. Crockett, *A Narrative*, p. 211.
13. Shackford, in David Crockett, *A Narrative*, p. xvi.
14. Blair, "Six Crocketts," p. 211.
15. Don C. Seitz, *Uncommon Americans* (Indianapolis, Ind., 1925), p. 323.
16. Parrington, *Main Currents*, 2:173.
17. Crockett, *A Narrative*, pp. 3–4.
18. David Crockett, *Sketches and Eccentricities of Col. David Crockett* (New York, 1833), p. 164.

19. Richard Dorson, ed., *Davy Crockett, American Comic Legend* (New York, 1939), p. xv.

20. Ibid., p. xxii.

21. Crockett, *A Narrative*, p. 9.

22. Curtis Carroll David, "A Legend at Full-Length," *Proceedings of the American Antiquarian Society*, 69 (1959):170.

Chapter 7

1. Vernon L. Parrington, *Main Currents in American Thought* (New York, 1927), 2:167.

2. Edgar Allan Poe, "*Georgia Scenes*," *Southern Literary Messenger*, 2 (March 1836):288.

3. Ibid., p. 288.

4. Ibid., p. 288.

5. Ibid., p. 289.

6. Parrington, *Main Currents*, p. 172.

7. Poe, "*Georgia Scenes*," p. 289.

8. Ibid., p. 290.

9. Parrington, *Main Currents*, p. 172.

10. John Donald Wade, *Augustus Baldwin Longstreet* (New York, 1924), p. 182.

11. Franklin J. Meine, ed., *Tall Tales of the Southwest* (New York, 1930), pp. xviii–xix.

12. Bernard De Voto, *Mark Twain's America* (Boston, 1967), p. 96.

13. Ibid., p. 96.

Chapter 8

1. Frances Anne Kemble, *Journal of a Residence on a Georgian Plantation in 1838–1839*, ed. John A. Scott (New York, 1961), p. 138.

2. Frances Anne Kemble, *Records of a Later Life* (London, 1882), 1:67.

3. Kemble, *Journal*, p. 131.

4. Ibid., p. 121.

5. Ibid., pp. 60–61.

6. Ibid., p. 210.

7. Kenneth M. Stampp, *The Peculiar Institution* (New York, 1956), p. 335.

8. Kemble, *Journal*, p. 353.

9. Dorothie Bobbé, *Fanny Kemble* (New York, 1931), p. 272.

10. Kemble, *Journal*, p. lxi.

11. Ibid., p. liv.

12. Herbert Ravenel Sass, "Fateful Island," *Saturday Evening Post*, 216 (22 April 1944):92.

Chapter 9

1. Frederick Douglass, *Narrative of the Life of Frederick Douglass* (Boston, 1845), p. 9.

2. Ibid., p. 26.

3. Ibid., p. 27.

4. Ibid., p. 28.

5. Ibid., p. 38.

6. Frederick Douglass, *My Bondage and My Freedom* (New York, 1855), p. 107.

7. Douglass, *Narrative*, p. 42.

8. Ibid., p. 45.

9. Ibid., p. 45.
10. Ibid., p. 48.
11. Ibid., p. 107.
12. Ibid., p. 56.
13. Ibid., p. 57.
14. Ibid., p.,58.
15. Ibid., p. 60.
16. Ibid., p. 67.
17. Frederick Douglass, *Life and Writings* (New York, 1950), p. 20.
18. Douglass, *Narrative*, p. 84.
19. Ibid., pp. 87–88.
20. Ibid., p. 110.
21. Ibid., p. 155.
22. Robert L. Factor, *Black Response to America* (Reading, Mass., 1970), p. 9.
23. Douglass, *Life and Writings*, p. 63.
24. Douglass, *Narrative*, p. viii.
25. Ibid., p. xxiii.
26. Benjamin Quarles, *Frederick Douglass* (New York, 1968), p. 5.

Chapter 10

1. Ralph Lerner, "Calhoun's New Science of Politics," in John L. Thomas, *John C. Calhoun* (New York, 1968), p. 193.
2. Hamilton Basso, *Mainstream* (New York, 1943), p. 56.
3. Saul K. Padover, *The Genius of America* (New York, 1960), p. 140.
4. Richard Hofstadter, *The American Political Tradition* (New York, 1949), p. 69.
5. John C. Calhoun, *Works* (New York, 1870), 6:33–34.
6. John C. Calhoun, *Works* (Charleston, S.C., 1851–57), 4:411.
7. Ibid., 4:507–8.
8. Ibid., 1:55.
9. Ibid., 1:2.
10. Ibid., 1:7.
11. Padover, *Genius*, p. 151.
12. Hofstadter, *American Tradition*, p. 86.
13. Willard Thorp, ed., *Southern Reader* (New York, 1955), p. 443.
14. Padover, *Genius*, p. 153.
15. Holmes Alexander, *The Famous Five* (New York, 1955), p. 117.
16. Richard N. Current, *John C. Calhoun* (New York, 1963), p. 61.
17. Ibid., p. 62.
18. Ibid., p. 62.
19. Padover, *Genius*, p. 139.
20. Hofstadter, *American Tradition*, pp. 88–89.

Chapter 11

1. Earl Schenck Meirs, introduction, in Hinton R. Helper, *The Impending Crisis in the South* (New York, 1963), p. 7.
2. Hinton Rowan Helper, *The Impending Crisis in the South: How to Meet It* (New York, 1857), p. 84.
3. Ibid., pp. 21–22.
4. Ibid., p. 22.
5. Ibid., pp. 22–23.
6. Ibid., p. 54.
7. Ibid., p. 46.

8. Ibid., p. 76.
9. Ibid., p. 42.
10. Ibid., p. 147.
11. Ibid., p. 159.
12. Ibid., p. 43.
13. Ibid., p. 392.
14. Ibid., pp. 391–92.
15. Ibid., pp. 97–98.
16. James Ford Rhodes, *History of the United States* (New York, 1910), 2:419–20.
17. Meirs, introduction in Helper, *Crisis* (1963), p. 17.

Chapter 12

1. Broadus Mitchell, *Frederick Law Olmsted* (Baltimore, 1924), p. xi.
2. Laura Wood Roper, *FLO: A Biography of Frederick Law Olmsted* (Baltimore, 1973), p. 87.
3. Edmund Wilson, *Patriotic Gore* (New York, 1962), pp. 226–27.
4. Mitchell, *Olmsted*, p. 115.
5. J. E. Cairns, *The Slave Power* (London, 1863), pp. 96–97.
6. Frederick Law Olmsted, *A Journey in the Back Country* (New York, 1863), p. 374.
7. Ibid., p. 19.
8. Frederick Law Olmsted, *Journey Through Texas* (New York, 1857), p. 140.
9. Frederick Law Olmsted, *A Journey in the Seaboard Slave States* (New York, 1856), p. 110.
10. Wilson, *Patriotic Gore*, p. 226.
11. Olmsted, *Back Country*, p. 424.
12. Olmsted, *Seaboard Slave States*, p. 479.
13. Olmsted, *The Cotton Kingdom* (New York, 1862), 1:13.
14. Olmsted, *Back Country*, p. 407.
15. Ibid., p. 293.
16. Ibid., p. 447.
17. Ibid., p. 373.
18. Willard Thorp, *Southern Reader* (New York, 1955), p. 288.
19. Olmsted, *Back Country*, p. vi.

Chapter 13

1. Edward King, *The Great South* (Hartford, Conn., 1875), p. i.
2. Ibid., p. 33.
3. Ibid., p. 35.
4. Ibid., p. 91.
5. Ibid., p. 93.
6. Ibid., p. 419.
7. Ibid., p. 426.
8. Ibid., p. 468.
9. Ibid., p. 644.
10. Ibid., p. 132.
11. Ibid., p. 276.
12. Ibid., p. 341.
13. Ibid., p. 431.
14. Ibid., p. 270.
15. Ibid., p. 607.
16. Ibid., p. 596.

17. Ibid., p. 342.
18. Ibid., p. 602.
19. Ibid., p. 774.
20. Ibid., p. 99.
21. Ibid., p. 139.
22. Ibid., p. 777.
23. Ibid., p. 791.
24. Ibid., p. 269.
25. Ibid., p. 794.
26. Ibid., p. 793.
27. Edward King, *The Great South* (New York, 1969), p. v.

Chapter 14

1. Edward L. Tinker, "Cable and the Creoles," *American Literature*, 5 (January 1934):313.
2. Ibid., p. 313.
3. George W. Cable, *Old Creole Days* (New York, 1879), p. 1.
4. Louis D. Rubin, Jr., *George W. Cable* (New York, 1969), p. 49.
5. Philip Butcher, *George W. Cable* (New York, 1962), p. 35.
6. Cable, *Old Creole Days*, p. 63.
7. Ibid., p. 84.
8. Ibid., p. 115.
9. Rubin, *Cable*, pp. 45–46.
10. Tinker, *Cable*, p. 313.
11. Edmund Wilson, *Patriotic Gore* (New York, 1962), p. 567.
12. Tinker, *Cable*, p. 326.
13. *Dictionary of American Biography* (New York, 1929), 3:393.

Chapter 15

1. C. Alphonso Smith, *Southern Literary Studies* (Chapel Hill, N.C., 1927), p. 128.
2. Paul M. Cousins, *Joel Chandler Harris, a Biography* (Baton Rouge, La., 1968), p. 111.
3. Jay B. Hubbell, *The South in American Literature* (Durham, N.C., 1954), p. 787.
4. Smith, *Southern Studies*, pp. 142–43.
5. Julia Collier Harris, *The Life and Letters of Joel Chandler Harris* (Boston, 1918), p. xvii.
6. Van Wyck Brooks, *The Times of Melville and Whitman* (New York, 1947), p. 376.
7. Bernard Wolfe, "Uncle Remus and the Malevolent Rabbit," *Commentary*, 8 (July 1949):31–41.
8. Stella Brewer Brookes, *Joel Chandler Harris–Folklorist* (Athens, Ga., 1950), p. 72.
9. Adolf Gerber, "Uncle Remus Traced to the Old World," *Journal of American Folklore*, 6 (October–December 1893):245–57.
10. John Tumlin, introduction, in Joel Chandler Harris, *Uncle Remus* (Savannah, Ga., 1974), p. xx.
11. John Winterich, *Twenty-Three Books* (Philadelphia, 1939), pp. 103–4.
12. Smith, *Southern Studies*, pp. 151–52.
13. Hubbell, *South in American Literature*, p. 794.
14. Tumlin, introduction, in Harris, *Uncle Remus*, p. xxvi.

Chapter 16

1. Jay B. Hubbell, *The South in American Literature* (Durham, N.C., 1954), p. 822.
2. Mark Twain, *Life on the Mississippi* (New York, 1944), p. 120.
3. Ibid., p. vii.
4. Ibid., p. 3.
5. Ibid., p. 28.
6. Ibid., p. 35.
7. Ibid., p. 39.
8. Ibid., p. 65.
9. Ibid., p. 51.
10. Ibid., p. 53.
11. Ibid., p. 62.
12. Ibid., p. 56.
13. Ibid., pp. 83–85.
14. Ibid., p. 105.
15. Ibid., p. 72.
16. Ibid., p. 134.
17. Dudley R. Hutcherson, "Mark Twain as a Pilot," *American Literature*, 12 (November 1940):353–55.
18. Bernard De Voto, *Mark Twain's America* (Boston, 1967), p. 110.
19. Twain, *Life on the Mississippi*, pp. 184–85.
20. Ibid., p. 239.
21. Ibid., p. 272.
22. Ibid., pp. 272–73.
23. Ibid., p. 259.
24. Caroline Ticknor, "Mark Twain's Missing Chapters," *The Bookman*, 39 (1914):298–309.
25. J. W. Rankin, introduction, in Mark Twain, *Life on the Mississippi* (New York, 1923), p. xvi.
26. Albert Bigelow Paine, introduction, in Mark Twain, *Life on the Mississippi* (New York, 1929), p. xii.
27. Edgar Lee Masters, *Mark Twain, a Portrait* (New York, 1938), p. 152.

Chapter 17

1. Gerald W. Johnson, *The Man Who Feels Left Behind* (New York, 1961), pp. 68–69.
2. Ibid., p. 70.
3. Grace King, *Memories of a Southern Woman of Letters* (New York, 1932), p. 377.
4. Thomas Nelson Page, *In Ole Virginia* (Chapel Hill, N.C., 1969), pp. x–xi.
5. Theodore L. Gross, *Thomas Nelson Page* (New York, 1967), p. 26.
6. Arlin Turner, *Southern Stories* (New York, 1960), pp. xxi–xxii.
7. Paul H. Buck, *The Road to Reunion* (New York, 1959), p. 224.
8. Thomas Nelson Page, *The Novels, Stories, Sketches, and Poems* (New York, 1906), 1:xi.
9. Gross, *Page*, p. 33.
10. Theodore L. Gross, *The Heroic Ideal in American Literature* (New York, 1971), p. 112.
11. Jay B. Hubbell, *Virginia Life in Fiction* (New York, 1922), pp. 28–29, 53–54.
12. Page, *The Novels*, etc., 12:221.
13. Ibid., p. 346.
14. Hubbell, *Virginia Life*, pp. 27–28.

15. *South Atlantic Quarterly*, 30 (1931):178.
16. Page, *The Novels*, etc., 1:262.
17. *Georgia Review*, 20 (1966):350.
18. Gross, *The Heroic Ideal*, p. 117.
19. Page, *In Ole Virginia*, p. xxxv.

Chapter 18

1. Booker T. Washington, *Up from Slavery* (New York, 1901), p. 127.
2. August Meier, *Negro Thought in America, 1880–1915* (Ann Arbor, Mich., 1963), pp. 85–99.
3. Washington, *Up From Slavery*, p. 119.
4. Ibid., p. 122.
5. Louis Lomax, introduction, in Booker T. Washington, *Up from Slavery* (New York, 1959), p. 12.
6. Robert L. Factor, *The Black Response to America* (Reading, Mass., 1970), p. 166.
7. Ibid., p. 165.
8. Lomax, introduction in Washington, *Up from Slavery* (1959), p. 12.
9. Ibid., pp. 12–13.
10. Washington, *Up from Slavery*, p. 145.
11. Ibid., pp. 218–25.
12. Louis R. Harlan, *Booker T. Washington: The Making of a Black Leader* (New York, 1972), p. 204.
13. W. E. B. Du Bois, *The Souls of Black Folk* (Chicago, 1903), p. 59.
14. Merle Curti, *The Social Ideas of American Educators* (New York, 1935), p. 307.
15. Ibid., p. 306.
16. Meier, *Negro Thought*, p. 110.
17. Gunnar Myrdal, *An American Dilemma* (New York, 1944), p. 739.
18. Howard Brotz, *Negro Social and Political Thought* (New York, 1966), p. 12.

Chapter 19

1. August Meier, *Negro Thought in America* (Ann Arbor, Mich., 1963), pp. 190, 205.
2. W. E. B. Du Bois, *The Souls of Black Folk* (Chicago, 1903), p. 4.
3. Ibid., p. 2.
4. Ibid., p. 3.
5. Ibid., p. 5.
6. Ibid., p. 6.
7. Ibid., p. 10.
8. Ibid., p. 22.
9. Ibid., p. 36.
10. Ibid., p. 40.
11. William M. Tuttle, Jr., *W. E. B. Du Bois* (Englewood Cliffs, N.J., 1973), p. 11.
12. Du Bois, *Souls of Black Folk*, p. 42.
13. Ibid., p. 51.
14. Ibid., p. 52.
15. *Outlook*, 74 (1903):214.
16. Elliott M. Rudwick, *W. E. B. Du Bois* (New York, 1969), p. 70.
17. Du Bois, *Souls of Black Folk*, p. 91.
18. Ibid., p. 94.
19. Ibid., p. 188.
20. Ibid., p. 203.

Chapter 20

1. *Current Literature*, 38 (March 1905):153–54.
2. *Charlotte (N.C.) Observer*, 4 May 1905, p. 12.
3. *Georgia Review*, 11 (1957):333–40.
4. *New Republic*, 2 (20 March 1915):185.
5. Raymond A. Cook, *Thomas Dixon* (New York, 1974), p. 76.
6. *Journal of Southern History*, 36 (August 1970):353.

Chapter 21

1. Richard Hofstadter, "U. B. Phillips and the Plantation Legend," *Journal of Negro History*, 29 (April 1944):109.
2. Ulrich B. Phillips, *Life and Labor in the Old South* (Boston, 1929), p. 3.
3. Ibid., p. 35.
4. Ibid., p. 104.
5. Ibid., p. 111.
6. Ibid., p. 148.
7. Ibid., p. 146.
8. Ibid., p. 158.
9. Ibid., p. 188.
10. Wendell H. Stephenson, *The South Lives in History* (Baton Rouge, La., 1955), p. 82.
11. Phillips, *Life and Labor*, pp. 196–203.
12. Ibid., p. 185.
13. Herbert Aptheker, *American Negro Slave Revolts* (New York, 1963), p. 162.
14. Hofstadter, "U. B. Phillips," pp. 122–23.
15. Phillips, *Life and Labor*, p. 164.
16. Hofstadter, "U. B. Phillips," p. 110.
17. Phillips, *Life and Labor*, p. 348.
18. Fred Landon, "A Bibliography of the Writings of Professor Ulrich Bonnell Phillips," *Agricultural History*, 8 (October 1934):197.

Chapter 22

1. Benjamin B. Kendrick, "Agrarian Movements: United States," *Encyclopedia of the Social Sciences*, 1:509.
2. *I'll Take My Stand* (New York, 1962), p. vi.
3. John L. Stewart, *The Burden of Time* (Princeton, N.J., 1965), pp. 148–49.
4. *I'll Take My Stand* (1962), p. xix.
5. Ibid., p. 12.
6. Stewart, *Burden of Time*, p. 154.
7. *I'll Take My Stand* (1962), p. 14.
8. Ibid., p. 47.·
9. Ibid., p. 69.
10. Ibid., p. 224.
11. Ibid., p. 234.
12. Stewart, *Burden of Time*, p. 169.
13. *I'll Take My Stand* (1962), p. 177.
14. Ibid., p. 188.
15. Ibid., p. 200.
16. Stewart, *Burden of Time*, pp. 169–70.
17. *I'll Take My Stand* (1962), p. 328.
18. Ibid., p. 358.
19. Ibid., p. xiii.

20. Ibid., p. xv.
21. *Nation*, 132 (14 January 1931):48.
22. *I'll Take My Stand* (1962), p. 93.

Chapter 23

1. *Washington Post*, 14 November 1954, p. 4B.
2. *New York Times Book Review*, 23 June 1936, p. 3.
3. Gerald W. Johnson, *The Wasted Land* (Chapel Hill, N.C., 1937), p. 73.
4. *Social Forces*, 33 (March 1955):207.
5. *Journal of Southern History* 24 (August 1958):305.
6. Ibid., p. 307.
7. *American Sociological Review*, 20 (April 1955):237.

Chapter 24

1. William E. Dodd, *The Cotton Kingdom* (New Haven, Conn., 1919), p. 24.
2. Edwin M. Yoder, "W. J. Cash After a Quarter Century," in Willie Morris, *The South Today* (New York, 1965), pp. 89–99.
3. C. Vann Woodward, *The Burden of Southern History* (Baton Rouge, La., 1960), p. 19.
4. Joseph L. Morrison, *W. J. Cash: Southern Prophet* (New York, 1967), p. 3.

Chapter 25

1. C. Vann Woodward, *Origins of the New South, 1877–1913* (Baton Rouge, La., 1951), p. x.
2. *New York Herald Tribune Weekly Book Review*, 28 (23 December 1951), p. 3.
3. *Nation*, 174(17 May 1952):484.
4. Woodward, *Origins of New South*, pp. 310–11.
5. Ibid., p. 50.
6. Ibid., p. 50.
7. Ibid., p. 51.
8. Ibid., p. 22.
9. Ibid., p. 105.
10. Ibid., pp. 319–20.
11. Ibid., p. 349.
12. Ibid., p. 368.
13. Ibid., p. 406.
14. *Report of U.S. Commissioner of Education, 1911*, pp. 255–56.
15. Woodward, *Origins of New South*, p. 481.

Bibliography

BARTRAM, WILLIAM (1739–1823)

Travels Through North and South Carolina, Georgia, East and West Florida, the Cherokee Country, the Extensive Territories of the Muscogulges, or Creek Confederacy, and the Country of the Chactaws. Philadelphia: James and Johnson, 1791.

BYRD, WILLIAM (1674–1744)

History of the Dividing Line Betwixt Virginia and North Carolina, first published in *The Westover Manuscripts: Containing the History of the Dividing Line Betwixt Virginia and North Carolina; A Journey to the Land of Eden, A.D. 1733, and A Progress to the Mines. Written from 1728 to 1736, and Now First Published.* Petersburg, Va.: Printed by E. and J. C. Ruffin, 1841. *Secret History of the Line,* first published in William Byrd's *Histories of the Dividing Line Betwixt Virginia and North Carolina,* edited by William K. Boyd. Raleigh: North Carolina Historical Commission, 1929.

CABLE, GEORGE WASHINGTON (1844–1925)

Old Creole Days. New York: Scribner, 1879.

CALHOUN, JOHN CALDWELL (1782–1850)

A Disquisition on Government, and A Discourse on the Constitution and Government of the United States. Charleston, S.C.: Press of Walker and James, 1851.

CASH, WILBUR JOSEPH (1901–1941)

The Mind of the South. New York: Knopf, 1941.

CLEMENS, SAMUEL LANGHORNE (1835–1910)

Life on the Mississippi. Boston: J. R. Osgood, 1883.

CROCKETT, DAVID (1786–1836)

A Narrative of the Life of David Crockett of the State of Tennessee, Written by Himself. Philadelphia: E. L. Carey and A. Hart, 1834.

Best modern edition, Knoxville: University of Tennessee Press, 1973.

DIXON, THOMAS (1864–1946)
The Clansman, an Historical Romance of the Ku Klux Klan. New York: Doubleday, Page, 1905.

DOUGLASS, FREDERICK (1817?–1895)
Narrative of the Life of Frederick Douglass, an American Slave. Boston: Anti-Slavery Office, 1845.

DU BOIS, WILLIAM EDWARD BURGHARDT (1868–1963)
The Souls of Black Folk. Chicago: A. C. McClurg, 1903.

HARRIS, JOEL CHANDLER (1848–1908)
Uncle Remus, His Songs and His Sayings: The Folklore of the Old Plantation. New York: Appleton, 1880.

HELPER, HINTON ROWAN (1829–1909)
The Impending Crisis of the South: How to Meet It. New York: Burdick Brothers, 1857.

JEFFERSON, THOMAS (1743–1826)
Notes on the State of Virginia. Paris, 1784–85. Definitive edition, London: J. Stockdale, 1787. First American edition, Philadelphia: Prichard and Hall, 1788.

KEMBLE, FRANCES ANNE (1809–1893)
Journal of a Residence on a Georgian Plantation in 1838–1839. London: Longman, Green, 1863. New York: Harper, 1863. Best modern edition, New York: Knopf, 1961.

KING, EDWARD (1848–1896)
The Great South: A Record of Journeys in Louisiana, Texas, the Indian Territory, Missouri, Arkansas, Mississippi, Alabama, Georgia, Florida, South Carolina, North Carolina, Kentucky, Tennessee, Virginia, and Maryland. Hartford, Conn.: American Publishing Co., 1875.

LONGSTREET, AUGUSTUS BALDWIN (1790–1870)
Georgia Scenes, Characters, Incidents, &c., in the First Half Century of the Republic. Augusta, Ga.: S. R. Sentinel Office, 1835.

ODUM, HOWARD WASHINGTON (1884–1954)
Southern Regions of the United States. Chapel Hill: University of North Carolina Press, 1936.

OLMSTED, FREDERICK LAW (1822–1903)

The Cotton Kingdom: A Traveller's Observations on Cotton and Slavery in the American Slave States. 2 vols. New York: Mason Brothers, 1861. Abridged from *A Journey in the Seaboard Slave States* (1856), *A Journey Through Texas* (1857), and *A Journey in the Back Country* (1860).

PAGE, THOMAS NELSON (1853–1922)

In Ole Virginia; or, Marse Chan, and Other Stories. New York: Scribner, 1887.

PHILLIPS, ULRICH BONNELL (1877–1934)

Life and Labor in the Old South. Boston: Little, Brown, 1929.

SMITH, JOHN (1580–1631)

The Generall Historie of Virginia, New-England, and the Summer Isles with the Names of the Adventurers, Planters, and Governours from Their First Beginning, Anno: 1584 to this Present 1624. With the Proceedings of Those Severall Colonies and the Accidents that befell them in all their Journeys and Discoveries. Also the Maps and Descriptions of all those Countryes, their Commodities, people, Government, Customes, and Religion yet knowne. London: Printed by I. D. and I. H. for Michael Sparkes, 1624.

TWELVE SOUTHERNERS

I'll Take My Stand: The South and the Agrarian Tradition. New York: Harper, 1930.

WASHINGTON, BOOKER TALIAFERRO (1859–1915)

Up from Slavery: An Autobiography. New York: A. L. Burt, 1901.

[WEEMS, MASON LOCKE (1759–1825)]

The Life and Memorable Actions of George Washington, General and Commander of the Armies of America. Philadelphia: George Keatinge, [1800?].

WOODWARD, COMER VANN (1908–)

Origins of the New South, 1877–1913. Baton Rouge: Louisiana State University Press, 1951.

Index

Twain, Mark, 81, 162; *Huckleberry Finn*,
165; *Life on the Mississippi*, 165–75;
Tom Sawyer, 165
Twichell, Joseph H., 166

U
Uncle Remus, Harris, 156–64
Union Sulphur Company, 265
United Confederate Veterans, 264
United Daughters of the Confederacy,
264
Up from Slavery, Washington, 186–96

V

Van Buren, Martin, 72
Vance, Rupert B., 246, 248
Van Tassel, David D., 59
Vardman, James K., 243, 267
Villard, Oswald Garrison, 216
Virginia Company of London, 4, 6, 8, 9,
12

W
Wade, John Donald, 80, 235
Wake Forest College, 209
Ward, Artemus, 164
Warren, Robert Penn, 185, 234
Washington, Booker T., 197, 202–4,
267; *Up from Slavery*, 186–96

Washington, George, 52, 56–60
Watson, Thomas E., 243
Webster, Daniel, 101
Weems, David, 52
Weems, Mason Locke: *Life of Washington
the Great*, 51–62
Wharton, Henry, 14
White, Edward D., 269
Whitman, Walt, 211
Whitney, Eli, 221
Wilberforce College, 198–99
Wilson, Alexander: *American
Ornithologist*, 47
Wilson, Edmund, 129, 155
Wilson, Woodrow, 209, 216, 243, 269
Wingfield, Edward, 4, 6
Wister, Fanny Kemble, 85
Wolfe, Bernard, 161
Wolfe, Samuel, 124
Wolfe, Thomas, 255
Women, Southern, 146
Woodward, C. Vann: *The Burden of
Southern History*, 258; *Origins of the
New South*, 259–69
Wroth, Lawrence C.: *Parson Weems*,
54–55

Y
Yellow fever, 146
Yoder, Edwin M., Jr., 257–58
Young, Stark, 185, 235